Tom Traves

The State and Enterprise:
Canadian Manufacturers and
the Federal Government, 1917-1931

UNIVERSITY OF TORONTO PRESS

TORONTO BUFFALO LONDON

© University of Toronto Press 1979
Toronto Buffalo London
Printed in Canada

Canadian Cataloguing in Publication Data

Traves, Tom, 1948-
  The state and enterprise
  (The state and economic life)
  A revision of the author's thesis, York University.
  Includes index.
  ISBN 0-8020-5445-5 bd.   ISBN 0-8020-6353-5 pa.
  1. Industry and state – Canada. 2. Canada – Manufactures. I. Title. II. Series.
  HD3616.C22T74   338.971   C78-001565-7

Contents

TO MY FATHER AND MOTHER

Acknowledgements

It gives me real pleasure to thank the many people who helped while I was writing this book. An earlier draft of the manuscript was presented as a doctoral dissertation at York University and I wish to express my appreciation to my supervisors, Ramsay Cook and Viv Nelles, who offered sound criticism and valuable assistance at each stage in this project's evolution. I would also like to thank Jack Saywell, Bob Cuff, Jack Granatstein, and Willard Piepenburg who also read parts or all of the manuscript and whose response I valued. At the University of Toronto Press Gerry Hallowell saved me from many pitfalls. Finally, I owe a special note of appreciation to my friends Paul Craven and Stan Pollin with whom I spent many hours discussing the ideas that form the heart of this book.

Over the past few years I have presented drafts of several chapters to different research groups and I would like to thank all those who participated for their interest and their comments. These forums play a vital role in the scholarly life of our community and I would like to acknowledge them here: York University History Department Research Group, York University Social Science Division Work in Progress Seminar, the Annual Meetings of the Canadian Historical Association, the University of Toronto-York University Historical Research Group, and the Economic History Workshop at the University of Toronto. I would also like to thank the editors of the Canadian Historical Review and Canadian Public Administration who published earlier drafts of parts of this manuscript.

This book has been published with the help of a grant from the Social Science Federation of Canada, using funds provided by the Social Sciences and Humanities Research Council of Canada, and a grant to the University of Toronto Press from the Andrew W. Mellon Foundation. The staff at the Public Archives of Canada, the Queen's University Archives, and the

Public Archives of Ontario also deserve praise for the splendid job they perform in support of historical research in Canada. I wish also to thank the Secretarial Services Department at York University and Mrs Shirley Ormsby who typed this manuscript. Finally, I would be remiss if I did not take this opportunity to thank my friends Ruth and Perry Coodin who kindly offered accommodation and companionship during my numerous visits to the Public Archives in Ottawa.

My last acknowledgement and my deepest gratitude are reserved for my wife, Karen, who always supported and encouraged me when I needed it most.

Tom Traves
York University

THE STATE AND ENTERPRISE

1
Economic change and regulation

The idea that the Canadian economy developed under the protective wing of the state is by now a familiar notion. Tiny markets, heavy overhead costs, persistent foreign competition, and the external control of necessary development capital and technological innovations impelled the state to sponsor measures to expand the reach of Canadian enterprise. Although the most persuasive accounts of the state's role focus on the resource sector and transportation improvements, the manufacturing sector offers no exception to the prevailing view.[1] The history of Canadian manufacturing cannot be understood outside the context of the complex institutional arrangements that businessmen and legislators created to promote, protect, and regulate industrial enterprise. At the same time, these arrangements deserve attention for the light they throw on the overall role of the state in a mature capitalist political economy. These concerns, the causes and consequences of the federal government's intervention in the Canadian economy between 1917 and 1931, constitute the basis of this study.[2]

1 The most useful discussions of these studies are found in W.T. Easterbrook, 'Recent Contributions to Economic History: Canada,' *Journal of Economic History*, 19, 1 (1959), and Glenn Porter, 'Recent Trends in Canadian Business and Economic History,' *Business History Review*, 47, 2 (1973).
2 It is necessary to distinguish between the state, the government, and the political system. The best discussion of these issues is found in Ralph Miliband, *The State in Capitalist Society* (London 1969), 49-55. The state system, as Miliband argues, is composed of the government, the public service, the military and police, the judicary, sub-central governments such as provincial and municipal institutions, and various local, provincial, and national legislative assemblies. The government is composed of those political factions which formally control the state executive offices by virtue of their ability to gain majority support within the legislative assembly. Only the government is formally invested with state power, and only the government can speak in the name of the state, but that does not mean that the government always effectively

Long-term changes in the structure of industrial capital in Canada created new problems and fresh demands for state intervention in the economy during and after the First World War. Traditionally, Canadian manufacturers depended on the state to help them protect established markets and expand into new areas of enterprise.[3] Tariffs, patent regulations, bonuses, and subsidies were the standard means to these ends. The growth of big business during the years following the introduction in 1879 of Sir John A. Macdonald's National Policy, moreover, led to increased pressure to continue these stimuli. Yet as the Great War drew to a close it became apparent to many leading businessmen that traditional policies alone would not suffice. The emergence of giant corporations, characterized by enormous fixed costs and oppressive long-term debts, had greatly increased the risks of economic instability, and passive measures like the tariff provided scant reassurance that record wartime profits would continue during the reconstruction period ahead.

Large corporations had dominated the industrial sector increasingly since the turn of the century. Although Canadian manufacturing was characterized by relatively small, regionally based enterprises at the time of Confederation, by 1890 the census recorded the beginning of a profound change in the country's industrial structure. Improved transportation facilities, attendant upon the completion of Canada's first transcontinental railroad in 1885, and a decade of extremely high tariff protection coincided with modest population increases since the 1860s to produce the Canadian industrial revolution. In addition to a tremendous expansion in the number of manufactories, from 38,402 to 70,123 between 1870 and 1890, the extent to which leading firms grew in terms of both assets and sales suggested a tendency towards industrial concentration as well as specialization.[4] During the next twenty years this trend became a permanent feature of the Canadian economy as businessmen strained to take advantage of the tremendous opportunities generated by immigration, increased export

controls all aspects of that state power. The degree of the government's control over the state system varies from moment to moment and from place to place. Finally, the state system is not synonymous with the political system, which includes formal political institutions such as parties and pressure groups, and institutions such as corporations, the mass media, the churches, and so on, which participate informally in the political system.

3 See H.G.J. Aitken, 'Defensive Expansion: The State and Economic Growth in Canada,' in Aitken, *The State and Economic Growth* (New York 1959), and W.T. Easterbrook, 'The Climate of Enterprise,' *American Economic Review, Papers and Proceedings*, 39 (1949)

4 Gordon Bertram, 'Historical Statistics on Growth and Structure of Manufacturing in Canada, 1870-1957,' Canadian Political Science Association, *Conference on Statistics*, 1962

capacities, further railroad construction, rapid urbanization, and the miraculous technological innovations associated with the introduction of hydroelectric power and, later, the internal combustion engine. As demand grew many firms naturally expanded, but certain producers (aided and abetted by a new breed of industrial stock promoters) sought a short cut to growth through corporate mergers. Between 1909 and 1913 the first great merger movement in Canada resulted in the consolidation of 221 firms, with over $200 million of assets, in 97 mergers. A host of huge new enterprises such as the Steel Company of Canada, Dominion Canners, Canada Cement, Canadian Cottons, and Dominion Glass Company appeared as a result.[5] The consequences of these developments were soon apparent. Between 1901 and 1921 the number and importance of big companies (characterized as those with over one million dollars in sales) grew steadily, from 39 in 1901, to 150 in 1911, and then to 410 by 1921. Collectively, the impact of these firms was enormous; together they accounted for 15 per cent of the total value of manufactured output in 1901, 31 per cent in 1911, and more than 51 per cent in 1921.[6]

The growth of big business in Canada featured two other noteworthy tendencies besides concentration: geographical centralization of the economy with concomitant regional underdevelopment, and the integration of the country's industrial leadership into the established commercial and financial élite which had long dominated the Canadian economic and political system. These two developments were of enormous importance subsequently in determining the evolution of the role of the state in the economy.

Shortly after the extension of the national transportation system, central Canadian manufacturers had expanded quickly to dominate both western and Maritime markets. Greater local opportunities, superior financial resources, better access to established capital markets, and favourable freight rates produced a decisive advantage for Montreal and Toronto manufacturers over their competitors in the Canadian hinterland.[7] By the 1920s the impact of this

5 See J.C. Weldon, 'Consolidations in Canadian Industry, 1900-1948,' in L.A. Skeoch, ed., *Restrictive Trade Practices in Canada* (Toronto 1966); R.T. Naylor, *The History of Canadian Business, 1867-1914*, II (Toronto 1975), chap. 14; and A.E. Epp, 'Cooperation among Capitalists: The Canadian Merger Movement, 1909-1913, Ph D thesis, Johns Hopkins University, 1973

6 Public Archives of Canada (PAC), Advisory Board on Tariff and Taxation Papers, RG36-11, vol. 64, file 0-70-8, table VI, Distribution of production between establishments of given sizes in 1901 and 1911; and Dominion Bureau of Statistics, *Canada Year Book, 1931* (Ottawa 1931), 363

7 D.J. Bercuson, ed., *Canada and the Burden of Unity* (Toronto 1977). The articles in this collection by E.R. Forbes, T.W. Acheson, and T.D. Regehr are especially noteworthy. See also T.W. Acheson, 'The Social Origins of Canadian Industrialism: A Study in the Structure of Entrepreneurship, unpublished Ph D thesis, University of Toronto, 1971

onslaught was clear. Interregional trade absorbed about 29 per cent of central Canadian production.[8] At the same time, the Maritimes had suffered a relative decline in both primary and secondary manufacturing. In 1900 the three Atlantic provinces had accounted for 9.9 per cent of national manufacturing output, but by 1926 this proportion had declined to 4.3 percent. Prairie producers fared somewhat better over the same period, increasing their share of national output from 3.1 per cent in 1900 to 6.9 per cent in 1926, but the region's output still lagged far behind its share of over one-fifth of the country's population.[9] Many western firms, moreover, operated as subsidiaries of Ontario or Quebec enterprises.[10]

As central Canadian manufacturers tightened their stranglehold on the country's industrial system, they gradually established binding alliances with powerful financial and commercial interests. By the outbreak of the war, according to T.W. Acheson, the character of Canada's industrial leadership had changed markedly in the direction of a modern corporate élite as compared to the small producers with narrow interests who had prevailed prior to the introduction of the National Policy. 'Members of the later elite tended to be organization men or financiers rather than individuals who, through heroic personal efforts, created major concerns. They tended, as well, to be found in those major cities in which the consolidation movements of the period had centred control of most manufacturing industry. And since industrial skills – in all but the newest technologies – were no longer a significant element in the industrial success of the entrepreneur, the industrialists of 1910 were far more likely to be lawyers, or high school graduates with some commercial training, than master machinists or journeyman clerks.' Economic integration also produced growing social cohesion among the industrial élite, who daily gathered 'in the board rooms of most major industrial corporations and met to discuss their mutual problems in the lounges of those exclusive social organizations which more than anything else symbolized their growing stature within the national community.'[11] Stephen Leacock's penetrating portrayal of the mem-

8 W.A. Mackintosh, *The Economic Background of Dominion-Provincial Relations* (Toronto 1964), 150
9 Bertram, 'Historical Statistics,' 120-1
10 Acheson, 'Social Origins of Canadian Industrialism,' chap. 5
11 Acheson, 'Changing Social Origins of the Canadian Industrial Elite, 1880-1910,' in G. Porter and R.D. Cuff, eds., *Enterprise and National Development* (Toronto 1973), 77-9. For discussions of the contemporary corporate elite, see John Porter, *The Vertical Mosaic* (Toronto 1965), and Wallace Clement, *The Canadian Corporate Elite* (Toronto 1975).

bers' activities at the Mausoleum Club in Plutoria provides a vivid picture of the social consequences of these meetings.[12]

Concentration, centralization, and socio-economic integration, however, did not prevent or hide the crisis confronting industrial Canada towards the end of the First World War. During the decade prior to the war the development of a western wheat boom and the construction of two new transcontinental railway systems led to rapid – too rapid – growth in the industrial sector. By 1913, when the wheat economy faltered and railway expansion collapsed, the serious overextension of the manufacturing sector drove many firms to failure. Although war contracts led to recovery by 1915, the Armistice would bring the threat of renewed instability. The peace so long desired was also feared, for it promised international economic chaos, increased foreign competition at home, and an end to guaranteed Allied markets abroad.

In the face of excess capacity and increased competition Canadian manufacturers began to cast about for fresh approaches to their problems, and, hesitantly, they initiated a search for the means to continued economic security through political regulation of the market. Wartime mobilization efforts provided the model for reconstruction planning. By 1917, at which time its wartime economic mobilization was completed, Canada had entered fully into the revolutionary maelstrom of modern warfare. 'War,' A.R.M. Lower has observed, 'as the greatest of economic forces, works many changes in men and affairs. It erases old, well worn patterns of behaviour and sets up new ones. It destroys old associations and establishes new. It shakes to its roots every institution, ancient or modern. By forcing the pace of technological invention, it changes the very environment in which men have to live.'[13] Undoubtedly the most significant innovation during the First World War was the development of the regulated society, not only in the armed services, but in the mine, the wheat field, the factory, the board room, and, ultimately, in the market-place. Regulation was the product of a drive towards order, which itself was an outcome of the need to organize complex social institutions so as to prosecute efficiently the war. But efficiency, rationality, and orderly regulation of complex phenomena were the hallmarks of the modern corporation, which also sought to marshal its forces to vanquish the uncertainties of the competitive struggle. The extension of wartime economic regulatory techniques seemed to provide the fresh approach needed for the reconstruction period.

Expanded institutional control of the economy, however, raised the question of political power in a new light. For economic regulation normally involves the

12 Leacock, *Arcadian Adventures of the Idle Rich* (New York 1914)
13 Lower, *Great Britain's Woodyard* (Montreal 1973), 45

use of state power to transfer wealth from one sector of the economy to another, or from one class to another. In short, regulation transforms competitive market relations into explicit political contests. But after 1917, national politics in Canada were far from simple. The breakdown of the established two-party system in the movement towards a Union government in 1917 blurred traditional loyalties and opened the door wide for other experiments in political organization. Although Union government promised the principles of business efficiency in public organizations, other interest groups in Canada also struggled to assert their power within the state apparatus. As many businessmen soon learned, regulation produced a good deal of frustration even while it offered hope.

The increased social cohesion of the Canadian 'haute bourgeoisie' described by Acheson masked a far from stable social order. Interregional, intersectoral, intra-industrial, and marked inter-class conflict prevailed on all fronts. While the Laurier and Borden governments strove mightily to integrate these conflicting interests into the established political system, their task was daunting. Uneven rates of regional development, against a backdrop of increased metropolitan dominance, produced sharp attacks upon national economic policies from both the western and eastern hinterlands. By 1917, western protests had crystallized in the Canadian Council of Agriculture's demand for a New National Policy. A few years later easterners also mobilized to seek 'better terms' under the banner of the Maritime Rights Movement.

While hinterland interests struggled to gain a larger share of the nation's wealth, the central Canadian business community was riven by internecine conflicts over economic policy. The struggle between the Canadian Manufacturers' Association and railway interests over freight rates and regulations, for example, resembled sectional grievances on this score.[14] Tariff policy also occasionally pitted one manufacturer against another. Although all agreed on the need for a 'living profit' and an 'equitable' tariff towards that end, many producers harboured suspicions that their suppliers could easily bear a modest tariff reduction in order to reduce the cost of factor inputs.[15] Thus, although class unity prevailed among industrialists in the face of challenges to either property or management rights, conventional politics still turned on the more immediate question of whose ox was gored.

Under these circumstances the state could not be either the businessman's abject servant or his all-powerful master. Naturally, manufacturers hoped to use

14 John English, *The Decline of Politics: The Conservatives and the Party System, 1901-20* (Toronto 1977), 51
15 Michael Bliss, *A Living Profit* (Toronto 1974)

the state to advance their interests, and, in the long view, it is clear that government decisions favoured manufacturers' interests over those of farmers, workers, or consumers. Such decisions also produced dividends for government leaders, of course, who were always anxious to secure the financial and political support of the business community. But political success did not depend exclusively on business support. Politicians like prime ministers Borden, Meighen, King, and Bennett responded to a broad range of forces in shaping their policies. The rise of the Union government movement in 1917, the meteoric advance of the farmers' Progressive party after 1920, and the vitality of the labour movements popularly associated with the Winnipeg General Strike of 1919, made political management especially difficult as new issues and new social forces challenged the patience and the ingenuity of traditional political leaders. Canada had changed dramatically during the first two decades of the century, and its politics reflected these changes.[16] As new issues -- for instance, the sympathetic general strike or the high price of important consumer and durable goods such as sugar and automobiles – began to exercise the public imagination, politicians had to tread carefully between powerful corporate interests and outraged public opinion. Of course, when the business community united behind a specific policy its influence was often decisive. The longevity of the National Policy tariff despite long-standing opposition from other interest groups stood testimony to that. But businessmen often divided on economic issues, and when they did the politician enjoyed greater independence and authority. Throughout the period from the war to the Great Depression, as manufacturers persistently advanced their claims upon the power of the state, politicians of necessity weighed each demand in balance against standards of national interest and political circumspection, with the latter usually determining the definition of the former. This point is crucial, for despite the ideological sympathies of leaders and their parties at this time there was never a simple translation of economic might into political power.

The businessman's desire to control his fate by regulating his environment proved exceptionally difficult under these circumstances. As W.T. Easterbrook has argued:

Entrepreneurial strategy in general may be described in terms of techniques designed to reduce uncertainty to the level of risks against which appropriate action may be taken; that is, in terms of a principle of 'conservation of certainty.' In the study of long-run change, however, the concept must be broadened to embrace the whole range of uncertainties that bear on entrepre-

16 English, *The Decline of Politics*

neurial decision making, not only those associated with economic competition, price fluctuations, income changes, but also those present in political unrest, social instability, problems of sanctions. The so-called 'competitive struggle,' then, takes the form of grappling with uncertainties rooted in economics, politics, and society, and for that matter, in the psychology of the individual.[17]

Following this line of thought it is clear that business behaviour cannot be understood simply as a response to market forces. In subsequent chapters, as we explore the interplay between the political, social, and economic factors that determined the environment within which Canadian manufacturers sought freedom of enterprise, this point will be clarified.

While the drive to control fractious elements within the political economy was constant throughout the period under review, it took many forms as changing conditions eliminated or promoted one or another strategy. These conditions and forms may be summarized briefly.

During the war and reconstruction period manufacturers and politicians tried a host of new techniques to organize the national economy. At first, the government's efforts stemmed from the need to mobilize and integrate Canadian efforts into the broader strategies adopted by the British and Americans. Mobilization, however, institutionalized political control of the economy and discounted market forces which hitherto had predominated. Since most manufacturers believed that the Armistice period promised general adversity and instability, many supported the reconstruction policies advocated by powerful organizations such as the Canadian Manufacturers' Association and the Canadian Reconstruction Association, which supported some form of continued economic regulation in the hope that government support would cushion the impact of the expected recession.

The appointment of the Board of Commerce in 1919 represented the culmination of this search for security through regulation. Manufacturers who supported the board, such as the sugar refiners, hoped that it would legitimize rising prices during inflationary periods and check precipitous price declines when deflationary pressures prevailed. However, not all producers supported the board. Such opposition to regulation within the business community reflected differing structural requirements, as well as a pervasive concern about the expanding role of the state in the economy. Not all producers feared disruption, for threat perception varied with the structure of the businessman's industry and the stability of his market. In some cases, fortunate manufacturers, such as the

17 Easterbrook, 'Uncertainty and Economic Change,' *Journal of Economic History*, 14 (1954), 349

pulp and paper producers, saw regulation as a check rather than as an inducement to enterprise. These producers opposed the Board of Commerce in the reconstruction period and its predecessor agencies, such as the Paper Controller, during the war years. For others, the prospects of continued political control of the economy prompted a sense of uneasiness about the future. To those whom Rotstein and Nelles call 'homesteaders on Bay Street,' increased regulation exacted a cost in terms of 'status, in conceptions of the self, in freedom to make certain traditional decisions, [and] in the disruption of once familiar and stable areas of managerial discretion.'[18]

The collapse of the Board of Commerce in 1920, and the increased political strength of hostile interest groups such as the farmers during Mackenzie King's minority administrations from 1921 to 1926, seriously reduced the manufacturers' prospects of checking the ravages of deteriorating market conditions. The twenties began and ended with a sharp recession, although the period from 1925 to 1929 produced record production and profit levels. Under such fluctuating circumstances, industrialists coped as best they could. Businessmen usually try to reduce costs and restrict competition during difficult periods and Canadian manufacturers followed this strategy closely during the twenties. In particular, many producers tried to reduce labour unrest, and hence restrict a major production cost, through the adoption of a host of so-called factory welfare programmes and company union schemes. A renewed merger movement and increased tariff protection offered the best hope of curtailing competition given the absence of more active regulatory mechanisms to control destructive conflict.

The government's extremely lenient anti-trust laws provided no obstacles for the merger movement, but the tariff question was a much less tractable issue. Farmers and liberal economists had long denounced the tariff as the 'mother of the trusts,' and the birth of the Progressive party, the 1919 provincial victory of the United Farmers of Ontario, and the emergence of a popular farmer-labour coalition in Nova Scotia in 1921 presaged a new, more powerful assault on the tariff in the future. Manufacturers responded to this challenge with a vigorous campaign designed to rally public support behind the historic National Policy. At the same time, they also sought to insulate the tariff against direct attack by promoting the establishment of a 'scientific' tariff board, which they hoped would 'take the tariff out of politics.' However, although the King government appointed an Advisory Board on Tariff and Taxation in 1926, the new agency

18 Robert E. Lane, *The Regulation of Businessmen* (Hamden, Conn. 1966), 35; Abraham Rotstein and H.V. Nelles, 'Canadian Business and the Eternal No,' in Rotstein, *The Precarious Homestead* (Toronto 1973)

did not provide a safe haven for Canadian industry. Like the Board of Commerce, the tariff board was only a mechanism to deal with uncertainty; it could not guarantee stability or prosperity. This became clear towards the end of the twenties, for although the radical attack waned with the return of prosperity, tariff questions still posed many problems for manufacturers. Put simply, the small Canadian market could not support extensive foreign competition as well as large-scale domestic production. Accordingly, many producers such as the automobile and primary steel manufacturers agitated for major tariff revisions in order to enlarge the effective demand for their own output. Needless to say, after the 1930 recession reduced business activities drastically these demands increased sharply. Although the Bennett government subsequently granted many of these requests, tariff changes alone could not curtail the impact of what rapidly became the worst economic disaster in Canadian history.

Finally, the study of business-government relations naturally prompts questions concerning the nature of the political economy and the role of the state in Canada. For example, is the state in a capitalist society the tool of the capitalist class? How are competitive corporate interests reconciled with broader class interests? How does the state promote social cohesion between competitive classes? What role do regulatory agencies play in this process? And, finally, how are these functions reflected in the structure of the state itself? These questions will be taken up in the concluding chapter of this study.

PART ONE

WAR, RECONSTRUCTION, AND ACTIVE REGULATION

2
The Canadian
Reconstruction Association

As war-weary Canadians pondered the meaning of their efforts during the Great War, many looked forward to the birth of a 'new era' in Canada. Clergymen, professors, and politicians all offered a reading of the past and hopes for the future that sometimes bordered on the utopian. Businessmen, too, responded to the rebirth of idealism. In part, their attitudes were conditioned by a deep-rooted faith in the material promise of the so-called 'gospel of efficiency.' At the same time, however, the businessman's assessment of the future reflected his perceptions of prospective economic conditions and his understanding of the wartime lessons about the possibilities of institutional change through national mobilization. More and more, as businessmen looked forward, government intervention in the economy figured prominently in their plans. Indeed, many had flocked to Prime Minister Borden's Union government in 1917 precisely because it promised to realize their demands for change. As Borden's biographer has commented, '... Big Government did come to Ottawa during the war. And there are not a few indications that at least some members of the second Borden government, including the Prime Minister, desired that Big Government, regulatory government, managerial government, should continue after the war. In basic objectives, in the interests of efficiency and management and development of the economy, Borden and many businessmen were in agreement.'[1] Perhaps no other business organization agreed more with Borden than the Canadian Reconstruction Association.

1 J.O. Miller, ed., *The New Era in Canada* (Toronto 1917), and R.C. Brown and R. Cook, *Canada, 1896-1921: A Nation Transformed* (Toronto 1974), chap. 15; Samuel Haber, *Efficiency and Uplift: Scientific Management in the Progressive Era, 1890-1920* (Chicago 1964); R.C. Brown, 'The Political Ideas of Robert Borden,' in Marcel Hamelin, ed., *The Political Ideas of the Prime Ministers of Canada* (Ottawa 1969), 94-6: see also John English, *The Decline of Politics: The Conservatives and the Party System, 1901-20* (Toronto 1977)

In March 1918 the provisional executive of the Canadian Home Manufacturers' Association (CHMA) decided to revive its moribund organization, dormant since the successful campaign against the 1911 Canadian-American reciprocity agreement. As proof of its renewed vitality, the association redefined both its purpose and its image. The executive adopted a new name, the Canadian Reconstruction Association (CRA), and the slogan 'Unity – Stability – Prosperity' became its goal as well as its motto. More specifically, the association demanded 'that the Government should make definite pronouncement on all public questions regarding industry, to overcome the uncertainty which exists throughout the industrial and financial centres of Canada.'[2] The policies of the CRA were nothing if not idealistic, for the association's leaders believed that the public interest would best be served through the achievement of 'Cooperation between employers and employed, between East and West, and between field and factory in a common national policy that will develop alike agriculture and industry, keep Canadians at home, attract immigration and make Canada more self-reliant and more capable of carrying its war burden.'[3] Despite the usual dose of humbug inherent in such pronouncements, the CRA was grimly serious about its mission – the future of industrial capitalism in Canada.

The uncertainty that troubled the leaders of industrial Canada stemmed from three sources. In the first place, economic prospects looked bleak. For the past four years the nation's productive energies had been directed to one goal, the supply of required munitions and supplies. In welcome contrast to the sharp recession of the immediate prewar period most plants operated near full capacity and businessmen earned record profits in most sectors and regions.[4] The imminent end of the war, however, threatened to terminate this prosperity. Peace would bring the end of munitions contracts, decreased exports, and increased foreign competition, unprecedented problems reintegrating thousands of soldiers into the labour force, and enormous war debts. Unless the transition

2 Public Archives of Canada (PAC) Minutes of the Canadian Reconstruction Association (hereafter cited as CRA Minutes), book II, p. 1, Meeting of Provisional Executive Committee, 14 March 1918; book III, p. 15, Executive Committee Meeting, 9 Dec. 1918. The association initially called itself the Canadian Industrial Reconstruction Association, but changed its name shortly afterward to reflect its broader purposes.
3 PAC, Sir John Willison Papers, MG30D14, vol. 12, file 52, 4198-4200, Willison to H.R. Thompson, 18 Nov. 1918
4 F.H. Brown, 'The History of Canadian War Finance, 1914-1920,' in Canadian Institute of International Affairs, *War Finance in Canada* (Toronto 1940), 17; K.A.J. Hay, 'Early Twentieth Century Business Cycles in Canada,' *Canadian Journal of Economics and Political Science*, 32 (1966); Edward J. Chambers, 'Canadian Business Cycles since 1919: A Progress Report,' *ibid.*, 24 (1958)

to a peacetime economy was carefully planned, reconstruction would spell economic chaos.

Economic problems were compounded by the prospect of increased social and political unrest across the country. Organized labour, for example, was caught up in a desperate battle between syndicalist and conservative craft union forces. At the same time, the rate of strikes in Canada increased markedly as working people struggled to keep up with the ever-rising cost of living. Moreover, as class tensions rose, so did sectional grievances. The farmers' movement, which the CHMA had helped to defeat so decisively in 1911, had regrouped politically to mount yet another campaign for lower tariffs.[5]

The CHMA executive doubted whether other businessmen's organizations possessed either the policies or the political resources to defeat these challenges. The Canadian Manufacturers' Association (CMA), for example, was tainted by its record as a narrow interest group, a reputation it had justly earned in past battles with farmers and unions alike. Indeed CMA leaders had established the CHMA in 1911 precisely in order to escape that stigma. Similar motives prompted the establishment of the CRA in 1918. As its president, the noted publisher, royal commissioner, and publicist, Sir John Willison, complained about a fellow executive member who had long ruled in the councils of the CMA: 'No leader among the grain growers or low tariff element will cooperate with [W.J.] Bulman. His only idea is conflict while I believe that cooperation is the only policy which this Association can pursue until it is convinced that cooperation will produce no results.'[6]

The CRA did not serve simply as a front group for the CMA, however. Although the members of the CRA executive committee – John F. Ellis, Huntley Drummond, W.K. George, C.H. Godfrey, W.J. Bulman, and Sir Augustus Nanton – achieved prominence in the CMA, real tensions existed between the two organizations. For one thing, the CRA raised substantial revenues by a one dollar per employee tax on manufacturing companies and by negotiating contributions with the banks, railroads, and trust companies, thus reducing the availability of funds to the CMA. More importantly, the CRA represented somewhat different interests than the CMA. At bottom, the CRA spoke only for

5 Stuart M. Jamieson, *Times of Trouble: Labour Unrest and Industrial Conflict, 1900-66*, Task Force on Labour Relations, under the Privy Council Office, Study no 22 (Ottawa 1968), 159; W.L. Morton, *The Progressive Party in Canada* (Toronto 1950), chaps 1 and 2

6 Brown and Cook, *Canada, 1896-1921*, 1.81; Willison Papers, vol. 24, file 100, 8638-9, Willison to H.R. Drummond, 15 Nov. 1918. Precisely the same point seems to have been at issue between the *Financial Post* and the CMA. See Floyd S. Chalmers, *A Gentleman of the Press* (Toronto 1969), 225.

big business interests in Canada. It did not have to cater to the smaller businessmen who numerically dominated the CMA and who demanded a much more narrowly defined and combative approach to the rights of property. Subtle bureaucratic conflicts and differences of interest thus informed Willison's complaint that 'the truth is that certain people in the Canadian Manufacturers' Association think it would be better to carry on their publicity over the Association's name and have never liked the creation of an independent organization not responsible to the Canadian Manufacturers' Association officers.'[7]

Willison's independent organization developed three major policies to mitigate the problems of the reconstruction period. In the first place, the association demanded significant expansion of government promotional and regulatory assistance in order to minimize the impact of the expected postwar recession. Next, the CRA recommended that Canadian businessmen undertake a full-scale review of their industrial relations practices with a view to mollifying their increasingly disaffected employees. Finally, the association wanted to prevent major tariff revisions in the postwar era.

During the war Canadian industry profited from guaranteed sales to government agencies and their suppliers, but during the reconstruction period businessmen expected a renewal of competition both at home and abroad. Moreover, as a CRA pamphlet explained, many Canadians anticipated the worst of this competition:

The development of industry in Canada ... is taking place under competition from probably the most highly organized industrial country in the world, proficient in mass production, with powerful manufacturing concerns distributed over the entire length of a 3000-mile boundary line, making the same classes and styles of goods that are used in Canada, and ready for any opportunity to cut into the Canadian market. Many of those industries in the United States are still protected in their home market by high tariff duties, and to some extent at least they use Canada as a dumping ground for their products. In addition there is competition from the United Kingdom and other countries, and these competitors for the most part have industries well established and plants provided at pre-war costs.[8]

7 CRA Minutes, book II, p. 2, and Willison Papers, vol. 71, file 273, 26408, Willison to
   W.E. Rundle, National Trust Co., 15 July 1919; S.D. Clark, *The Canadian Manufacturers'
   Association* (Toronto 1939), 66-7; Willison Papers, vol. 24, file 100, 8658-9, Willison to
   Drummond, 29 March 1920
8 Canadian Reconstruction Association (CRA), *Buy Canadian Products*, May 1921

In order to withstand such competition the CRA argued that Canadians must improve their products, rationalize their production systems, and reorganize their sales efforts. For one thing the events of the last decade had demonstrated clearly that scientific research held the key to economic progress. 'It is not too much to say,' declared a CRA pamphlet, 'that Germany's commercial position before the war was due to the association of science and industry.'[9] In the postwar period, Canada's most serious competitor also would benefit from this association. 'The truth is,' Sir John Willison commented, 'that German efficiency at its best will be outrun by American efficiency. Fifty industrial companies in the United States are spending from $25,000 to $500,000 a year in research. The Mellon Institute, the Massachusetts School of Technology, Harvard, Columbia, Wisconsin and other American universities have an incomparable equipment. Their services to American industry are beyond estimation. If the investment is heavy the returns are commensurate.' Few Canadian firms, however, possessed sufficient resources to finance their own research programmes, and only Canadian governments could organize and finance such projects. Accordingly, the CRA proposed that the federal government establish a bureau of standards to study processes and materials used in industry and a research bureau to supervise basic scientific projects. They also advocated increased assistance for the University of Toronto and McGill University to support post-graduate and research work in the country's two main science faculties.[10] Despite the apparent urgency of these proposals, however, they received little government support. Although the Advisory Council for Scientific and Industrial Research, the predecessor of the National Research Council, was established in 1916, it received minimal assistance and most of its activity amounted to campaigning for additional aid. Government parsimony, internal rivalries in the tiny Canadian scientific community, and bureaucratic conflicts between the universities and government agencies seriously restricted the prospects for the CRA's proposals.[11]

The benefits of organization and specialization were another important lesson which the CRA had gleaned from the war experience, for Canadian producers had obviously achieved substantial benefits by combining their efforts in the interest of economic rationalization and efficiency. Willison argued that

9 CRA, *Ways to National Prosperity*, 1 June 1920
10 CRA, *A National Policy*, 17 July 1918, speech by Sir John Willison
11 Mel Thistle, *The Inner Ring: The Early History of the National Research Council of Canada* (Toronto 1966), and Peter Oliver, 'Government, Industry and Science in Ontario: The Case of the Ontario Research Foundation,' in his *Public and Private Persons* (Toronto 1975)

continued co-operation and organization would produce similar results in the postwar era:

There could be no clearer evidence of the genius and resourcefulness of Canadian manufacturers and the skill of Canadian labor than what had been achieved under the Imperial Munitions Board ... If it be true that without definite direction and organization these results could not have been achieved it is also true that the manufacturers and workmen who have made these results possible are not lacking in skill, enterprise or courage. Under likewise direction and organization the industries of Canada should be as effective in the era of construction as they have been in the era of destruction.

The CRA tied most of these arguments in favour of industrial rationalization to the requirements of the export trade. The implications of these arguments for domestic economic activity were profound, however. 'Canadian manufacturing establishments have been largely dependent upon our relatively small home market and there has been a notable lack of specialization,' the association reported. 'There is need in Canada that manufacturers of similar products should be brought together; that an agreement should be reached upon limitation of the number of lines that they will produce; and that they should look to the foreign market as well as to the home market so that the obvious advantages of quantity production may be obtained.' The CRA illustrated this point by regular reports on American standardization efforts and also commissioned studies of the possibilities of Canadian co-operation in this respect.[12]

These efforts to promote industrial efficiency were but a small part of a much larger scheme to establish export combinations under the aegis of the state. The CRA argued that agencies modelled on the War Trade Board, which had been established in 1918 to organize and facilitate Canadian sales through US war boards, should assume the power to fix prices and prorate available export production among member firms. 'If we are to have an adequate share in the rebuilding of the ruined nations,' Willison proclaimed, 'Canadian industries must organize with vigor, foresight and courage. They must cooperate to secure the necessary knowledge of conditions abroad. They must establish joint selling agencies.' These proposals clearly implied a marked reduction in domestic competition as well as foreign competition. It could not be otherwise, and the

12 CRA, *Confidential Bulletin no 1*, 2 Dec. 1918, and *Standardization and Specialization*, 25 March 1918. Before 1913 Canada exported about 7 per cent of its total manufactured output. Between 1916 and 1918 exports rose to over 40 percent of total output. Brown and Cook, *Canada, 1896-1921*, 234

CRA anticipated and welcomed this result. Looking abroad, Willison noted approvingly: 'In the Mother Country the sacred doctrine of individualism is treated with violence; in the United States industrial combination is no longer regarded as the sum of social and political villainy.' The 'flight from competition,' which had proceeded at a rapid pace for several decades, appeared to reach a new peak of intensity during the war years.[13]

The CRA's proposals for economic reorganization raised important questions about the relationship of the war experience to the development of industrial capitalism in Canada. Robert Cuff has argued that in the United States:

Administrators believed that their task in industrial mobilization included saving and strenghtening the country's industrial structure for the postwar years ... With their emphasis on economic stability, rationality, efficiency and industry-wide cooperation, these men sought to expand through state organization the values associated with modern corporate capitalism. During the war they experimented with national institutional arrangements which Presidents Hoover and Roosevelt would enlarge upon twenty years later in their efforts to save capitalism itself. The war served an important function in educating the new public administrators to the relationships which could be established among different kinds of private organizations and then combined in turn with public power.[14]

Clearly the values promoted by the CRA bore a striking resemblance to those described by Cuff. On the other hand, Michael Bliss has compared Canadian and American businessmen at war and concluded that 'we are dealing with men holding different values, operating in differently structured economies at different stages of development.' To illustrate this point Bliss cited Imperial Munitions Board chairman Sir Joseph Flavelle's view 'that emergency measures necessary for the war are not applicable to peace time.'[15] This illustration, however, glosses over the crucial experiences of 1919-20, which saw first the

13 CRA, *Confidential Bulletin no 3*, 22 Jan. 1919. For a discussion of the War Trade Board, see R.D. Cuff and J.L. Granatstein, *Canadian-American Relations in Wartime* (Toronto 1975), chap. 3, and O. Mary Hill, *Canada's Salesman to the World: The Department of Trade and Commerce, 1892-1939* (Montreal 1977), 177-80. See Michael Bliss, *A Living Profit* (Toronto 1974), chap. 2, for a discussion of the preceding phase of what he calls 'the flight from competition.'
14 Cuff, 'Organizing for War: Canada and the United States during World War I,' Canadian Historical Association, Historical Papers, 1969, p. 153
15 Bliss, 'A Canadian Businessman and War: The Case of Joseph Flavelle,' in J.L. Granatstein and R.D. Cuff, *War and Society in North America* (Toronto 1971), 36, 23

extension of state regulation and then its retraction. It also fails to acknowledge the political significance of the low-tariff movement's challenge to the hegemony of industrial interests in Canada.

Following the Armistice the Union government extended wartime price and production controls over a wide range of commodities. In some cases, such as the newsprint industry, the powers of wartime controllers were simply extended; in other cases, a new agency, the Board of Commerce, brought the appearance of order to peacetime markets. While businessmen generally supported these controls as a temporary measure, most hesitated before committing themselves to such a programme as the basis of a permanent new economic and political order. For one thing, businessmen feared that desperate politicians might sell their interests short in order to maintain power. Moreover, while regulation promised a measure of stability overall, in some industries producers found their freedom of enterprise too closely checked for comfort. In the long run, these hesitations hardened into outright opposition. As newsprint prices doubled and then tripled after the war, for example, pulp and paper producers protested vigorously that the paper controller's order to sell newsprint to Canadian publishers at reduced prices was an unwarranted interference with the rights of property. For their part, Canadian sugar refiners suffered grievously when the cabinet annulled an order issued by the Board of Commerce to establish a floor price under the collapsing sugar market. Both the paper makers and the refiners recognized that the government would not listen sympathetically to their problems so long as more pressing political interests claimed its attention.[16] Ultimately businessmen came to realize that political stability was essential for the success of any programme promising long-term, state-supported economic stability. Organizations such as the CRA, therefore, dropped their ambition to achieve security through regulation and took up the more fundamental problem of stemming the rising tide of social and political unrest across the country.

The CRA believed that low-tariff agrarian interests posed the greatest threat to industrial Canada in the postwar period. Although the CRA tried to find common ground between industrial and agrarian interests, the conflict over tariff policy provided little room for compromise. Needless to say, the association advanced the usual argument that 'there is a natural economic relationship between agriculture and industry which makes home market development advantageous to farm and factory.' But export-oriented farmers put little stock in domestic sales opportunities. Quite realistically, they preferred to reduce their costs by promoting freer trade. The CRA, like the CHMA before it, would not tolerate such tampering with the National Policy and concluded: 'It is

16 These two cases are discussed in detail in Chapters 3 and 4.

thoughtlessly suggested that after four years of war, with the universal disturbance and dislocation which the war has produced, there should be revolutionary fiscal changes which at any time and under the most favourable conditions would be infinitely perplexing and disturbing. It is inconceivable that the Grain Growers would press their revolutionary demands at this time if they had ever seriously considered the certain consequences of their proposals.'[17] To counteract the farmers' influence in Ottawa the CRA proposed that the government establish a 'scientific' tariff board, whose purpose would be 'to take the tariff out of politics.'

The CRA and the CMA believed that a tariff board would insulate the tariff schedule against politically expedient piecemeal revisions. Demands for such a board dated back to the 1890s when it appeared that low-tariff Liberals might succeed to authority within the state.[18] Subsequently, when the Liberals proved their loyalty to the National Policy, these demands abated, but they were revived whenever the government's support for protection seemed to waver. In addition, by 1918 American experience appeared to confirm the political value of the tariff board. 'Fortunately at Washington they have a Tariff Board which informs Congress and ensures that legislation for or against the industries of the country will not be rashly enacted," the CRA observed. 'We need some such Board in Canada, not to instruct, but to inform Parliament, and not representing any single interest, but concerned to provide facts and show actual conditions.' More specifically, advocates of the board wanted it to 'make a scientific study of the Canadian Customs Tariff and the tariffs of other countries with whose products Canadian producers are forced to compete, familiarize itself with costs of production at home and abroad, [and] investigate the nature and probable national effect of all requests for tariff changes.'[19] Of course, this board could not prevent low-tariff interests from dismantling the National Policy if they gained complete ascendancy in Parliament. But in the more likely event that a multi-interest party tried to hang on to power by selective tariff reductions, a tariff board would provide a bureaucratic check to prevent politicians from throwing over isolated manufacturing interests one by one. The CRA hoped that a tariff board which was sympathetic to its industrial constituency could serve as a shield against unfavourable political deals.

To promote its views, the CRA mounted a major public relations campaign across Canada. A flood of pamphlets, pay envelope cards, newspaper advertise-

17 *Ways to National Prosperity*; CRA, *Co-operation or Conflict*, 18 March 1919
18 Bliss, *A Living Profit*, 127
19 *Co-operation or Conflict; Industrial Canada*, July 1922, p. 132, resolution of the 1922 CMA general meeting

ments, and industrial movies everywhere proclaimed the need for a continuation of the National Policy and the desirability of creating a tariff board. Although the association made periodic attempts to address agrarian interests, most of its propaganda was directed towards the industrial workingman and his recently enfranchised wife. Both were warned that 'economic theories provide neither jobs nor wages. If the worker is to have both without any disastrous interruptions in industrial activity it must be through a continuation of the National Policy which has built up Canada.'[20]

The CRA's efforts to woo the workingman reflected its analysis of rapidly shifting political conditions in Canada. As sectional and class conflicts became more intense the political system began to buckle under the strain. By mid-1919, when Agriculture Minister Thomas Crerar broke with the government, agrarian interests seemed irrevocably committed to an independent course in politics.[21] The CRA feared that workingmen might follow a similar path. When the United Farmers of Ontario and the Independent Labour party allied to form a new provincial administration in Ontario after the general election of 1919 these apprehensions appeared to have been warranted. "I do not like the alliance here between the United Farmers and Labor,' Willison observed. 'It may last or it may not. If we lose labor the industrial system of this country cannot survive.'[22]

The CRA pursued two major policies to bind labour more tightly to the country's 'industrial system.' First, the association tried to reduce class tensions by improving industrial relations in Canada.[23] To this end the CRA urged businessmen to drop their unreasonable opposition to union organizations and to recognize the chosen representatives of their employees. While the CRA preferred and advocated the establishment of company unions, it recognized that in some cases events had moved too swiftly for such conservative proposals and that broadly based collective bargaining was inevitable. Willison expressed the association's views on this point most forcefully:

The separation between employers and employees seems to be a necessary result of modern industrial conditions. The old and ideal relationship between the master and his journeyman has gone forever. There has come the great factory and the great industrial corporation, great systems of transportation, great financial and corporate combinations. The workman goes in and out of these

---

20 *Industrial Canada*, Oct. 1921, p. 50; see also CRA, *Progress Bulletin no 11*, 18 April 1919
21 Morton, *Progressive Party*, 96
22 Willison Papers, vol. 5, file 42, 3574, Willison to W.J. Bulman, 27 Oct. 1919
23 This issue is discussed in more detail in Chapter 5.

huge establishments, a stranger to the manager and ignorant, often, of the very names of the boards of directors. The tools with which he works are not his own, the machine he tends, the engine he drives, the ship he directs belongs to a corporation whose stocks are on the Exchange and whose investments too often are their concern. Their relationship with labor is impersonal and remote; their interest in dividends personal and direct. Under such conditions the organization of labor is natural and necessary and occasional misunderstanding and conflict are inevitable.

Along with union recognition, the CRA suggested that Canadian industrialists attempt to co-opt organized labour with factory welfare programmes and some semblance of co-operation and consultation on peripheral issues such as plant safety, accident compensation, and insurance schemes of various kinds.[24] Willison concluded that 'such a co-operative relation would go far to establish the complete identity of interest between capital and labor, and to defeat the devices of demagogues, and to steady the social forces.' These policies appear to confirm the CRA's big business orientation since interest at this time in factory welfare plans and company unions was concentrated mainly in larger firms.[25]

In addition to its public policies, the CRA initiated a covert campaign designed to commit individual unions and the Trades and Labor Congress (TLC) to support both protection and the establishment of a tariff board. While many elements in the labour movement naturally supported the National Policy, its organizations were far from united on the issue. During the 1911 election, for example, labour councils in Winnipeg and Montreal expressed approval of the government's reciprocity agreement with the United States.[26] In 1919 labour's position was still unclear. As Willison complained, 'with organized farmers committed to a definite policy of radical tariff reduction and with the present association between the farmers and labor in Ontario and other provinces, it is hard to determine exactly where labor leaders stand on the whole question.'[27] If labour could be persuaded to unite behind the business community's demand for a tariff board, however, the CRA and the CMA could promote their policy as one which transcended both class and sectional divisions in Canada.

24 CRA, *Tariff, Labor and Unity*, speech by T.A. Russell. This point is dealt with in greater detail in Chapter 5. For an interesting case study, see Bruce Scott, 'A Place in the Sun: The Industrial Council at Massey-Harris, 1919-1929,' *Labour/Le Travailleur*, 1 (1976).
25 H.C. Pentland, *A Study of the Changing Social, Economic and Political Background of the Canadian System of Industrial Relations*, Task Force on Labour Relations, Project no 1a (Ottawa 1968), 100
26 Charles Lipton, *The Trade Union Movement of Canada* (Toronto 1973), 158
27 Willison Papers, vol. 66, file 253, 24933, Willison to George Pierce, undated

Willison explained the CRA's covert campaign briefly to the president of Stelco, Robert Hobson:

We have spent thousands of dollars among labor leaders in the hope of getting a satisfactory judgement at the Dominion Trades and Labor Congress now meeting in Hamilton. Whatever that judgement may be many labor unions have been induced to pass resolutions in favour of a tariff commission and fiscal stability, and something has been done to strenghthen the resistance of moderate Labor leaders to the One Big Unionists. Here is a story which cannot be told in a letter, which in many of its details is necessarily confidential, but the Committee acted on assurances that certain results would be secured and I have carried out the judgement of the Committee as best I could and in so far as resources were available.

The committee that directed Willison's actions was composed of T.P. Howard, W.J. Bulman, and C. Howard Smith, all past and future presidents of the CMA, W.A. Black, who headed Ogilvie Flour Mills, and Edward Beatty of the CPR. George Pierce, a labour journalist, was the association's contact in the union movement. Pierce was editor of the *Canadian Railroader*, a monthly magazine published by a committee of international union officials associated with the conservative running trades brotherhoods.[28]

The CRA's ends and means were quite simple. As T.P. Howard explained: 'I have kept in touch with these [union] people from the start and am quite convinced that they are working steadily towards the desired end of the appointment of a Scientific Tariff Board and will pass a resolution to this effect at the Annual [TLC] Convention in Hamilton ... Consequently it is my opinion that with a little careful handling, we will have these people with us, whereas in the past, they were certainly against us.' To assist and encourage Pierce and his associates in their efforts the CRA agreed to pay $5000 immediately, and another $25,000 in nine monthly instalments. Subsequently, the CRA agreed to increase the final total payment to $50,000. Although initially dubious about this agreement, Willison finally concluded in October 1919 that 'this work, I know, is of far more importance than anything else in Canada.'[29]

Despite their efforts the CRA's hopes did not materialize precisely as desired. It is true that in January 1920 Pierce and Paddy Draper, secretary-treasurer of

28 *Ibid.*, vol. 41, file 151, 15337, Willison to Hobson, 25 Sept. 1919; vol. 42, file 156, 15746, Howard to Willison, 21 July 1919; vol. 33, file 253, 24942, G.D. Robertson, minister of labour, to Sir Henry Drayton, minister of finance, 22 Jan. 1920
29 *Ibid.*, Howard to Willison, 21 July; 15740, Howard to Willison, 7 July; 15744, Willison to Howard, 18 July; 15758, Willison to Howard, 16 Oct. 1919

the TLC, lobbied the government to appoint a tariff board. Moreover, several months later, the TLC convention unanimously passed a resolution to the same effect. As TLC president Tom Moore explained: 'We believe that Parliament should retain the right to finally pass upon any Tariff Regulations, but only after the fullest and most scientific investigation by a competent Board, and which should be constituted, because of the vital importance to wage earners, so as to have at least one of their chosen representatives upon such a Board.'[30] The government, however, was unmoved by these efforts. Fierce opposition to the tariff board in western Canada could not be ignored.

As the Unionist government desperately clung to office by playing off one set of interests against another, the leaders of the CRA gradually lost hope in their enterprise. The collapse of the most important reconstruction agency, the Board of Commerce, in October 1920, and the growing strength of the Progressive party throughout 1921, doomed their cause. In due course it became clear that propaganda alone would not suffice and businessmen transferred their energies from the CRA's campaigns to more traditional partisan political activities. Although the association spent over $213,000 on its activities to October 1919, during the next year expenditures declined by $100,000, and funds became increasingly scarce. In January 1921 the CRA closed its Winnipeg and Montreal offices, leaving only Toronto, and in November, a month before the federal election, Sir John Willison resigned from the presidency of the association. By that time Willison and other CRA leaders had concluded that only a straight party fight could stem the tide of agrarian radicalism. Following the disastrous results of the 1921 election, from which Mackenzie King emerged as the leader of a minority Liberal administration dependent for its survival upon the Progressive party, which captured sixty-five seats, fifteen more than the protectionist Tories, the CRA executive finally gave up the ghost, paid off its debts, and turned the association's remaining funds over to a trustee.[31]

Gabriel Kolko once described the outcome of business-government relations in the United States during this period as the 'triumph of conservatism,' and argued that big business interests in the United States aspired to and partially succeeded in using political institutions to attain stability, predictability, and security in the economy in order to rationalize the entire social order. Stability was defined as freedom from competition and economic fluctuations; predictability as the ability to establish corporate plans on the basis of reasonably

30 PAC, Tariff Commission, 1920 Papers, RG36-8, vol. 9, file 27, p. 5675; testimony of Tom Moore, 3 Jan. 1921
31 CRA Minutes, book III, p. 39, 21 Nov. 1919; p. 46, 27 Oct. 1920; p. 51, 21 Jan. 1921; p. 54, 28 Nov. 1922; pp. 57-8, 7 June 1922

calculable expectations; and security as freedom from attack by other interest groups embedded in the political structure. Kolko concluded: 'I do not give rationalization its frequent definition as the improvement of efficiency, output or internal organization of a company, I mean by the term, rather, the organization of the economy and the larger political and social spheres in a manner that will allow corporations to function in a predictable and secure environment permitting reasonable profits over the long run.'[32]

As we shall see, one critical difference distinguished the Canadian experience from the American. Organizations such as the CRA clearly espoused the same values and promoted policies similar to those pursued by American businessmen. Understandably, leading industrialists in Canada were extremely sensitive to the need for economic stability and predictability. Indeed, large corporations with substantial fixed costs could hardly survive under any other circumstances. But despite their aspirations Canadian businessmen obviously failed to rationalize either the economy or the social order in the reconstruction period. They failed principally because they did not achieve political security. To escape agrarian, labour, and small business interests, which usually expressed themselves most forcefully at a local level, American corporate leaders turned to their national government to provide favourable legislation and protection. In Canada this tactic proved impossible. Agrarian interests were a major force in national as well as provincial politics, and organizational and institutional differences between the Canadian and American political systems prevented Canadian corporate interests from prevailing after the fashion of their southern counterparts.[33] Failure, however, cannot be equated with want of trying.

The policies promoted by the CRA at the end of the Great War correspond to big business perceptions of political and economic conditions. By 1918 Canada's industrial system was highly centralized. At the same time, though, the national market was quite small, foreign competition was fierce, and industrial prosperity was closely tied to the level of staple exports. Thus, despite their wealth and power, Canadian industrial leaders were extremely vulnerable to economic dislocation. The measures which the CRA proposed were designed to minimize this danger. Political and economic developments, however, did not favour the association's programme. Ultimately the CRA retreated and regrouped to protect its most important position, the tariff. 'Reconstruction' was forgotten amid the fray that followed, but the economic imperatives that demanded increased state regulation remained, and in the decades that followed another depression and another war would provide a fresh impetus to renewed action.

32 Kolko, *The Triumph of Conservatism* (London 1963), 3
33 For a similar conclusion, see Christopher Armstrong and H.V. Nelles, 'Private Property in Peril: Ontario Businessmen and the Federal System, 1898-1911,' in G. Porter and R.D. Cuff, eds., *Enterprise and National Development* (Toronto 1973).

3
The regulation of
the newsprint industry

The Great War provided the spark for many fresh departures from established custom in Canada. Female suffrage, prohibition, and conscription stand out most sharply in this respect. The rapid proliferation of wartime economic regulatory agencies, however, was an equally critical departure from the norm. Between 1916 and 1918 the federal government created the National Service Board, the Acting Commissioner re Cost of Living, the Board of Grain Supervisors, Food, Fuel, and Paper Controllers, and the War Trade Board to serve alongside the Imperial Munitions Board, which had been appointed in 1915.[1] Many of these agencies were established to facilitate the integration of Canadian war production into the increasingly bureaucratized mobilization efforts of American and British administrators, but it is important to appreciate that regulation also provided opportunities for some businessmen to secure readjustment of the terms of trade between suppliers, producers, and consumers in their industry by virtue of their political power within the new regulatory institutions. The newsprint industry provides a striking case in point.

The modern newsprint industry in Canada developed mainly to supply the demands of American newspaper publishers. By 1917, 86.4 per cent of all Canadian newsprint production was exported, mostly to the United States.[2] Naturally, price and production policies in Canada varied directly with changes in American consumption habits. Although Canadian domestic demand was a marginal factor in the industry's overall development, however, Canadian consumers nevertheless attempted periodically to subvert market forces to control the domestic price of Canadian newsprint. Under normal circumstances,

1 J.A. Corry, 'The Growth of Government Activities in Canada, 1914-1921,' Canadian Historical Association, *Historical Papers*, 1940
2 C.R. Coughlin, 'The Newsprint Industry in Canada,' unpublished MA thesis, McGill University, 1939, p. 65, table 11

of course, marginal consumers have little bargaining power; but in the newsprint industry consumers wielded power well beyond the ordinary. Since they controlled the principal means of mass communication, newspaper publishers tried to use their political influence to force the government to support their desire for favourable newsprint contracts. The leaders of the giant newsprint industry, however, also possessed considerable economic and political influence, and late in 1916 this conflict between producers and consumers came to a head when Canadian publishers formally demanded federal regulation of the newsprint industry.

The outbreak of war had failed to interrupt the steady expansion of Canadian newsprint production. By 1916 Canadian output had climbed roughly 70 per cent above the production level of 1913. Before the war ended production climbed another 21 per cent; and by 1920 Canadian producers increased their output by a further 19 per cent (see Figure 3.1). These phenomenal increases in production were prompted by an apparently limitless American demand for newsprint. The mergence of mass markets had provoked a steady expansion in newspaper advertising, which in turn had caused an inexorable increase in the size of American newspapers.[3] While demand increased, however, American production lagged because of dwindling pulpwood reserves and rising costs. After the turn of the century the American industry began to turn north, and increased Canadian production levels followed. These developments were reinforced by a variety of legislative enactments during the first two decades of the century including the removal of the American tariff on newsprint imports and a Canadian embargo on pulpwood exports by the Ontario and Quebec governments, which wanted local production of provincial resources.[4]

Despite these increases in production, however, demand completely outstripped the rate of supply towards the end of 1916, and newsprint prices began to increase rapidly, from $2.00 per cwt. in 1916 to $3.50 in 1917, an increase of

3 *Ibid.*, 233, app. A, table 1; see also the *Financial Post*, 24 Sept. 1920, for a contemporary perspective. American newsprint consumption rose from 8 pounds per capita in 1890 to 30 pounds in 1913, and to 62 pounds in 1929. See V.W. Bladen, *An Introduction to Political Economy* (Toronto 1956), 166-7

4 For the extent of American involvement in this process, see J.T. Saywell, 'Economic Council of Canada, Draft Report, Pulp and Paper to 1918,' July 1973, unpublished, York University. For the legislation, see J.A. Guthrie, *The Newsprint Paper Industry* (Cambridge, Mass. 1941), 44-6; see also H.V. Nelles, 'Empire Ontario: The Problems of Resource Development,' in Donald Swainson, ed., *Oliver Mowat's Ontario* (Toronto 1972).

Figure 3.1
Production, value of production , and price of Canadian newsprint, 1913-23

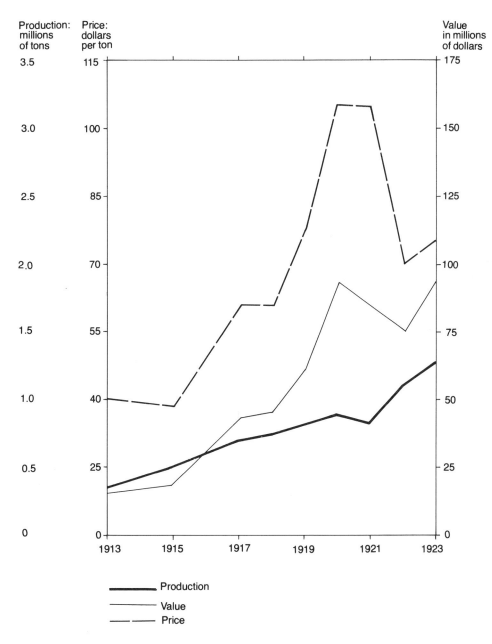

Production:
millions
of tons

Price:
dollars
per ton

Value
in millions
of dollars

Production
Value
Price

Source: compiled from C. R. Coughlin, 'The Newsprint Industry in Canada,' unpublished MA thesis,
McGill University, 1939, p. 162

61 per cent.[5] Naturally, Canadian paper makers, who were blessed with cheap raw materials, extremely efficient plants, and modest transportation costs, scrambled to place every ton they produced up for American bids.[6] If Canadian publishers could not match these bids the newsprint manufacturers saw no reason to continue to supply them.

On 6 October 1916 the Canadian Press Association (CPA) called a special meeting to consider the 'sudden prospect of a desperate increase in the price of white paper, which we suspected to be wholly unjustified by cost of manufacture.' The next day the association's Special Paper Committee placed its problem before Finance Minister Thomas White, who immediately arranged a meeting in his office between the publishers and the paper makers. The newspaper publishers announced that they could tolerate a 25 cents per cwt. advance over the $2.00 they had paid at the beginning of 1916; the newsprint manufacturers, however, demanded $3.25 per cwt. This price, the publishers feared, would put many of them out of business:

We pointed out difficulties in the way of our increasing our revenue materially at an early date. We contended that the newspaper industry, a much larger one than the paper-mill industry as regards the number of persons employed, but hard pressed by war conditions in general, was entitled to decent treatment by another Canadian industry which was making enormous profit out of war conditions by selling 80 per cent of its product abroad at an unprecedently high price; and we argued that if the paper manufacturers, whose own industry and pockets had benefited greatly by national legislation in the past, failed to treat the newspaper industry with consideration, the newspaper industry was now entitled to protection also by national legislation.[7]

5 Guthrie, *ibid.*, 247, table 14. In addition, after 1916, pricing in the industry changed from f.o.b. delivery room to f.o.b. mill, and publishers had to absorb the costs of transportation. *Ibid.*, 119

6 On supply and efficiency conditions, see Bladen, *Introduction*, 170, n 11, and PAC, W.L.M. King Papers, Memoranda and Notes, MG26J4, vol. 192, file 993, C94440-1, Memorandum for the Chairman: Export of Raw Materials, Pulpwood, Wood Pulp and Paper Industry, 2 Aug. 1928.

7 The CPA account is taken from Canadian Press Association, Inc., Bulletin no 317, 8 Jan. 1917, found in PAC, Robert L. Borden Papers, MG26H, vol. 212, file 1087(1), (same volume and file numbers throughout this chapter) 119715. The committee consisted of P.D. Ross, Ottawa *Journal-Press* (chairman); J.F. MacKay, Toronto *Globe*; J.E. Atkinson, *Toronto Star*; John R. Robinson, Toronto *Telegram*; G.F. Pearson, Halifax *Chronicle*; W.R. Givens, Kingston *Standard*; and W.E. Smallfield, Renfrew *Mercury*.

Meetings and bargaining between the publishers, the paper manufacturers, and the minister continued for three months, during which period each side balanced arguments of justice and necessity.Even the newspaper unions threw their weight into the fray as dozens of union locals sent in form letters to the prime minister protesting the high price of paper which, they claimed, threatened their jobs.[8] The negotiations, however, produced no acceptable compromise.

Finally, on 5 January 1917 the minister of finance, acting under the War Measures Act, imposed a settlement by advancing the price of newsprint in Canada 50 cents per cwt. The newspaper publishers accepted this settlement with good grace, admitting that they had won a great deal through government intervention:

An advance of 50 cents per 100 pounds over last year in the price of newsprint in Canada means a very heavy tax upon Canadian papers [said the CPA]. But it is to be noted that in default of Government action, there could have been no escape from a tremendously greater burden. We had absolutely no other chance short of Government action. The paper mills controlled the situation absolutely. They could sell every pound of their product in the United States at an increase of $1.00 or more per 100 pounds over last year's prices. There wasn't a ghost of a show of our escaping the same thing in Canada, except Government action.[9]

The newsprint manufacturers were less generous in their assessment of the situation. 'In the annals of Canadian politics,' the *Pulp and Paper Magazine of Canada* editorialized on 11 January 1917,

we know nothing that savors more of high-handed injustice than the action of Sir Thomas White in seeking to regulate the price at which newsprint shall be sold to Canadian publishers ... Everything the people of this country require, such as food, clothing, etc., has made enormous advances in cost, yet Sir Thomas White remains silent. Why then this outburst of piety and change of heart, this desire to cleanse the Aegean stables as represented by the paper industry? The reason is not hard to find. The press of the country have a tremendous influence, and Sir Thomas White who has his ear to the ground, and is credited with ambitions in the direction of a Premiership, wants to curry favor with the newspaper men of the Dominion. He will find that the newsprint industry is not in the hands of a lot of weaklings who will tamely submit to his whims and

8 See, for example, Borden Papers, 119658-72 and 119678-706
9 CPA, Bulletin no 317

caprices. They have just claims, and do not intend to have their rights over-ridden by Sir Thomas White or any other individual.

The minister's decision hardly settled the dispute. For one thing, the American price of newsprint continued to rise. For another, since the paper companies abhorred White's decision, they might well attempt to sabotage the order. In his announcement fixing the new prices White had suggested that the manufacturers and the publishers 'compose their differences ... and render unnecessary any [further] action on the part of the government.'[10] Under the circumstances, however, this was a vain hope. If prices were fixed, supplies also would have to be regulated, lest the paper mills simply refuse to fill the orders of Canadian customers.

These considerations pushed the government towards further regulation of the newsprint industry. On 16 April 1917 the government named R.A. Pringle, an Ottawa lawyer, to conduct a royal commission inquiry into 'the manufacture, sale, price and supply of news print paper' in Canada. Furthermore, under Section 6 of the War Measures Act, Pringle was appointed paper controller as a representative of the minister of customs, with the power to fix the quantity and price of newsprint to be delivered in Canada from 1 March to 1 June 1917.

Pringle maintained the current level of Canadian newsprint prices for several months after his appointment.[11] Rolled paper had to be sold at $2.50 per cwt. (f.o.b. mill) and sheet paper was fixed at $3.25 per cwt. At the same time Pringle ordered all the mills in Canada to supply 11 per cent of their rated capacity tonnage to domestic consumers. This order was based on the ratio of current Canadian consumption to current production. Further, since some mills were better situated than others to supply Canadian consumers economically, Pringle ordered that under-quota mills reimburse over-quota mills with supplies of paper or by the differential between Canadian and American prices.[12]

During the period covered by these initial regulations Pringle conducted an extensive investigation to establish the basis of equitable prices in the newsprint

10 Cited in *ibid.*, W.T. White to George Chahoon, Jr., president, Laurentide Co. Ltd., 5 Jan. 1917
11 For Pringle's appointment and powers, see PCO 1059, 16 April 1917, in Borden Papers, 119725, and PCO 1060, 16 April 1917, in PAC, Arthur Meighen Papers, MG261, vol. 10, file 54 (same throughout this chapter), 5468. Pringle's authority to fix prices and regulate supplies was reconfirmed on 3 November 1917 when he was appointed paper controller. See PCO 3122, 3 Nov. 1917, Meighen Papers, 5469-72
12 See Royal Commission re: Inquiry into the Manufacture, Sale, Price and Supply of Newsprint in Canada, 'Interim Report,' R.A. Pringle, commissioner, 18 Jan. 1918, in Borden Papers, 119741-70. No final report was ever submitted.

industry. All the newsprint mills in Canada were ordered to furnish the commissioner with information regarding their production and exports, their costs and selling prices in Canada and the United States, their capital stock and bonded indebtedness, and their profits. The commission's accountant, Geoffrey T. Clarkson, audited this evidence, and subsequently representatives of the Canadian Press Association were invited to cross-examine individual paper mill managers at a series of public hearings conducted by Pringle.

The commission discovered that it was very difficult to determine precisely the exact costs of all the mills. Pringle and Clarkson tried to establish three principal accounting items to cover all costs: material costs, conversion costs, and general expenses, which included taxes, depreciation, administration, and return on investment. Under the first item, wood costs were a major expense, but as paper company spokesmen pointed out, pulpwood was often cut two or three years before it reached the mill, and losses during the drive to the mill, which usually ranged beteeen 5 per cent and 20 per cent of the wood cut, had to be calculated into the original costs. These conditions posed serious estimation problems and Pringle found that wood costs from mill to mill varied by as much as seven to nine dollars a cord in 1916 and 1917. The commissioner also found that hydro power, a major item under conversion costs, was often supplied to the paper mill by a subsidiary corporation. In such cases the accountants found it difficult to determine if paper profits were being disguised and diverted by way of excessive hydro charges. Finally, Pringle discovered that it was extremely difficult to establish the basis of a fair return on investment. Although the commission ultimately agreed that the replacement cost of an integrated newsprint mill was about $30,000 per ton capacity, and that 8 per cent was a fair return on such an investment, Clarkson pointed out that 'the actual capital investments of the manufacturers are in nearly all cases obscure, for the reason that the companies have either been formed through amalgamations or assets have been purchased by the issue of shares and securities.' For these reasons, the commission's accountant concluded that 'any figures prepared as to their costs can be made the subject of criticism and enquiry.'[13]

Despite these difficulties Paper Controller Pringle had to make a decision and to act upon it. Although costs varied by as much as $15 per ton from company to company, Clarkson estimated an industry-wide average cost of $51.98 per ton, exclusive of any interest charges or allowance for a fair return on

13 PAC, Royal Commission on Cost of Newsprint Papers, RG33-53 (hereafter Pringle Commission), vol. 9, file: Correspondence: Clarkson, no 1, Clarkson to Pringle, 21 Jan. 1918. All the information in the analysis of cost problems comes from this letter and from the 'Interim Report,' *ibid.*

investment. These additional items added $8 per ton to the final charge. The findings suggested that newsprint prices be increased to $60 per ton. The newspaper publishers, however, questioned these figures, and at one point they went so far as to withdraw from the public hearings in protest against Pringle's rulings. Nevertheless Pringle decided that prices must go up, and on 18 January 1917 he announced that effective the beginning of February newsprint rolls must sell for $57 per ton. Subsequently Clarkson noted that 'your figure of $57, therefore, allows a leeway of $3 towards meeting items objected to by the publishers.'[14]

By the time Pringle fixed the Canadian price at $57 per ton, American prices had been pegged at $60 by order of the Federal Trade Commission. The FTC had begun to supervise American price levels as part of a broad agreement reached between the American paper producers, American publishers, and the attorney-general. Under threat of anti-trust action the leading American paper makers, who included in their number the agents of major Canadian firms that sold in the United States, agreed to a voluntary regulation of their industry by the FTC for the duration of the war and the three months that followed. As of 1 January 1918 the FTC ruled that American prices must be maintained at $60 per ton until 1 April 1918. However, the FTC regulation covered only the leading producers who were party to the agreement with the attorney-general. Unregulated prices were consistently higher than those subject to controls.[15]

Since there was an obvious relationship between Canadian costs and American prices, Canadian paper producers feared that the Pringle Commission's findings would form the basis of future FTC decisions. For many paper makers this fear far outweighed their concerns about the profitability of the Canadian market. As one paper executive wrote Pringle:

The Canadian newspapers have on several occasions stated that even if we did make a loss by supplying newspapers in Canada at $50 a ton, we could easily recover this from the large profits we made in the States. Whether this is quite a fair way to look at it, in view of our relation with the States as Allies in this war, I leave to you to judge, but this contention can no longer apply if a price less than $60 a ton is fixed for Canadian prices, because *undoubtedly the Federal*

14 CPA, Bulletin no 366, 26 June 1917, in Borden Papers, 119729. The price of newsprint sheets was not changed since 'no evidence has been presented to justify ... making a change in these prices.' 'Interim Report.' Pringle Commission, *ibid.*, Clarkson to Pringle, 21 Jan. 1918
15 For details on the American case, see E.O. Merchant, 'The Government and the News-Print Paper Manufacturers,' *Quarterly Journal of Economics*, 32 (Feb. 1918), and 34 (Feb. 1920).

Trade Commission will fix a price not much, if any, more than the Canadian price, and if this should be less than $60 a ton, then we should not be able to survive.[16]

Pringle's decision to force a two-price system on the newsprint industry, like Finance Minister White's decision before him, was only half the solution to the Canadian publishers' problem. On top of what they regarded as fair prices, the publishers also needed regular supplies. Pringle's system of supply quotas and price differential payments between the under- and over-quota mills was designed to resolve this difficulty. From the beginning, however, the system did not work smoothly, and as time went on it failed completely.

Two major problems undermined Pringle's distribution system. First, although long-term contract prices generally were regulated in both Canada and the United States, irregular sales at 'spot prices' to desperate American publishers seeking newsprint tonnage at almost any price could not be controlled. Accordingly, it was often in the interests of the paper companies to refuse Canadian orders, pay the price differential on their unfilled quota, and then sell their freed surplus tonnage for spot prices in the United States. A situation of excess demand over supply in conjunction with controlled prices, then, led to the formation of what was in essence a black market, and this in turn compounded the difficulties of regulation.

The second problem for Pringle's system derived from the production function in the newsprint industry. As in many other capital-intensive, flow-process industries,[17] demand and price did not always exclusively determine output in the paper business. Up to a point, because their costs reflected heavy fixed overhead charges and hydro power rates based on maximum capacity utilization, newsprint companies placed a premium on volume rather than marginal price increases.[18] Moreover, since they produced an undifferentiated product, the paper makers were always anxious to establish good relations with customers who might then enter into regular long-term contractual relationships with them. Thus, in the period prior to the war, when Canadian companies struggled to enter the American market, they were willing and anxious to take on local Canadian business. Subsequently, however, as the American market boomed and the Canadian mills gained a growing share of that market, Canadian demand became less important. By 1917 the Canadian paper makers believed that the

16 Pringle Commission, vol. 7, file: Correspondence S1, P.B. Wilson, Spanish River Pulp
   and Paper Co., to Pringle, 9 Nov. 1917 (my emphasis)
17 R.T. Averitt, *The Dual Economy* (New York 1968), 24-6
18 Coughlin, 'Newsprint Industry,' 19-20 and 88, and Guthrie, *Newsprint Paper Industry*,
   154

quota system threatened to divert tonnage from potential American customers to relatively undesired Canadian consumers. Under these circumstances, they often preferred to pay differential charges to other companies rather than jeopardize their chances for further American business by diverting supplies to Canadian publishers. The complaint of Spanish River Pulp and Paper Mills president, G.H. Mead, was typical of this view:

Since Mr. Backus [of the Fort Frances Pulp and Paper Company] is keeping his tonnage in its regular channels, and supplying his regular trade, it is entirely unfair that he should make a demand upon us for tonnage which we must take from our regular customers and which he proposes to distribute as surplus to his customers.

It is now impossible for us to give up tonnage as suggested but in order to give you every possible assistance in dealing with the situation we are willing as already offered in your presence to give Mr. Backus seven dollars per ton on the excess tonnage he is shipping.[19]

Pringle's efforts to set prices met many obstacles too. Following his decision to raise prices effective 1 February 1918 from $50 to $57 per ton, the newspaper publishers called upon the cabinet to rescind the order. The politicians, torn by the conflicting forces, vacillated. Finance Minister White advised further talks: 'I think another effort should be made to get the manufacturers and publishers to agree as there is really a solidarity of interest between them.' This line of reasoning had considerable appeal within the cabinet, but it was a hopeless position. Three weeks later the cabinet reluctantly modified Pringle's January order. The revisions reflected the government's uncertainty. The cabinet temporarily supported the price increase to $57. At the same time, however, they allowed the paper manufacturers to receive only $50 per ton, the remainder going in trust to Controller Pringle, who was to hold these funds for distribution to the manufacturers or for refund to the publishers subject to subsequent cabinet decisions upon this issue.[20]

The paper companies naturally objected to these revisions, just as they had objected to the original order setting the price at $57. So far as they were

19 Pringle Commission, vol. 7, file: Correspondence: S1, Mead to Pringle, 28 April 1917; telegram, Mead to Pringle, 27 April 1917

20 Borden Papers, 119772, memorandum, White to Borden, 23 Jan. 1918; Meighen Papers, 5473-5, PCO 408, 18 Feb. 1918. The cabinet Subcommittee on Paper was composed of White, Maclean, Carvell, Calder, Doherty, Meighen, Reid, and Rowell. Borden Papers, 119893, telegram, Borden to Glyn Osler, 22 Oct. 1918

concerned, 'they [were] still being used as pawns in the game of politics.' To circumvent this 'game,' the paper makers demanded the establishment of a court of final appeal from the paper controller's orders. The precedent for such a court existed in the American control regulations and Pringle had also supported the need for an appeals procedure in his initial interim report. Despite the objections of the publishers, who understandably preferred political to judicial review of the controller's decisions, the government finally agreed on 16 September 1918 to establish a Paper Control Tribunal, consisting of Justices W.E. Middleton, Charles Archer, and A.S. White.[21]

The Paper Control Tribunal received its first case only ten days after it was established. On 26 September Pringle had responded to rising US prices for paper and rising Canadian wood and labour costs by increasing the basic price of Canadian newsprint to $69 per ton. This price was to apply retroactively to all contracts in force since 1 July 1918. Pringle's order followed hard on the heels of a decision by the US Second Circuit Court of Appeal which had ruled against an FTC decision to fix the price for April 1918 at $62 per ton and raised it to $70. Shortly thereafter the FTC fixed May and June prices at $72.65 per ton and the post-June 1918 rate at $75. Since these regulated prices covered only 50 per cent of American consumption, in some places spot prices ranged even higher than $75. None the less, the Canadian publishers immediately appealed Pringle's ruling. The Paper Control Tribunal, however, did not deliver its findings on this appeal immediately and in the interim Pringle's orders continued to stand, subject to judicial revision.[22]

Pringle's ruling remained in force until 17 December 1919 when he announced yet another round of price increases. By this time FTC regulation of the American industry had lapsed, war conditions having ceased, and American contract prices were quoted at $90 per ton, while spot prices hovered around the $100 level. In these circumstances the paper makers became increasingly restive under Pringle's regulations, and Price Brothers, for one, refused to continue negotiations with the controller prior to his December decision. Pringle's new ruling contained two important features. First, he increased Canadian prices from $69 to $80 per ton for newsprint rolls and $92 per ton for sheets, effective January first. Second, the paper controller announced the imminent end of the

21 Borden Papers, 119812, pamphlet, issued by the Newsprint Section of the Canadian Pulp and Paper Association, 'The Government and the Newsprint Paper Manufacturer'; and 119844-6, PCO 2270, 16 Sept. 1918
22 PAC, Board of Commerce Files (hereafter BCF), RG36-6, vol. 32, file 17-3-6, Memorandum in Regard to the Fort Frances Pulp and Paper Co. undated (FFPP memo), and Merchant, 'The Government,' 34, pp. 314-16

Canadian two-price system! Pringle declared that as of 1 July 1920 he would abandon his independent price-fixing efforts; thereafter the lowest Canadian export price would establish the level of all contracts within the domestic market. However, in the months that followed Pringle's announcement American prices continued to soar, and by mid-1920 newsprint contracts reached the unprecedented level of $130 per ton.[23]

Pringle's announcements did not stifle the growing resistance by the paper makers to the controller's orders, nor did they ensure regularity of supplies for Canadian publishers. Quite the opposite, for within a month Pringle's entire system of regulation teetered on the edge of disaster, while the controller himself decided to abandon his post for greener pastures, becoming a legal representative for the newsprint producers' association!

The failure of the controller's guaranteed supply system was responsible for this crisis. By 1920 Canadian publishers consumed 12.7 per cent of Canadian production capacity, while other newsprint users boosted Canadian consumption to 15 per cent of maximum production levels. The bulk of Canadian orders were shipped in rolls, sheet sales accounting for only 7000 out of 124,000 tons shipped. To guarantee these shipments, Pringle consulted with both the publishers and paper makers and then ordered the distribution of Canadian tonnage as shown in Table 3.1.

All the producers except Price Brothers and Fort Frances agreed to accept these arrangements. Price Brothers was shipping only 2465 tons per annum to Canadian publishers when Pringle ordered the company to increase its supplies to roughly 8500 tons. However, since Price Brothers had refused to be a party to the negotiations leading to Pringle's first of January orders, they subsequently refused to be bound by his directions. Sir William Price explained his company's position to the press in the following terms: 'As businessmen, the whole question for us is as to whether we, manufacturers of paper, of all other producers, are to be restricted in our constitutional right of dealing with whom we choose and of retaining our right of freedom of contract. We base our refusal upon the total absence of jurisdiction in the Ottawa authorities and in the Paper Controller in the premises, and we will seek by all legal means at our disposal to resist the carrying out of the orders given.'[24] Price proceeded to take his grievance to the Supreme Court which heard his case on 17 March 1920.

23 BCF, vol. 31, file: Newsprint: Orders in Council, PC2586A and 2586B, 17 Oct. 1917; Merchant, *ibid.*, 315-16; Guthrie, *Newsprint Paper Industry*, 247-8; and Coughlin, 'Newsprint Industry,' 113, table 11
24 Quoted in *Canadian Annual Review, 1920*, 184

TABLE 3.1
Newsprint industry and the Canadian market, 1920 (tons)

	Rated capacity per annum	15 percent Canadian quota	Current shipments	Required additional shipments
Abitibi Power and Paper Company	72,000	10,800	8425	800
Belgo-Canadian Pulp and Paper	60,000	9000	14,420	
J.R. Booth Company	45,000	6750	3680	5815
Brompton Pulp and Paper Company	30,000	4500	225	2410
Canada Paper Company	10,500	1575	1771	
Donnacona Pulp and Paper Company	30,000	4500		3600
E.B. Eddy Company	15,000	2250	2000	
Fort Frances Pulp and Paper Company	45,000	6750	15,700	
Laurentide Company	67,500	10,125	10,002	
News Pulp and Paper Company	9000	1350	1350	
Ontario Paper Company	67,500	10,125	10,000	5330
Pacific Mills Limited	60,000	9000		350
Powell River Pulp and Paper Company	66,500	9975	12,529	
Price Brothers and Company	75,000	11,250	2465	6047
Spanish River Pulp and Paper Mills	145,000	21,750	5455	16,451
St Maurice Paper Company	30,000	4500	1400	2260

Source: Meighen Papers, vol. 10, file 54, 5614-21, Memorandum Regarding Canadian Newsprint Situation, 30 Jan. 1920

In the interim the government took steps to ensure the obedience of the dissident firms. On 5 January the cabinet reaffirmed the paper controller's authority to refuse export licences to delinquent mills, and it also granted him power to requisition and seize paper, if necessary, in order to ensure the continued flow of supplies to the country's newspapers.[25] These measures were then brought to bear upon the Price Brothers and Fort Frances companies.

By January 1920 the Fort Frances Pulp and Paper Company case was extremely confused. Because of its location only two hundred miles southeast of Winnipeg, Fort Frances had become the major supplier of western Canadian publishers. Their demands, however, far exceeded the Canadian quota allotments expected of the Fort Frances mill. Moreover, because of its location vis-à-vis its timber and power supplies, the Fort Frances mill had extraordinary costs which appeared to require some sort of special treatment in price-fixing decisions.[26]

25 Meighen Papers, 5497-9, PCO 25, 5 Jan. 1920; see also *ibid.*
26 Fort Frances' paper mill was on the Canadian side of the border while its power and timber supplies were situated on the American side. The location of its timber supplies

Pringle initially responded to these problems by arranging compensation in paper or cash for Fort Frances' excess Canadian shipments and by allowing the Fort Frances company a higher price for its paper. These arrangements, however, were challenged by the other mills and by the publishers, and accordingly cases were launched before the Paper Control Tribunal.

The publishers objected to two aspects of Pringle's pricing policy. First, they believed that the controller's order of 26 September 1918 which raised prices for all mills to $69 per ton permitted excessive profits for the paper companies. They also believed that Pringle was mistaken when he agreed to allow the Fort Frances company to charge an additional $4 per ton so long as it faced uniquely higher costs. However, steps were taken to reduce these extraordinary charges and Pringle ordered Fort Frances to rebate the extra payments to the publishers. When the company stalled on these rebates, because of an argument with Pringle about the precise amounts involved, the publishers had no choice but to take their rebate claims to the Paper Control Tribunal.

The tribunal delivered its rulings on both these disputes on 18 August 1919. The judges agreed that the prices fixed for the five months from 1 July to 1 December 1918 were too high and they ordered that all contracts for this period be reduced from $69 to $66 per ton. The tribunal further ruled that the Fort Frances company should also receive only $66, and the judges directed the publishers to apply to Pringle for a final order regarding the payment of rebates.

Pringle disagreed with the tribunal's rulings and immediately took steps to counter their effects. First, he claimed that in view of the tribunal's findings, prices fixed for the period prior to 1 July 1918 should also be reviewed, and accordingly he refused to order the rebate payments. Next, on 24 December 1919, shortly after he had fixed the price for 1920 contracts at $80 per ton, Pringle announced that the Fort Frances company must pay the $7 rebate covering the period from 1 July to 1 December 1918. At the same time, however, Pringle also declared that the price previously set for 1 January to 1 July 1918 at $57 had been reviewed and raised to $67 per ton, and thus the publishers must also arrange price revisions. Finally, Pringle ruled that the Fort Frances price from 1 December 1918 to 31 December 1919 was now to be fixed at $73 per ton and that all the other mills should receive $69 per ton for shipments made during the same period.

involved extra transportation costs, and, in addition, Fort Frances, alone amongst the Canadian paper companies, had to import its sulphite supplies on which it paid duty. BCF, FFPP memo: the information in the following paragraphs comes from this memorandum.

Although the Fort Frances company appeared to be pleased with these arrangements, it received no satisfaction in its dispute with the other paper companies over long-standing claims for compensation for excess quota shipments. Initially the other mills had paid these claims from 1 March to 31 December 1917, but subsequently they appealed for relief to the Paper Control Tribunal and withheld payments pending a ruling. The other paper companies contended that since Fort Frances normally supplied the western Canadian market it should not now be paid what in effect amounted to a bonus merely to continue to supply its regular customers. Although some $200,000 was involved in this dispute Pringle refused to issue any further order in this area until the tribunal had established a basis on which to proceed.

As a result of these delays in differential payments and the prolonged dispute over prices, the Fort Frances Pulp and Paper Company became a very erratic source for western Canadian newsprint supplies. During 1918 and 1919 prairie publishers complained bitterly that they were unable to obtain any firm commitment about regular shipments. Finally, on 12 December 1919 the company pushed matters to a crisis with an announcement that henceforth it would ship only its regular quota, fourteen tons daily, instead of the fifty tons required by western publishers. Company spokesmen explained that they would not increase their rate of supply except to the extent that additional tonnage was placed at their disposal by other firms.

During the next month Pringle laboured unsuccessfully to resolve this dispute. On 24 December he believed that he had settled matters when he arranged for the Spanish River company, which was consistently under its quota, to ship roughly 172 tons per week to the order of the Fort Frances company. The two companies subsequently disagreed about the commencement date of this plan, however, and Fort Frances refused once again to ship paper to western publishers, unless of course they agreed to pay open market prices which were then $140 per ton.[27] By 5 January 1920 the crisis deepened as the three Winnipeg newspapers faced the immediate prospect of suspending publication due to paper shortages. Accordingly, five days later, Pringle ceased negotiations and ordered the company to proceed with western shipments regardless of all previous arrangements. He also guaranteed that he would see to it that Spanish River made up the difference on over-quota shipments. The paper controller telegraphed the warning that 'shipments must be resumed today on this basis

27 *Ibid.* See also Meighen Papers, 5503-4, B.G. Dahlberg, Fort Frances Pulp and Paper Co., to *Manitoba Free Press*, Telegram Printing Co., *Winnipeg Tribune*, 6 Jan 1920

otherwise I will instruct Commissioner Customs to place embargo on paper and also will have to commandeer.'[28]

Pringle's telegram used more paper than it produced. Since the Fort Frances company gave no indication of obeying the paper controller's directive, Pringle's assistant at the site, J.L. McNicol, notified the company that he would commandeer the necessary paper supplies on 12 January at 10 a.m. Later, he extended the commandeering order to 4 p.m. By the time he arrived with the local sheriff, the horse had already bolted through the open barn door. Taking advantage of their time extensions, the Fort Frances company immediately loaded all its paper on hand and readied it for shipment to the United States. Next, the company tore up the railway switch by which this paper, if seized, would be transferred to the CNR tracks to Winnipeg. Finally, when McNicol and the sheriff arrived on the scene Fort Frances officials denied their admittance to the premises and threatened forcible resistance if any seizure was attempted.[29]

During the next few days a considerable degree of confusion surrounded the captured Fort Frances trains. McNicol believed that he should enforce the embargo on all Fort Frances exports and that the paper should be commandeered. Pringle opposed any embargo since the Fort Frances company had supplied more than its 15 per cent quota of Canadian shipments. The minister of Finance, Sir Henry Drayton, however, ordered the embargo into effect on 14 January 1920.[30] Two days later, the harried controller resigned his office.

During the following week the Fort Frances Pulp and Paper Company refused to make any further shipments to western Canada until the embargo was lifted. As a result on 17 January the publishers' predictions were realized and all three Winnipeg dailies suspended publication for five days because of lack of paper. The pressure to resolve this long-standing dispute was accentuated at the same time by American protests about the embargo to the British Embassy at Washington.[31]

The government achieved a temporary settlement of the Fort Frances dispute a week after Pringle's resignation. On 22 January the cabinet appointed a finance

28 *Ibid.*, 5495, telegram, Vernon Knowles, *Winnipeg Telegram*, to Meighen, 5 Jan. 1920 (see also 5494, R.L. Richardson, *Winnipeg Tribune*, to Meighen, 5 Jan. 1920, and 5506-10, Memorandum Re Paper Situation, prepared by the *Winnipeg Telegram*, 6 Jan. 1920); 5531, telegram, Pringle to Fort Frances Pulp and Paper Co., 10 Jan. 1920
29 BCF, FFPP memo
30 *Ibid.*, telegram, Pringle to McNicol, 15 Jan., and McNicol to Pringle, 14 Jan. 1920
31 Meighen Papers, 5600-1, H.A. Prall-Pierce, customs collector, to R.R. Farrow, commissioner of customs, 16 Jan. 1920; 5595, British Embassy at Washington, to governor-general, 17 Jan. 1920; *CAR, 1920*, 182

department official, R.W. Breadner, to serve as the new paper controller, and he immediately ordered new shipments by both the Fort Frances and the Spanish River companies.[32] However, Breadner ignored the terms of Pringle's 10 January order and once again Fort Frances' shipments were tied to continuous prior shipments by Spanish River.[33] In an interview the new paper controller explained: 'In his opinion, the Fort Frances concern had hardly been given a square deal, prior to the beginning of his enquiry. He found that the "differentials" relating to prices to be paid for their product, had not been revised for about two years, and are still un-revised. He also found that almost 100% of the material used in the manufacture of their product comes from the South side of the International Boundary, on which side the bulk of their plant is also situated. The amount of Canadian raw material used, he considers negligible.'[34]

Although Breadner's order did get the paper trains moving for a short while, his critics complained that he had not come to grips with the quota and differential problems. Breadner's successor as paper controller later noted that Fort Frances' shipments continued in an erratic fashion as 'any local disturbance at Spanish River which delayed their shipments immediately resulted in the halting of Fort Frances shipments.' The Winnipeg publishers took a harsher view of the Breadner order: 'The tensity [sic] of the situation of that time was relieved, insofar as the Government of Canada is concerned, by Mr. R.W. Breadner's humiliating the Government and negotiating, in alien territory, a compromise which in effect not only sacrificed the interests of Western publishers but also threw bodily to the four winds the position that attitude taken by the Government in respect to the Fort Frances Company and defied by that corporation.'[35]

Breadner's tenure as paper controller was extremely short-lived. Whether his solution to the Fort Frances affair brought him into official disfavour, or whether his appointment was merely a stopgap measure brought on by Pringle's sudden resignation, is not clear, but one week after his appointment the cabinet

32 BCF, vol. 31, file: Newsprint Orders in Council, PCO 154, 22 Jan. 1920
33 Meighen Papers, 5610, Breadner's order, 24 Jan. 1920
34 BCF, vol. 31, file 7-1-1, letter, Re: Notes on interview with Mr Breadner, G. Linsell, Board of Commerce, to secretary, Board of Commerce, 31 Jan. 1920. A handwritten note at the bottom of this letter reads: 'It is suggested that you do not take B's statements at their face. The opinion here is that he is over credulous.'
35 Meighen Papers, 5044, James Murdock to Meighen, 6 March 1920; 5657-8, Knowles to Meighen, 22 March 1918

replaced Breadner with the Board of Commerce. The board subsequently claimed that it possessed power to regulate the newsprint industry on the basis of its declaration under the Combines and Fair Prices Act that newsprint was a 'necessity of life,' as well as by virtue of the power vested in it as the paper controller serving under the War Measures Act.[36] The legal basis of both these claims to power, however, was to be reviewed shortly by the Supreme Court in the Price Brothers case.

The fact that a judicial review of the board's authority was pending, and the apparently successful defiance of the law by the Fort Frances company, made it extremely difficult for the Board of Commerce to regulate the newsprint industry. 'The contumacy of Price Brothers has brought about a like attitude on the part of the other manufacturers,' declared the board's secretary, 'and there is at present a crisis which can only be removed by immediate and forceful action. The Board considers that it may be necessary to impose a general embargo in order to bring these manufacturers into a reasonable frame of mind.'[37]

The Board of Commerce faced the same difficulties as Pringle and Breadner had before. So long as Canadian prices were fixed below those prevailing in the United States, Canadian producers were loath to supply even their required quota of paper to Canadian publishers. As a result, western publishers continued to face shortages. Relations between the Spanish River and the Fort Frances companies remained strained and the latter mill persisted in its fractious behaviour. Between 19 February and 4 March the Board of Commerce struggled to find a new basis for the settlement of these old grievances. Finally it arranged to distribute the western Canadian demand between the Fort Frances company, the Spanish River company, and Pacific Mills Limited of British Columbia. However, even this solution was not entirely satisfactory. 'The arrangement is of most precarious tenure,' wrote the Winnipeg publishers, 'interim in character and designed merely to afford temporary relief. It gives no assurance nor guarantee of continuous or permanent supply, inasmuch as the representative of the Ocean

---

36 BCF, vol. 31, file: Newsprint Orders in Council, PCO 230, 29 Jan. 1920, and Board of Commerce Order no 17, 11 Oct. 1919. The Board of Commerce, established to administer the Combines and Fair Prices Act, was enjoined to investigate combines, cartels, and other price-fixing associations, and to prosecute them if unfair trade practices were uncovered. It was also empowered to control or prevent boarding and to limit undue and unscrupulous increases in the prices of the necessaries of life. A necessary of life was taken to include food, fuel, and clothing, and any products necessary to their production or derived from them. The Board of Commerce Act, 9-10 Geo. V, c. 45

37 Borden Papers, file 1087(2), 120002, W. White to Sir George Foster, acting prime minister, 16 Feb. 1920

Falls mill [Pacific] made it clear that his company feels constrained to continue shipments and obey the orders of the Board only during the currency of the Board's jurisdiction, which, he pointed out, is now challenged.'[38]

The paper makers' opposition to regulation reached new heights in mid-February when Price Brothers and Company declared that it would refuse an order by the board to increase its supplies to Quebec newspapers. The cabinet responded by issuing yet another order-in-council affirming the jurisdiction of the board and ordered Price Brothers to proceed with the required shipments.[39] By this time, however, the newsprint producers' continuous agitation had finally begun to produce results. On 18 February the Board of Commerce informed the publishers' association:

It is to be added that the motive of public policy for this unusual control of manufacturers for the benefit of one class of consumer which existed during the war does not now exist, and therefore, ruthless application in this matter of extraordinary and expiring legislation is not to be expected. The Board of Commerce cannot overlook the fact that there is a most extraordinary consumption of newsprint in Canada. It is most inconsistent to suppose that the now oppressive terms of the paper control orders and of the Fair Prices Act should be put into force merely to distribute among the public page after page of advertisements which encourage extravagance to a most excessive degree. Further, such a condition must be so profitable to the newspapers that price control of the raw material is incongruous.[40]

On 6 April 1920 control of the newsprint industry collapsed as a result of the Supreme Court's decision in the case of *Price Bros.* v *The Board of Commerce.* The court decided that such controls could not be justified on the basis of existing legislation.[41] As the secretary of the board explained:

The basis of the decision of the Supreme Court of Canada is that the war being, in fact, at an end the Governor-in-Council had not jurisdiction under that Act to vest in any newsprint controller or in the Board of Commerce of Canada as

38 BCF, vol. 31, file: Orders of Board of Commerce re Newsprint Control, Order 5, 19 Feb. Orders 6-8, 4 March 1920; Meighen Papers, 5669-70, Presentation to the Newsprint Committee of Cabinet by the Winnipeg Publishers, 12 March 1920
39 BCF, *ibid.*, Order 2, 6 Feb. 1920; PCO 444, 26 Feb., PCO 445, 26 Feb. 1920
40 *Ibid.*, file 17-2-1, Board of Commerce to Canadian Daily Newspaper Association, 18 Feb. 1920
41 In Re Price Brothers and Company and the Board of Commerce of Canada, *60 Can. S.C.R.*, 265

newsprint controller powers additional to those existing at the time of the new grant of power by reason of or in reliance upon the War Measures Act, which Act must be deemed inoperative as authorizing the conferring of new jurisdiction as to newsprint paper. The decision does not involve the power of Parliament over newsprint. As a subsidiary matter the Court decided that the Board of Commerce as such had not jurisdiction with respect to profit control over newsprint because newsprint could not be considered a necessary of life appearing in the Combines and Fair Prices Act.[42]

As the board's secretary suggested, although the Supreme Court decision voided existing paper regulations, it did not restrict the right of Parliament to consider other measures to that end. Accordingly, even though the tide had now turned in favour of the paper manufacturers, the publishers continued to press for controls. Winnipeg publishers, for example, complained that some of the manufacturers refused even to respond to their requests for contract quotations. The government was prepared to consider these grievances but no easy solution presented itself. The only plan which was seriously considered was a proposal to impose export controls. 'I think I am justified in saying to you,' Interior Minister Arthur Meighen wrote to a publisher, 'that one plan immediately under consideration is an export licence system looking to such control thereby as will insure the provisioning of Canadian newspapers with their reasonable requirements at market rates. I am not hopeful that anything beyond this can be expected, and I say that after the most thorough and earnest thought and consultation with my colleagues.'[43]

A number of problems stood in the way of such a system of export controls. Perhaps the most serious was the possibility that the United States might object to such controls and retaliate in kind. For at this time the American Senate was occupied with legislation which threatened trade restrictions if the old embargo, by which Ontario and Quebec restricted exports of pulpwood cut on crown land, was not suitably reviewed.[44] In all their discussions of the newsprint situation the Canadian cabinet showed a marked sensitivity to this aspect of the case. As A.E. Kemp, the minister of overseas forces, wrote Borden:

It seems to myself as well as to some other members of the Council that we should try to avoid putting onto the statute Books any such legislation for the

42 BCF, vol. 31, file 17-2-2, W. White to Messrs Davis and Mehr, Toronto, 16 April 1920
43 Meighen Papers, 5725-7, Knowles to Meighen, 17 April, Meighen to Knowles, 20 April 1920
44 L.E. Ellis, *Print Paper Pendulum* (New Brunswick, NJ 1948), 120-2

reason that it would likely antagonize the United States and cause them to retaliate. I should hope that the question of newsprint might be settled without any bill whatever being passed. If, however, a bill should have to be passed it should be in general terms and not refer to any particular commodity along the lines of the owners of certain natural products of Canada being obliged to supply all Canadian consumers at prices not necessarily lower than those which they receive from foreign buyers.[45]

Despite these hesitations, the government finally acted as paper shortages spread across the country. By 1920 spot prices of newsprint ranged between $220 and $320 per ton. On 29 May a large delegation of Ontario publishers crowded into the finance minister's office to protest that one-quarter of all the daily newspapers in the country were without any assurances of paper after 1 July. A few days later, the Canadian Daily Newspapers Association passed unanimously a resolution appealing 'for legislation requiring each newsprint manufacturer unwilling to do so to supply his proportion of the domestic requirements of newsprint at prices not higher than the current contract prices for export to foreign countries.' The prime minister finally responded to this pressure on 16 June 1920 by introducing a bill to regulate the export of newsprint paper.[46]

Borden's bill essentially renewed the system of controls in force prior to the Supreme Court's ruling on the Price Brothers case. All newsprint manufacturers were required to obtain export licences and the granting and renewal of such licences was to be subject to their agreement to supply domestic newsprint needs at prices fixed by the minister of finance. This bill did not reach final reading, however. When Parliament referred the issue to a house committee for further scrutiny, the paper makers voluntarily agreed to guarantee supplies for the Canadian market. As spot prices ranged ever higher the newsprint producers undoubtedly were anxious to avoid further controls on the industry. The Canadian Pulp and Paper Association and the J.R. Booth Company each agreed to supply or guarantee the supply of one-half of domestic needs, and the government willingly agreed to drop the whole scheme of continued regulation of the industry.[47]

45 Borden Papers, 1087(2), 120028-9, Kemp to Borden, 18 May, Borden to Kemp, 20 May 1920. Borden replied that he agreed entirely with Kemp's views.
46 Ellis, *Print Paper Pendulum*, 371; *CAR, 1920*, 185; and Borden Papers, *ibid.*, Copy of Resolution Passed Unanimously by a Special Meeting of Canadian Daily Newspapers Association, held at Ottawa, 5 June 1920; 120100-1, An Act to Regulate the Exportation of Newsprint Paper
47 *CAR, 1920*, 186. See also the objections to the act by the Canadian Pulp and Paper

Ironically, in the months that followed, this agreement proved unnecessary, for the newsprint market, like so many others, finally broke during the recession that began late in 1920. By April 1921 several of the largest mills, including Price Brothers and Abitibi, had shut down operations temporarily for lack of sufficient business. The industry's ratio of operations to mill capacity dropped from 95.5 per cent in 1920 to 73.5 per cent in 1921. With the mills desperate for business, Canadian publishers had no difficulty finding adequate supplies; by the end of 1921 contract prices fell to $80 per ton, fifty dollars less than the price that prevailed at the beginning of the year.[48]

It is striking that even though the newsprint producers consistently objected to regulation in their industry their profits between 1917 and 1920 reached record levels. Spanish River saw its profits, after all deductions save common shareholders' dividends, climb from $1.1 million in 1917 to $2.2 million in 1920. Abitibi increased its profits from $270,000 to $3.6 million in the same period. Price Brothers, Brompton, St Maurice, and indeed almost all the other paper companies, also experienced profit levels which by 1920 had doubled or even tripled those of 1917.[49]

The impact of these returns had far-reaching consequences for the newsprint industry in the years to follow. In 1920 Abitibi paid a common share dividend equivalent to 30 per cent, and Laurentide paid 18 per cent. In 1919 Price Brothers paid 10 per cent plus a 39 per cent stock dividend, while in 1920 10 per cent was paid once again and another 22 per cent stock bonus was proffered. Other firms presented similar, if slightly less striking, records. Investors and financiers naturally scrambled to associate themselves with what must have seemed a guaranteed stake in the prosperity of the future. In 1919 and 1920 newsprint company shares led the way on the Montreal Stock Exchange to new record levels of trading. During the first nine months of 1920 MSE sales climbed 40 per cent over 1919, and in September 1920 paper company stocks held the first four places in terms of the number of stocks traded and two other paper firms held the eighth and eleventh positions as well. In subsequent years, in light of their ease of access to the expanding Canadian and American capital markets, many newsprint companies were tempted to refinance and expand their capacity

Association, Borden Papers, *ibid.*, 120096-9, A.L. Dawe, secretary for the association, to Borden, 21 June 1920

48 *Financial Post*, 20 May 1921: see also Carl Wiegman, *Trees to News* (Toronto 1953), 76; Coughlin, 'Newsprint Industry,' 82, table 16; 95, table 20

49 Profit and loss statements to be found in various issues of W.R. Houston, ed., *Annual Financial Review, 1917-22* (Toronto 1918-22)

by absorbing ever-increasing annual fixed debt charges.[50] However, towards the end of the decade, as prices tumbled and excess capacity mounted, industry leaders must have looked back ruefully to a *Pulp and Paper Magazine* editorial of 4 January 1917, written 'to warn paper men and the public of the danger and injury which will come to the whole pulp and paper industry if the chief interest in paper making is to be centred in the stock market end. Paper must be made at the mills in Northern Ontario and Quebec, and not in financial houses on St. James Street.'

The profitability of the newsprint industry resulted from market conditions, not regulation. In theory, government regulation was supposed to act as a brake upon the industry and a check upon its appetite for excessive profits. In the United States, control was imposed in response to charges that monopoly profits were being taken. In Canada, regulation was designed to ensure a 'fair' relation between costs and selling prices and adequate supplies for domestic consumers. Yet there is much evidence to suggest that the regulators failed to meet these aims completely in either country. In the United States, E.O. Merchant pointed out that a judicial decision to fix return on investment rates at 15 per cent of $40,000 per ton estimated capitalization costs resulted in profit margins during the regulation period ranging from $9.50 to $19.43 per ton, with an average of $14.50 per ton. However, FTC investigations revealed that in the period prior to 1917 no company ever earned as much as $10 per ton profit! Merchant concluded that in the United States the regulation experience represented a 'complete victory for the manufacturers.' Under FTC control the paper makers escaped prosecution under the Sherman Act, and eventually, Merchant argued, they obtained prices that equalled those that would have prevailed without regulation.[51]

In Canada there is no doubt that prices and profits would have been higher without some form of regulation. Yet it is significant that the Canadian paper controller eventually adopted the same accounting principles that prevailed in the United States. The Board of Commerce discovered that Pringle's regulations allowed as much as $17.50 per ton profit on Canadian sales. In 1916 Price Brothers, a low cost mill, had commented that a profit of $5.64 per ton was 'most satisfactory.'[52] Although restrained somewhat, the paper companies clearly did not do badly on their Canadian sales.

50 *Financial Post*, 7 Oct. 1921, 8 Oct. 1920. For an analysis of the implications of increasing fixed debt charges, see *ibid.*, 31 Aug. 1923.
51 Merchant, 'The Government,' 34, pp. 324-6, 327
52 BCF, vol. 66, file: Pulp and Paper-Canada, Lewis Duncan to secretary, Board of Commerce, 16 Feb. 1920; vol. 33, file: Price Brothers, Report for 15 Months ending 28

Despite these profit increases, the newsprint manufacturers did not share the same enthusiasm for government regulation which prompted some producers to urge the appointment of the Board of Commerce. The paper makers, however, were concerned about expanding export markets, not marginal domestic consumers. Their reaction against regulation stemmed from economic need, not laissez-faire ideology, which, of course, never made sense in an industry founded on provincial timber grants and government embargos against pulpwood exports. When paper company owners such as Sir William Price invoked their 'constitutional right of dealing with whom we choose and of retaining our right of freedom of contract,' their statements embodied a curiously American tone. The American influence, of course, indicated the true source of the paper manufacturers' concern. In the past the great American newspaper chains had regularly attempted to bind the government to their viewpoint and to their interests in disputes with the paper producers.[53] Regulation of the newsprint industry in Canada obviously served as a precedent for similar action in the United States. Moreover, the export embargo enacted against the Fort Frances company and the one threatened against Price Brothers demonstrated that marginal local concerns could seriously disrupt more important trade patterns. Under such circumstances regulation ceased being simply an irritant and became a real threat.

The Canadian government's response to Canadian publishers' demands reinforced the paper makers' fears about continued regulation. The publishers, of course, merely reacted to market forces when they demanded continued price controls on their traditional suppliers. Although the market pitted manufacturer against manufacturer, in the absence of controls the contest for domination was most uneven. Despite the overwhelming economic importance of the newsprint industry, however, the publishers' political power was sufficiently great to weight the balance in their favour. Although the federal government was otherwise anxious to expand export sales and maintain foreign exchange reserves,[54] in this case it failed to advance the interests of the newsprint industry. Rather than intervene diplomatically to influence American price-fixing efforts,

Feb. 1916. Price Brothers was considered to be one of the two lowest cost mills in Canada.
53 For a discussion on this point, see Ellis, *Print Paper Pendulum*
54 This point was made repeatedly by the Canadian Pulp and Paper Association. See Borden Papers, 119812, 'The Government and the Newsprint Paper Manufacturers,' and 120096-9, A Statement from the Canadian Pulp and Paper Association, 21 June 1920. For the wider considerations involved in this question, see R.D. Cuff and J.L. Granatstein, 'The IMB-Ordnance Agreement of 1917,' in *Canadian-American Relations in Wartime* (Toronto 1975).

Canadian officials co-operated in attempting to stabilize prices. At every step of the way, then, narrow political considerations determined the course of regulation in the newsprint industry.

Regulation in this case points to more general considerations regarding the regulatory process during the war period. It is clear, for one thing, that private interests, not the government, forced the issue that led to regulation. As J.R. Baldwin has argued, 'the essential nature of the conflict that gives rise to a regulatory agency is the refusal of one of the parties concerned to accept the optimum that might be established via bargaining, given the existing structure of legal rights.' Under wartime conditions, however, traditional legal rights bowed to mobilization considerations in numerous areas of life, ranging from prohibition to economic regulation. Legal rights, in short, were subordinated to political necessity, and under these circumstances the newspaper publishers pushed their cause with the full knowledge that their product, propaganda, was more important to the government than newsprint production. The federal government, however, could not ignore legal rights completely, since one case set precedents for other industries. At the same time, the government had no desire to risk totally alienating the newsprint producers, since they counted amongst their number very important Canadian and American businessmen with numerous interests on both sides of the border. Just this kind of dilemma prompted Baldwin to conclude that 'regulatory agencies must, therefore, not only arbitrate a compromise but also arrange for side-payments to those who suffer negative effects.'[55] In this case, the paper controller tried to arrange regular supplies for the publishers, but ultimately they paid the going rate for paper contracts. For their part, the paper producers lost a few potential customers, but the controller's price regulations never seriously disturbed their more important relations with American consumers, who also had achieved price regulation by the Federal Trade Commission. In short, Canadian publishers bowed to broader continental considerations in exchange for security of supply, while newsprint producers tolerated regulation so long as it did not disturb the smooth operation of their continental markets. To the federal government, hemmed in by partisan considerations and the desire to avoid a major confrontation with American interests, this trade-off between security of supply and higher profits represented the optimum solution to a potentially dangerous conflict.

55 John R. Baldwin, *The Regulatory Agency and the Public Corporation: The Canadian Air Transport Agency* (Cambridge, Mass. 1975), 7; John H. Thompson, ' "The Beginning of Our Regeneration" : The Great War and Western Canadian Reform Movements,' CHA, *Historical Papers*, 1972

When newsprint prices fell and excess capacity mounted at the end of 1920 the structural requirements of the newsprint industry changed. Yet the paper producers did not then turn to the government to stabilize prices through continued regulation of their industry. Since only 15 per cent of the continental market for Canadian output was subject to Canadian regulation, even if government price-fixing had been possible or desirable it would not have saved many of the paper companies that stumbled or fell in 1921-22. Moreover, such a price-fixing programme was not possible by late 1920, for the Board of Commerce, which alone possessed the power to enact such regulations, had recently perished in its first and only attempt to impose price supports.

4

The Board of Commerce and
the sugar refining industry

The appointment of the Board of Commerce in the fall of 1919 represented the most serious attempt yet by business and government leaders to achieve economic security through state regulation of a major sector of the economy. From the outset, however, the board reflected several contradictory views of its goals and outlook. On the one hand, consumers might take heart from the board's declaration that it was 'the last and only resource and recourse of the consumer.' Indeed the board's powers to limit undue price increases and unfair trade practices appeared essential if the government was to prevent further uprisings similar to the Winnipeg General Strike which erupted in the spring of 1919. As one opposition critic warned the Borden administration, 'If nothing is done [to control rising prices] the peace that will be signed shortly in Paris will mean nothing for Canada, for war between classes will have started and no one can predict where it will stop.' Yet the board's powers in this respect were ambiguous, for besides its power to limit price increases it also appeared to have the authority to prevent price declines during periods of rapid deflation. In this connection, leading businessmen could take heart from a declaration by the board's most powerful member to the effect that 'a quick fall [in prices] is far more disastrous than a quick rise; it means failures and bankruptcy. In such a predicament, I said, it would be the duty of the Board to keep the prices up; that might conceivably happen.'[1] The establishment of the Board of Commerce

---

1 Dominion of Canada, 'Annual Report of the Board of Commerce of Canada,' 31 May 1920, *Sessional Papers*, no 205., unprinted, p. 53, PAC, RG14D2, vol. 74; *Can. H. of C. Debates*, 11 March 1919, p. 394, speech by F.J. Pelletier (Liberal). As Stuart Jamieson observed, 'One of the most important factors underlying the mounting unrest of the late war and post-war years was the inflationary price spiral. The cost of living index had remained virtually unchanged until the end of 1915. It jumped from then on, by 8% in 1916, more than 18% in 1917, and 13½% in 1918.' *Times of Trouble:*

thus brought together a host of conflicting expectations and demands: lower prices for consumers and higher prices for producers, increased regulation and stability for some businessmen, and outright opposition to controls and demands for freedom of enterprise from other producers such as the newsprint manufacturers. Under these circumstances the board's regulatory efforts proved an extremely trying task. Ultimately its attempt to regulate the sugar refining industry produced such sharp conflicts of interest that the board, together with the manufacturers' vision of security through regulation, perished beneath a wave of public outrage.

The three members of the board, Chairman H.A. Robson, Assistant Chairman W.F. O'Connor, and Commissioner James Murdock,[2] confronted the problems of the price and supply of sugar immediately upon assuming office. For the most part, Canadian refiners[3] depended upon Cuban sugar producers for their supplies, but shortly before the board began operations the Cuban market was severely disrupted. During 1918-19 the American Sugar Equalization Board had successfully controlled American sugar prices by purchasing the entire 1918 Cuban crop. Canadian sugar refiners also had been supplied from this purchase. In 1919, though, the American government disbanded the Sugar Equalization Board and Cuban commodities sold freely in the world market. The immediate result of these actions was a steady increase in the price of raw sugar,[4] an increase reflected in the domestic price of Canadian refined sugar. By the fall these increases began to hamper many industries dependent on low sugar prices. When western fruit growers and canners appealed to the board to stabilize the refined sugar market, therefore, the board responded by fixing the maximum

Labour Unrest and Industrial Conflict in Canada, 1900-66 (Ottawa 1968), 159. The powerful board member was W.F. O'Connor, quoted in the *Toronto Star*, 12 Sept. 1919.

2 Robson was a Manitoba judge, O'Connor an Ottawa lawyer and former wartime cost-of-living commissioner (1916-18), and Murdock was the Canadian vice-president of the Brotherhood of Railroad Trainmen.

3 Listed in order of their share of total production, the six companies were: St Lawrence Sugar Refining Co., Montreal (24 per cent); Canada Sugar Refining Co., Montreal (19½); Atlantic Sugar Refineries, Montreal (16½); Dominion Sugar Co., Chatham, Ont. (16); British Columbia Sugar Refineries, Vancouver (12); Acadia Sugar Refining Co., Halifax (12).

4 For a discussion of American conditions, see R.G. Blakey, 'Sugar Prices and Distribution under Food Control,' *Quarterly Journal of Economics*, 32 (1918); Joshua Bernhardt, 'Government Control of Sugar' during the War,' *ibid.*, 33 (1919); and Bernhardt, 'The Transition from Government Control of Sugar to Competitive Conditions,' *ibid.*, 34 (1920).

retail price for sugar at 11 cents per pound; refiners were limited to a maximum profit margin of two-fifths of a cent per pound.[5]

By January 1920 changing circumstances forced the Board of Commerce to review its initial sugar regulations. The board noted that American retail prices had recently risen from 10 cents a pound to a range between 18 and 21 cents. The cause of these increases was traced to the rising price of Cuban raw sugar, the cost of which had almost doubled between September and January. Ultimately the market's instability was attributable to competitive bidding by European and American buyers, but, as the board noted, Canadian firms had managed to avoid this competition by stocking up on lower-priced raw sugars for the supply period from January to March 1920. None the less, the board believed that Canadian prices had to rise if they were to prevent refiners from selling their sugar contracts in the United States in order to grab a quick profit.

Consequently, by its Order no 38 the board raised the maximum retail price to 16 cents a pound and effectively limited refiners to a selling price of 13.775 cents. This regulation was to apply until 31 March 1920. In order to ensure sufficient Canadian supplies at the new price the commissioners also prohibited the refiners from selling their raw sugar contracts without the board's permission. According to the board, this action was taken to ensure that the refiners would be 'compelled to share in part with the Canadian people the benefits of the cheaper prices at which such refiners bought.' To justify this new arrangement to the public, the board released a statement of the 'actual cost of production at a Canadian refinery of one hundred pounds of granulated sugar at the present cost of raw sugar.'[6]

Cost of raw sugar f.o.b. Cuba	$11.50
Average freight to New York	.46
New York exchange	.95
Freight to Montreal and handling	.25
Duty	1.37
Manufacturing cost	2.10
Absorbed freight	.10
Total	$16.73

5 PAC, Board of Commerce Files (BCF), vol. 16, Board of Commerce Orders file, Order no 2, 28 Aug. 1919; Order no 3, 2 Sept. 1919
6 *Ibid.*, Order nos 38 and 38a, 8 Jan. 1920. Note that replacement rather than actual costs are cited.

The new order obviously changed the basis of price-fixing regulations. Initially the board had controlled profit margins; now it simply regulated selling prices. The board justified this change with the curious argument that since all six companies had purchased their raw sugars at different prices, profit margin controls alone would lead to fierce price competition. Ultimately, the board claimed, the consumer would suffer since lower-priced refiners would sell out their inventories first and raw sugars purchased at higher prices would be imported to replace them. This would lead to a sudden rise in the price of refined sugar across the country.

The board's logic and the effect of Order no 38 deserves further comment. The most telling point is that under the new regulations several refiners' profit margins rose quite significantly. Using the board's figures, cited above, it appears that refiners would have to pay at least 8.145 cents per pound for their raw sugar if profit margins were to remain stabilized at $.40 per cwt.

Selling price to wholesalers	$13.775/cwt.
Cost of converting raw sugar f.o.b.	
Cuba to refined sugar in Canada	
ready for sale ($16.73 - 11.50 see above)	-5.23
Profit of $.40/cwt.	-0.40
Difference	$8.145/cwt.

Obviously any sugar purchased below this price would produce an increased margin of profit equal to the difference between these two prices, and, of course, the converse would be equally true.

An analysis of the refiners' raw sugar contracts deposited with the board reveals that several firms stood to gain by the changed regulations. Atlantic Sugar Refineries, for example, purchased 32,000 long tons of raw sugar at 6.5 cents per pound, f.o.b. Cuba, 3000 long tons at 7.85 cents, and 6000 long tons at 11 cents, all to be delivered during the control period ending 31 March 1920. If sold on the basis of the board's calculations, these contracts would produce an additional $729,000 above the profits Atlantic might have expected given a margin of .40 cents per pound.[7] Although no other company fared as well as Atlantic, both Acadia and BC Sugar gained on their earlier profit margins, while St Lawrence broke even. Only Dominion Sugar lost ground, but just slightly. No data were available for Canada Sugar.

---

7 BCF, vol. 5, file 2-2C1. This total takes into account the weight loss due to refining.

Events, however, intervened to prevent the realization of these windfall profits. First, labour problems in Cuba prevented the shipment of the low-priced raw sugars, and Canadian refiners had to deal with other Latin American suppliers at much higher prices. Furthermore, the exchange rate on US currency, which was the basis of all sugar contracts, rose almost 150 per cent after 22 January, again increasing producers' costs. Under these circumstances the refiners were unable to obtain sufficient supplies at reasonable prices and in February many of them shut down temporarily. In the face of these events it was almost impossible to maintain price controls or profit restrictions, for as Commissioner Murdock observed on 12 February, Canada was 'daily going behind 3,000,000 pounds of sugar in its total supply.'[8] Two weeks later the board gave up its efforts to regulate sugar altogether, and Order no 38 was rescinded. No new controls replaced it.

Given the disturbed conditions of the international raw sugar market, and the lack of controls at home, refined sugar prices rose gradually throughout the spring and summer of 1920. The board did not attempt to reimpose order on the sugar market until 18 June 1920. At that time new regulations fixed the retail price of sugar at 23 cents per pound, plus freight costs, and limited the refiners' selling price to 21 cents. Although this new order was effective until 13 September, continued rising costs necessitated price changes before that date. In July 1920 retailers' prices were revised to 26 cents, plus freight costs, and the refiners' selling price rose to 24 cents.[9] These high prices persisted into August, but then the sugar market slowly began to give way.

Between August 1919 and August 1920, a period of rising costs and rising prices, the board's actions did not particularly hamper the refiners. For one thing, while raw material costs rose the board stabilized the industry by preventing price competition between refiners. For another, the board's regulations, such as Order no 38, did not unduly restrict corporate profits. Moreover, when Order no 38 was rescinded, the board made no effort to limit windfall gains under the new conditions which prevailed.

The board's policy regarding the resale of raw sugar contracts exemplifies its bias in favour of the refiners. Under Order no 38, of course, resales were prohibited. The board justified this policy to the industry by pointing out that 'if this Board had not made it so profitable to the refineries to bring in their raw sugars, as this Board did when it made its order of 8th January, this Board would not have imposed any terms with respect to resales.' The fact remains, however, that the refiners did make substantial profits on resales of their raw sugars.

8 Quoted in *Canadian Annual Review*, 1920, 197
9 BCF, vol. 16, Order no 82, 18 June; Order no 88, 20 July 1920

Atlantic Sugar, for example, netted $1,199,012.77 on resales. While it is true that these profits were made on contracts closed during the control-free period from 16 February to 30 April 1920, these materials still had to be replaced by higher-priced supplies. Yet the board, which earlier had promised to force companies 'to share in part with the Canadian people the benefits of the cheaper prices at which such refiners have bought,' made no subsequent effort to compel readjustments by any of the refiners.[10] Thus, the refiners gained all the benefits of their perspicacious low-priced purchases while the domestic price of sugar was in no way reduced by their speculative coup.

The refiners had every reason to be pleased with the performance of the Board of Commerce – they had urged its appointment in the first place! 'When the Financial Post asked the refiners their feelings as to the [first sugar] ruling there was no protest expressed; it was [their] general view that public opinion was so aroused over high costs, and suspicious of profiteering, that deference to this state of affairs demanded the fixing of a maximum profit.' As early as 1917 J.W. McConnell, president of St Lawrence Sugar, had proposed the establishment of an agency similar to the Board of Commerce, and McConnell had recommended that W.F. O'Connor should head it. Two years later McConnell again supported O'Connor's nomination to the board, and this time he had the full concurrence of all the other refiners. This strong lobby led at least one cabinet member, Labour Minister G.D. Robertson, to oppose O'Connor's appointment on the ground that he was too closely linked to the sugar refining industry. Robertson went on to object that 'other instances might be mentioned indicating that Mr. O'Connor has not been the champion of the people to the extent that the press and public opinion gave him credit for ...'[11] Senator Robertson no doubt would have been dismayed had he learned subsequently that the other members of the board agreed that O'Connor should dominate proceedings regarding the sugar industry. At one point H.A. Robson wrote his assistant chief to say that 'I will ... defer to your judgement as I must confess I am only superficially acquainted with the sugar business.'[12] Needless to say, under O'Connor's direction the board soon moved to regulations like Order no 38.

10 *Ibid.*, vol. 5, file 2-2A1, Secretary W. White to Acadia Sugar, 20 Jan. 1920; vol. 16, Order no 38a; Atlantic Sugar Refineries Ltd., Annual Statement, published in *Monetary Times of Canada*, 20 July 1920, pp. 46-8
11 *Financial Post*, 6 Sept. 1919; PAC, W.F. O'Connor Papers, MG30E12, no 122, vol. 30, file 3, McConnell to H.C. Becket, 9 May 1917; PAC, Robert L. Borden Papers, 76795, memo from Robertson to Borden, 9 Aug. 1919. The co-op movement also thought O'Connor was too closely allied to the refiners and wholesalers of sugar. See W.T. Jackman, 'Should the Board of Commerce Be Retained,' *Monetary Times of Canada*, 4 June 1920, pp. 5-8
12 BCF, vol. 5, file 2-2, memorandum, Robson to O'Connor, 7 Oct. 1919

Yet when the sugar market collapsed in August 1920 O'Connor was no longer a member of the board, and other people had to intervene to save the industry. By the end of June 1920 all three original members had resigned and the board had been reconstituted with the appointment of temporary commissioners. Robson had stepped down on 23 February declaring that he was 'out of sympathy with the Act.' By this he meant that it was almost impossible to bring down high prices by controlling profits, for it seemed obvious 'that high prices and small profits may and in fact do very often coincide.'[13] O'Connor and Murdock remained on for some months, but when the Supreme Court did not decisively reject a challenge to the board's right to set prices,[14] O'Connor resigned to return to private legal practice. Murdock's position then became untenable, for he realized that the government was not about to replace either Robson or O'Connor, and on 24 June he too resigned.[15] Pending a decision by the Privy Council on the Board of Commerce case, the government appointed William White, formerly secretary to the board, as acting chairman. Two senior civil servants, F.A. Acland, deputy minister of labour, and G.A. Dillon, purchasing agent for the Department of Justice, were seconded to serve with White.

The collapse of the sugar market was caused by the same forces which earlier had prompted its rise. North American sugar prices had initially climbed in response to American producers' belief that a world shortage was impending. This led to a willingness to pay higher prices and unusually heavy demand which resulted in a massive inflow of sugar into the United States from supplies which had previously been absorbed elsewhere. When the anticipated world sugar shortage failed to materialize, however, the American market was glutted. And as the banks decided not to extend credits to carry commodities, sugar dealers, both wholesale and retail, were forced to unload their inventories without regard

13 *Can. H. of C. Debates*, 3 March 1920, p. 86. For another view of Robson's resignation, see *ibid.*, 24 June 1920, pp. 4481-3 (Murdock's letter of resignation).
14 Some Ottawa clothiers affected by a board decision to limit the retail mark-up on men's clothing wished to establish two points: (1) whether the board had the power to limit the profit which could be taken on a specific commodity in a specified town; and (2) whether the board had the power to file its order in the Superior Court of the province affected for the purpose of utilizing the machinery of that court for the enforcement of the order so submitted. The Supreme Court divided three for and three against, upholding the board's power on the first point. For further details, see J.A. Ball, *Canadian Anti-Trust Legislation* (Baltimore 1934), 59, and Bora Laskin, 'Peace, Order and Good Government Re-examined,' *Canadian Bar Review*, 25 (1947), 1067-84; In Re the Board of Commerce Act and the Combines and Fair Prices Act of 1919, *60 Can. S.C.R.*, 456.
15 *Can. H. of C. Debates*, 17 June 1920, p. 3685, speech by Borden; 24 June 1920, pp. 4481-3 (Murdock's letter of resignation printed in full)

to price. In a short time the retail price of sugar dropped precipitously from over 20 cents to 11 or 12 cents a pound.[16] At this point Canadian wholesalers began to import, or at least threaten to import, American sugar (duty paid), and Canadian refiners faced enormous pressure to lower their prices to competitive levels.

The refiners' first reaction was to turn to the Board of Commerce to protect them against these drastically declining prices. As early as mid-August H.R. Drummond of Canada Sugar had written to White noting the consequences of the recent five- to six-cent drop in raw sugar prices. 'Having submitted to your wishes in regard to advancing prices,' he wrote, 'and postponed doing that at your request longer than we thought advisable, we venture to think that it is only fair that you should now give your support to the Refiners, in an endeavour not to be involved in heavy financial loss through sudden lowering of the price at the present time. A statement from you that the price asked was fair and reasonable, and that it had your approval and would not be altered until such time as equalizing the cost of raws would permit it, would have a very beneficial effect on the feeling of the country.' This request obviously influenced White, for shortly afterwards he negotiated only a two-cent decrease in the price of sugar. At the same time he announced that prices could not decline further without large inventory losses for the refiners. 'The reduction effected by the cooperation of the Canadian refiners,' he said, 'is in face of the fact that the refiners have been heavily stocked with sugar purchased at high prices, though not of course at the highest prices, and the selling price fixed becomes possible only by certain proportions of these stocks being sold at considerable loss.'[17]

American prices continued to fall through September and October, and sugar refined in the United States began to enter the Canadian market despite duty and exchange costs. On 9 October 1920 the BC Sugar Refineries cabled the following query to the board: 'Cannot you protect us against competition American granulated now being forced upon the market.' By this time, however, the eastern refiners appear to have given up on the board, at least for the moment. On the same day that BC Sugar cabled the board, the easterners called on the prime minister to impose the anti-dumping clauses of the Customs Act against American sugar exports. This request proved impossible to grant,

16 PAC, Arthur Meighen Papers, vol. 49, file 201 (same throughout chapter), 27778-81, copy of an unsigned letter, presumably from an American sugar dealer, to McConnell, 7 Oct. 1920
17 BCF, vol. 6, file 4-2, Drummond to White, 3 Aug. 1920; White quoted in *CAR, 1920*, 201

however, for the simple reason that American companies were not guilty of dumping under the provisions of the act.[18]

The refiners were soon desperate for support. On 11 October they converged upon Ottawa to discuss their plight with Prime Minister Arthur Meighen, Justice Minister C.J. Doherty, and Customs Minister Sir George Foster. The refiners' spokesman at this meeting was W.F. O'Connor, recently recruited to their ranks as legal counsel.[19] Although the content of these talks was not revealed, the *Montreal Daily Star* the next day reported that it understood that the stability of the banking system, the country's credit position, and the problems of sugar financing were all discussed. This impression seems credible since on that very day Sir Vincent Meredith, president of the Bank of Montreal, wrote the prime minister that 'should failures result, it would be very strongly against Canada's best interests at this particular time.' The refiners also argued that since government control had earlier protected consumers against rising prices, government control should now be exercised to protect producers against a falling market. These points sufficiently moved Doherty and Foster so that next day they carried the refiners' case to the cabinet, which in the prime minister's absence decided to hand the whole business back to the Board of Commerce. That evening the refiners, the board, and those 'members of the Government left in the city' considered the whole problem once more; the next day, 13 October, Order no 92 was issued.[20]

Under its new regulations the Board of Commerce fixed the retail price of sugar at 21 cents, plus freight, and maintained the refiners' price at 18.5 cents. The board also moved to ban all imports of cheaper foreign sugar in order to preserve this new rate structure. Canadian refiners were compelled to sell only to Canadian wholesalers, manufacturers, and retailers, and these customers were compelled to buy sugar only from Canadian suppliers. The board justified these

18 BCF, vol. 5, file 2-2B1, telegram, BC Sugar to White, 9 Oct. 1920; *Montreal Star*, 11 Oct. 1920

19 It is ironic that O'Connor appeared as counsel for the sugar refiners. During his period on the Board of Commerce he once chastised R.A. Pringle, former paper controller, for appearing before the board as counsel to Price Brothers Ltd. 'Mr. O'Connor asked Mr. Pringle whether he was appearing before the board as counsel for the interested manufacturers, and on receiving an affirmative reply asked whether he did not feel embarrassed ... ' 'You are embarassing me,' said Commissioner O'Connor. 'You are saying things as counsel for a newsprint manufacturer that I feel I should take up with you, as the previous Paper Controller.' 'Mr. O'Connor said that his guiding principle had been not to touch anything in one capacity that he had been connected with in another.' *Globe*, Toronto, 6 March 1920

20 Meighen Papers, 27794, Meredith to Meighen, 11 Oct. 1920; *Montreal Star*, 13 and 15 Oct. 1920

decisions by declaring that it was simply implementing 'the undertaking being set out in an order on the 11th day of June last to which no exception was taken and which reads as follows: the Board will not recognize prices based on replacement values on a rising market. It will be its duty in good times as it hopes to as carefully protect the trader on a falling market by permitting him to average his cost down as it must now carefully protect the consumer in compelling the trader to average his costs up.' This commitment was an obvious extension of O'Connor's view, cited above, that 'a quick fall is far more disastrous than a quick rise; it means failures and bankruptcy. In such a predicament ... it would be the duty of the Board to keep the prices up; that might conceivably happen.'[21]

Happen, of course, it did, but public opinion put little stock in past promises. Many people disputed the refiners' claims. Michael Dwyer, president of the Wholesale Grocers' Guild of Nova Scotia, declared 'that during the first six months of this year the refiners made profits unparalleled in their industry. They advanced their prices from 12 cents in the month of January to 24 cents in the month of July. When the fixed price was not satisfactory to them and they anticipated an advance in price, they withdrew from the market and refused to sell to their customers.' Other interested parties put their claims more bluntly. The confectionery manufacturers, for example, stated simply that if they were forced to use higher-priced sugar than their American competitors they would be totally wiped out in the forthcoming competition for the Christmas trade.[22]

At the political level, a flood of protests descended upon the government. Church groups, chambers of commerce and boards of trade, labour unions, and outraged consumers cabled their opposition to Order no 92. Mackenzie King denounced the order as an 'iniquitous thing,' while a Unionist organizer warned the prime minister: 'I feel it my duty to inform you that there is a general outburst of indignation (even from our own people) in North Ontario here, against the ruling of the Board of Commerce: and would say that if this ruling is permitted to stand as at present, no candidate of yours could ever hope to win this riding.'[23]

The hapless Meighen government was shaken by these protests and the prime minister reacted decisively. First, the government suspended the offending order pending a public hearing to be held on 20 October 1920. Then the government

21 BCF, vol. 16, Order no 92, 13 Oct.; vol. 7, file 4-5, White to Meighen, 22 Oct. 1920; O'Connor quoted in *Toronto Star*, 12 Sept. 1919.
22 *Montreal Star*, 15 Oct. 1920; Dwyer quoted in *CAR, 1920*, 202-3
23 PAC, W.L.M. King, Transcript Diaries, MG26J13, vol. 10, 14 Oct. 1920, p. G3408; Meighen Papers, 27804, N.D. Mackinnon, Cannington, Ont., to Meighen, 13 Oct. 1920

tried to dissociate itself from both the board and its regulations. The cabinet publicly expressed its doubts as to whether the statutes applicable to the board gave it the power to pass Order no 92. Furthermore, even if the board was acting within its constitutional limits, government leaders declared that it was acting against the interpretation held by Parliament when the enabling legislation for the creation of the board was passed.[24]

The government's prompt reaction suggests that it was rather surprised by the scope of the board's ruling. Such a charitable view shifts the focus of attention away from the government and back to the board itself. To begin with, it appears that White was an extremely weak chief commissioner. Shortly after White's appointment, former commissioner Murdock wrote to Borden and expressed his surprise. Murdock claimed that White had been appointed as the board's secretary only because he had formerly employed Judge Robson, and the judge felt 'disposed to assist him on that account.' The ex-commissioner concluded: 'I am quite ready to assert that the new Chairman is one of the most pleasant, but most hopelessly useless old gentleman in a business way that it has been my good fortune to meet, and so far as my judgement goes, is not competent to perform the exacting duties required of so important a position as that of Chairman of the Board of Commerce of Canada. In addition to his age incapacitation, he is temperamentally unfit for the position due to the fact that he is incapable of taking issue with any person on any question ...' Certainly White was no match for O'Connor and the sugar refiners in the negotiations leading to Order no 92. Just such a thought led Sir George Foster to note in his diary that 'this order finished the B. of C. so far as confidence or usefulness mainly from the malign and mischievous influence of O'Connor.'[25]

Whatever its reasons, the government's decision to suspend the sugar regulations placed the industry in a difficult situation. In an attempt to sway the government at the appeal hearing, and perhaps to assuage public outrage, the refiners drew up an extremely bleak picture of their industry. After citing the board's promise of 11 June 1920 to help them, and charging that their earlier profits had been greatly diminished by board regulations, the refiners argued that the government was doubly responsible for the plight of their industry. For another government creation, the Canadian Trade Commission, earlier in the year had prohibited the refiners from exporting their product; this, they said, had prevented them from competing for sales in more profitable foreign markets. The refiners concluded that collectively they stood to lose almost $8

24 BCF, vol. 5, file 2-2, 14 Oct. 1920, PCO 2529
25 Borden Papers, 8249-50, Murdock to Borden, 5 July 1920; PAC, Sir George Foster Papers MG26IID7, Diary, vol. 9, 7 Oct. 1920

million by the application of Order no 92. If the government did nothing to aid them, losses would climb to over $21 million. At that rate, they declared, they would all go under, creating a panic situation, 'the magnitude and sympathetic consequences of which it will be impossible to overestimate.'[26]

That the refiners would lose money few doubted, but many rejected their claims that the government was responsible for this situation. The claim that the Canadian Trade Commission prevented exports for a short period seems to be beside the point. An anonymous memorandum in the Board of Commerce files, written after a July meeting with the Montreal refiners, stated that '... I do not think that the sugar refiners will dispose of their stocks for export for the good reason that they, in normal times, depend upon the home trade for their business, and it would place any one company in a very bad position to refuse to supply the wholesale trade at present for the reason above mentioned.'[27]

Far more to the point is the fact that the refiners misread market conditions and assumed a continuing strong demand for sugar at high prices. As the board of directors of Atlantic Sugar subsequently commented on the forces that ultimately brought about the collapse of their market, 'they were deep and not discernible beneath the mass of artificial cover.'[28] Under such circumstances was it entirely the government's fault that the refiners were caught by surprise with high-priced inventories? The editors of the *Financial Post*, on 5 May, thought not: 'A certain portion at least of responsibility must be shifted upon the refiners themselves, as in such case one might reasonably conclude that even without government control they would have stocked up heavily in raws at high figures to anticipate the normal demand that failed to be realized.'

Despite these counter-arguments, the refiners' case was impressive, or at least effective, since government leaders were prepared to admit privately that they had been influenced. Prime Minister Meighen wrote to former finance minister Sir Thomas White that he 'could not but be impressed with the strength of the case made by the refiners and I fear their condition is much worse and the effects of a possible failure more far-reaching than the public is disposed to believe.' None the less, despite these views, Meighen and his government could not, or would not, step in to support the industry. 'I cannot say, of course, whether the industry will be able to generally stand the situation or not,' wrote Meighen, 'but we do not feel there was justification in law or policy for the

---

26 BCF, vol. 5, file 2-2, Memorandum in Regard to the Present Condition of the Canadian Sugar Refining Industry
27 *Ibid.*, vol. 7, file 2-2-8, unsigned memorandum, 12 July 1920
28 Atlantic Sugar Refineries Ltd., 1920-21, Annual Report, published in W.R. Houston, ed., *Annual Financial Review, 1922* (Toronto 1922), 167

action taken by the Board and consequently we stepped in at once.'[29] Clearly, public opinion was not to be ignored.

The appeal hearing set for 20 October was short and to the point. Neither BC Sugar nor Dominion was represented. The former had a private raw sugar supply from its holdings in the Fiji Islands, and it was reasonably well placed to weather the storm. Dominion also was not pressed, for as it wrote the government: 'This Company did not purchase raw cane sugar further than their immediate requirements and are now operating all plants in the manufacture of [cheap, Canadian-produced] beet sugar.'[30] The four remaining companies were re-presented by H.R. Drummond of Canada Sugar, who acted as their spokesman.

As Drummond read the refiners' opening statement he declared that they did not dispute the legality of the government's suspension of Order no 92, for that, he admitted, was clearly within its powers. What he wished to present was a moral and historical case which, he felt, bound the government to help them. At this point, however, the prime minister, who was chairing the meeting, made an announcement. He said that since the refiners admitted the legality of the point at issue, he could see no further purpose to continuing. So far as he was concerned, the case was closed. With this judgement, no other briefs were necessary, and the meeting was quickly adjourned.[31]

Given the lack of support from either the government or the public, the Board of Commerce collapsed almost immediately following the public hearing. By 22 October 1920 all three temporary commissioners had resigned. No effort was made to replace them, pending the outcome of the appeal to the Privy Council. Even before that decision was announced, all the staff of the board were discharged. As of 31 January 1921 only White remained on as secretary, and he was kept simply to reply to correspondence addressed to the Board of Commerce. As for the sugar refiners, their fate was not so final, although it certainly was drastic.

Government circles believed that only the Montreal refiners would be badly hit by the decision to repeal the regulations of the Board of Commerce. Foster confided to his diary that 'The Dom [inion] beet is all right – B.C. also and Acadia has a small loss being too poor to have had big transactions. The Atlantic has speculated in raws but it is badly hit. Redpath Canada is at present prices wiped out and St. Lawrence in a bad way also.' Almost immediately rumours

29 Meighen Papers, 27998, Meighen to White, 15 Oct., 27887, Meighen to J.A. MacKelvie, 15 Oct. 1920
30 *Ibid.*, 27979, C.H. Houson, Dominion Sugar, to R. Boudreau, clerk of the Privy Council, 16 Oct. 1920
31 *Montreal Star*, 20 Oct. 1920

began that the government would still take action to save these companies, but reports in the Montreal papers indicated that the refiners were not too hopeful.[32]

Two proposals were offered. One was that the government should give the sugar companies a rebate of the duty on raw sugar. The other proposed that a loan should be arranged to tide the companies over their difficulties. On 22 October 1920 the refiners met with Sir Henry Drayton, the minister of finance, to discuss relief, but their talks came to nothing. It was rumoured that two conditions would have to be agreed to by any company seeking government aid: they would have to open their books to government accountants, and assistance, if any, was to be based on actual losses sustained as a direct result of government control.[33] The reasons for the failure of these talks are not clear. However, even if some agreement had been reached, the refiners would have had difficulty in demonstrating successfully that their losses were a result of government control rather than misjudgement on their part.

The collapse of these talks did not bring sugar matters to a halt. In the months that followed the repeal of Order no 92 the sugar refiners' major problem was to find sufficient working capital to weather the deflationary storm. It appears that desperation bred desperate plans. The Montreal refiners planned to sacrifice Atlantic Sugar as a pawn in order to lure government aid. On 1 December 1920 Drayton passed on the following note to Meighen: 'The Atlantic Sugar matter is at a standstill. I now learn that both the Montreal companies want it to remain at a standstill, that they want this company to fail, and that they want to be in the position after having obtained control of it through interests friendly to themselves at a sacrifice price, to come again to the Government, make further representations and ask if we want both of them ruined, and that they think they will be able to come back with a very much stronger case not only with probable difficulty, but with an absolute failure, attributable to Government officials.' Atlantic's problems were confirmed a year later, when its annual financial statement was issued, but the company did not fail at this time. Operating losses and losses on account of depreciation of inventory amounted to $8.5 million. These losses were offset somewhat by a past balance of $178,000 in the profit and loss account and by reserves amounting to $3.1 million, but these credits still left a deficit of almost $5.2 million. Rather than go under, however, the management secured new capital through a major bank loan and by the sale of a considerable portion of the company to English and American interests.[34] Since neither of these interests was associated with the other two

32 Foster Diary, vol. 9, 24 Oct. 1920; *Montreal Star*, 20 Oct. 1920
33 *Ibid., Star*, 23 Oct. 1920
34 Meighen Papers, 28121, Drayton to Meighen, 1 Dec. 1920; Atlantic Sugar, 1920-21, Annual Report, 167; *Financial Post*, 14 Jan. 1921

Montreal companies, the efforts of St Lawrence and Canada Sugar to secure government aid failed, and they were forced to turn to their own resources to survive. It is not possible to explain how they managed this, since data on these privately held corporations are not available.

The brief career of the Board of Commerce was not a happy experience for the Unionist government. Obviously it alienated many businessmen while at the same time it failed to establish the government in the public's mind as the consumer's champion. Yet contemporary observers concerned with social unrest and social integration believed that some good came from its actions. J. Castell Hopkins concluded: 'it was carried on amid difficulties which from the first were almost insuperable; yet some good was accomplished in detail while in a general sense public opinion was soothed and the people carried more smoothly over the rocky road of war prices and reconstruction problems than would otherwise have been the case.'[35]

The regulatory experience in the sugar refining industry provides an interesting contrast to the experience in the newsprint industry. Basically, newsprint was an export commodity and a producers' good, while sugar was sold domestically as a finished product. These distinctions produced a different response to regulation in each case. Caught between rising raw material costs and consumers' resistance to rising prices, the sugar refiners accepted regulation as a means to legitimize pricing policies and to ensure an orderly transition from war prosperity to peacetime recession. The newsprint producers, however, never accepted regulation in their industry. Because they sold to other producers, newsprint manufacturers were less concerned about outraged public opinion. Although the publishers pressed the government strongly, there was little public comment on newsprint prices. Moreover, since the paper manufacturers' principle interest was the export market, which promised seemingly unlimited growth prospects, they wanted only to be left alone to exploit the possibilities that confronted them. For the sugar refiners uncertainty and insecurity stemmed from the state of the market-place; government regulation appeared to provide a bulwark against precarious conditions. In the newsprint industry a bustling confidence about the market predominated, and uncertainty and insecurity arose not from a fear of anticipated collapse but from the threat of continued government regulation. Different environments thus produced markedly different responses to regulation.

For the government, the regulation of the newsprint industry was quite a different matter from the case of the sugar refiners. In the latter instance the government mediated the contest between producers and consumers largely through symbolic gestures. The Board of Commerce was unable to affect fundamentally the causes of rising prices and the government never intended that the board should arbitrarily favour consumers over producers. As Hopkins observed, however, merely by appearing to stand as an impartial umpire the board seemed to give evidence of governmental concern and action. In the newsprint case producers and consumers were much more evenly matched in terms of their knowledge of conditions and of their ability to move the levers of power. As a result the conflict over regulation here was sharper and more persistent.

Under these circumstances the Canadian Reconstruction Association's decision to abandon its efforts to achieve security through regulation seems quite explicable. Following the sugar hearings, Huntley Drummond bitterly informed his CRA colleague Sir John Willison: 'Certainly I am rid of any possible illusions as to what the result of Government control must mean, and I may add, also, entirely satisfied as to the absence of any such quality as gratitude.'[36] Experience, not ideology, turned manufacturers against continued government regulation of the economy.

Returning to Kolko's argument in favour of the 'triumph of conservatism,' one is tempted to conclude that Canadian and American businessmen drew strikingly different conclusions about the value of their wartime experiments. A more recent study of the American case by Robert Cuff, however, demonstrated that 'the keynotes of business-government relations during the war are complexity, hesitancy, and ambiguity.' Cuff argued that previous studies by Kolko, Weinstein, and Weibe, for example, which stressed the 'acceleration of centralizing, consolidating, integrating trends' in America and conceptualized 'the political economy of the war years as a fully integrated institutional order ... exaggerates the modernity of America's response to the crisis of World War I.'[37] These observations seem to apply equally to the Canadian experience. In the concluding chapter of this study we shall explore further why manufacturers and government leaders failed to press on with their apparent desire to create the state institutions necessary to prevent economic instability and political chaos. First, however, the manufacturers' attempts to survive without active regulation during the 1920s must be examined in order to appreciate more fully the array of class forces, market conditions, and political institutions that shaped the political economy of this period.

36 PAC, Sir John Willison Papers, vol. 12, file 100, 8670, Drummond to Willison, 23 Oct. 1920
37 R.D. Cuff, *The War Industries Board* (Baltimore 1973), 6-7, 274; see also Gabriel Kolko, *The Triumph of Conservatism* (London 1963); Robert H. Wiebe, *The Search for Order* (New York, 1967); and James Weinstein, *The Corporate Ideal in the Liberal State, 1900-1918* (Boston 1969)

PART TWO

COMPETITION AND PASSIVE REGULATION

5
Security without regulation

In spite of the collapse of the Board of Commerce, which crippled all hopes of achieving security through regulation, manufacturers continued to feel the need for institutional protection against the impact of rapid socio-economic change. During the 1920s the problems highlighted by the Canadian Reconstruction Association persisted, especially the necessity to minimize the vicious effects of competition, the desire to reduce the economic losses and control the psychological unease that resulted from serious labour unrest, and the essential need to guard against the possible implementation of policies promoted by the radical new political parties spawned by the farmer and labour movements. But as the economic recession that began in the fall of 1920 lengthened into the long-expected postwar recession, and the new minority government led by Mackenzie King cast about trying to lure the votes of the radical parties following the 1921 federal election, manufacturers realized that they possessed rather limited resources to deal with the continuing crisis of industrial Canada.

Three solutions stood out as the best means to achieve environmental control and economic security. First, since manufacturers no longer counted on active government regulation to control input and output prices, they tried to increase their own control over such factors, either through informal price-fixing or trade associations or by more formal arrangements such as mergers. Second, since wages and salaries accounted for almost 40 per cent of their total manufacturing costs,[1] producers tried to control them by reducing industrial unrest and increasing labour productivity through the promotion of a host of so-called factory welfare programmes and company union schemes. Finally, as excess

1 Dominion Bureau of Statistics, *Canada Year Book, 1922* (Ottawa 1924), 420-1. This figure is based on wages and salaries as a percentage of the net value of manufactured products, excluding material costs.

capacity mounted in the face of persistent foreign competition, Canadian manufacturers demanded extensive revisions of the tariff schedule in order to guarantee the domestic market for local producers. Although active regulation was impossible, manufacturers still looked to the federal government for passive support like the tariff. But before the government could increase such protection, manufacturers had to find a way to side-step the violent objections of consumers and the low-tariff Progressive party. Once again, following the example set during the reconstruction period, industrial Canada rallied behind the demand to appoint a tariff board in order to remove the tariff from the political arena.

THE CONTROL OF COMPETITION

As Adam Smith observed long ago, 'People of the same trade seldom meet together even for merriment and diversion, but the conversation ends in a conspiracy against the public, or in some contrivance to raise prices ... But though the law cannot hinder people of the same trade from sometimes assembling together, it ought to do nothing to facilitate such assemblies; much less render them necessary.'[2] Yet during the reconstruction period the federal government countenanced, indeed sometimes even ordered, such meetings on a regular basis. In particular, the week before the war ended, the Department of Trade and Commerce created the Canadian Trade Mission to co-ordinate and finance private efforts to establish foreign trade outlets. Led by the former chairman of the War Trade Board, Lloyd Harris, who had spent the final year of the war promoting and organizing Canadian exports to the United States, the mission set up headquarters in London to organize the postwar assault on Europe. At home, the government created a Canadian Trade Commission which regularly urged manufacturers to combine their energies to secure the greatest possible export business. However, despite Harris' energetic efforts and his offers of extensive government credits to finance Canadian exports, he failed to drum up much business and in 1921 the government gave up on agencies such as the CTM and the CTC.[3] Individual manufacturers, however, continued to support the need for private export combinations long after the reconstruction period.

The Canadian Manufacturers' Association's president, C. Howard Smith, put the case for private export associations most forcefully. 'The individual firm is

2 Smith, *The Wealth of Nations* (New York 1937), 128
3 Peter E. Ryder, 'The Imperial Munitions Board and Its Relationship to Government, Business and Labour,' unpublished PH D thesis, University of Toronto, 1974, pp. 151-61, and O. Mary Hill, *Canada's Salesman to the World: The Department of Trade and Commerce* (Montreal 1977), 184-5

not a natural unit for international trade,' he explained, 'the national organization is. And now that practically every other exporting country has perfected, or is perfecting its national organization of exporters in every line of trade, Canada cannot cling to the old individualistic doctrine.' Smith believed that the facts supporting his position were both 'obvious and overwhelming.' 'Not only has [the individual Canadian exporter] nothing like the resources, the credit facilities, or the organization and the connections of great competitors with whom he must contend,' Smith reported, 'but he knows that he, unlike his competitors, is subject even in his foreign business to the competition of his own domestic fellow-producers.' Although critics might complain that associations between fellow-producers could not fail to have serious domestic consequences, the CMA's leader brushed aside these champions of the free market with contempt. 'All the old arguments,' he sneered, 'of the effects of such a combination upon internal trade, of the possibility of monopoly and tyranny and extortion upon domestic consumers are brought out and made to do duty whenever there is talk of forming an export trade combination in any industry.' 'However,' he warned, 'unless Canada follows the example of the United States and emerges similarly into the free air of a reasonable treatment of trade combinations, her export trade is doomed to play a very secondary part, if any part at all, in competition with the better directed and concentrated efforts of the American exporters.'[4]

Despite Howard Smith's disclaimers, considerable evidence existed to support the view that export combinations to rationalize price and production schedules merely served to legitimate the activities of price-fixing rings which already informally regulated large parts of the domestic market. By 1921, producers in over fifty industries gathered regularly as members of trade sections organized by the Canadian Manufacturers' Association. Although *Industrial Canada* described these trade associations' concerns as production costs, research, markets, trade terms and phrases, credit information, insurance, co-operative advertising and trade promotion, labour relations, and legislative matters pertaining to taxes, tariffs, and transportation, Adam Smith's caveat concerning 'a conspiracy against the public' produced the greatest reaction. The CMA's leaders complained that 'there are some captious critics who hold that the BE ALL and END ALL of trade organizations is to regulate prices.' The association hotly denied such charges, but did acknowledge that 'market conditions may be discussed with the greatest frankness. The effect on the market of what may be considered unwise sales policies may always be the subject of frank criticism, but

4 *Industrial Canada*, May 1923, pp. 50-1

to encourage by agreement any method of regulating prices is absolutely foreign to the Association's program.'[5] To an outsider, however, the distinction between 'frank criticism' and price-fixing appears a rather fine one. Certainly, by the decade's end, informal price agreements governed the sale of agricultural implements, beer, various iron and steel products, gasoline, sugar, canned goods, and textile products. More formal price and production agreements governed the output in industries producing fertilizers, leather, rubber footwear, tobacco products, and various kinds of hardware, plumbing, and heating equipment. As one trade association secretary remarked, 'manufacturers up here wouldn't be bothered with an association that couldn't control prices.'[6] Such price-fixing agencies ranged from price leadership by giant firms, through informal gentlemen's agreements, to formal, if not legally binding, cartel arrangements.

Price leadership was a feature common to industries dominated by a single firm that possessed sufficient resources to withstand and ultimately defeat any form of price competition. The gasoline, tobacco, and canning industries offered classic examples of such cases, for Imperial Oil, Imperial Tobacco, and Canadian Canners controlled roughly 75 to 80 per cent of their respective markets. In 1925 a special investigator for the Ontario government, G.T. Clarkson, pointed out the consequences of this domination in the gasoline industry: 'It was frankly stated by officers of the other companies that, inasmuch as the Imperial Oil Company Ltd. holds a predominant position in the trade in Canada, it has been and is their custom to follow prices set by it from time to time. Such a course was upheld by them on the ground that it is a common trade practice for the largest producer in any line of business to set prices and other dealers to follow him.' Given the price leaders' threats to discontinue supplying independent retailers that cut prices and the tendency in both the gasoline and canning industries to insist on exclusive '100 per cent accounts' with retail or wholesale dealers, the price leaders were able to control effectively both price and production levels within their industries.[7] Under these circumstances, government regulation to secure these ends was unnecessary.

Other industries depended on active organization rather than price leadership to regulate conditions among member firms. In many industries dominated by oligopolies, such as sugar, textiles, fertilizers, and railway supplies, informal

5 *Industrial Canada*, July 1923, p. 139; Nov. 1921, p. 71, editorial
6 Lloyd G. Reynolds, *The Control of Competition in Canada* (Cambridge, Mass. 1940), 8, table 2, quotation on p. 21
7 *Ibid.*, 12-15, Clarkson report to the government of Ontario, 11 Jan. 1926, quoted in n 9. The canning industry is discussed in T.D. Traves, 'Some Problems with Peacetime Price Controls: The Case of the Board of Commerce of Canada, 1919-20,' *Canadian Public Administration*, 17, 1 (1974), 92.

agreements were common.[8] In the sugar industry, for example, W.F. O'Connor reported that the refiners had persisted for nearly thirty years in maintaining informal price agreements. While serving as cost-of-living commissioner in 1917, O'Connor observed: 'It appears that the relations between the refineries and the wholesale grocery trade constitute resale price-fixing arrangements made by way of tacit agreement.'[9] Thus when O'Connor assumed formal powers to regulate the refiners he simply confirmed the long-established traditions that prevailed in the industry. In so doing he anticipated the explanation offered by a railway uniform manufacturer who described similar arrangements during the 1930s: 'We'll have to quote the same price in the end anyway, so we might as well do it at the beginning.'[10]

In some cases, however, informal agreements could not be maintained and more formal arrangements were adopted. In 1924, for example, the manufacturers of rubber footwear agreed to establish prices informally, but by 1931 they felt the need to enact strong sanctions against those tempted to break ranks. Under a formal agreement adopted by the eight firms in the industry, they passed regulations establishing uniform list prices, discounts, and terms of sale, provisions were agreed on for product standardization in order to curtail rivalry in quality, and each firm agreed to the allotment of a fixed share of the market based on previous production levels. Firms exceeding their monthly quota were taxed 25 per cent of the value of their sales, although each year quotas were reviewed for adjustment. Finally, each firm posted a cash bond ranging from $10,000 to $75,000 with the trade association's secretary, and he was empowered to punish any breach of the agreement by a fine ranging from $100 to the offender's full deposit.[11] Clearly, when manufacturers agreed voluntarily to such arrangements, government support was not required, and, as R.A. Pringle discovered with the newsprint industry, when they actively opposed restraints on trade, regulation was extremely difficult.

The newsprint industry persisted in its fractious behaviour throughout the twenties, and even when disaster stared the industry in the face it was impossible to secure a general agreement to control production and prices. In 1927, with excess capacity in the industry ranging between 15 and 20 per cent, several leading firms attempted to establish an industry cartel through the creation of a

8 Reynolds, *ibid.*, 15-16
9 Canada, Department of Labour, *Labour Gazette*, June 1917, pp. 482-7. Sugar prices had also been fixed as far back as the 1880s. See Michael Bliss, 'Another Anti-Trust Tradition: Canadian Anti-Combines Policy, 1889-1910,' *Business History Review*, 47 (1973), 42
10 Quoted in Reynolds, *Control of Competition*, 16, n 23
11 *Ibid.*, 18-19

joint selling agency, the Canadian Newsprint Company. However, many firms did not join the cartel, and with only 50 per cent of the industry's capacity under its control, Canadian Newsprint failed to achieve its goals and was dissolved in 1928. At that point, the Ontario and Quebec governments intervened to save their most important industry, and at their behest the Newsprint Institute was formed to prorate production and increase prices. Both governments threatened recalcitrant firms with increased royalties on timber cut on crown lands, but International Paper, the industry's largest firm, and one of its most efficient, refused to follow the premiers' orders, claiming fear of prosecution under the US Sherman Anti-Trust Act. As prices declined in 1930, a leading member of the Newsprint Institute, Canada Power and Paper, offered secret price cuts and a stock bonus to secure a contract with the giant Hearst chain of newspapers. This action made a mockery of all further efforts to control competition within the industry and the Newsprint Institute collapsed. By 1932, over one-half of the industry's capacity had passed into receivership or was forced into extensive financial reorganization.[12]

The failure of the Newsprint Institute points to many of the difficulties confronting manufacturers when they attempted to control competition privately. In some industries not all producers shared the same interests. In the newsprint industry, for example, International Paper was more efficient and more diversified than most of its competitors, with the result that it saw increased competition as a chance to capture a greater share of the market rather than as a threat to its survival. Similarly, in the hosiery industry, an elaborate cartel arrangement established between 1928 and 1932 ultimately broke down because producers of unbranded goods refused to accede to the demands of brand-name producers to establish a common price for branded and unbranded hosiery alike. In other cases, persistent excess capacity across the industry made it extremely difficult to keep all parties to a trade agreement in line since there was always a powerful incentive to accept below average prices in order to reduce the burden of fixed costs. The newsprint industry obviously suffered from such secret deals, as did the Canadian National Millers' Association, which attempted to regulate flour prices from 1920 on in the face of an industry-wide operating ratio of only 50 per cent of capacity. Finally, the big newspaper chains like the Hearsts certainly proved, as did the large department stores investigated by the Royal Commission on Price Spreads in 1934, that large buyers could

12 This case is discussed most fully in V.W. Bladen, *An Introduction to Political Economy* (Toronto 1956), chap. 7, and H.V. Nelles, *The Politics of Development* (Toronto 1974), 443-53

exert tremendous pressure on individual producers to cut prices secretly and break trade agreements in order to secure a really large order.[13]

Given the number of cases cited, it is obvious that Canadian anti-trust legislation was not regarded as a serious obstacle to attempts at industrial self-regulation. That is not to say that the federal government lacked a competition policy, to use the modern euphemism for official countenance of restraints on trade; it simply never bothered to apply the law vigorously. The principal provisions of Canadian anti-trust law had been established between 1889 and 1900, during which period the criminal code was amended to make it a criminal offence for any person to unduly limit competition to the detriment of the public welfare.[14] Apart from the problem of legally defining the public welfare and the specific nature of 'undue' restraints on competition, the criminal code contained no special provisions for the establishment of the investigative machinery necessary if complex economic issues were to be brought forward for public and legal scrutiny. In 1910, under extreme pressure from agricultural groups and small-town newspapers, the labour minister, Mackenzie King, introduced measures to provide such machinery under the aegis of the Combines Investigation Act.[15] Upon application from any six persons who believed an injurious combine to exist, a judge could order an investigation to be started. The minister of labour then appointed a tripartite board, representing all the interested parties, to investigate and report its findings to the minister, who must then publish these results. In the event of an adverse report, the combine was ordered to cease its activities or face fines and criminal charges; there was no penalty provided for past actions, although under an 1897 amendment to the Customs Act the government could reduce tariff duties on items produced by the combine, or revoke its patent rights. Between 1910 and 1919, when it was superseded by the Combines and Fair Prices Act, administered by the Board of Commerce, only one case reached trial under this new law. This is not surprising since the procedures adopted under the 1910 legislation clearly were cumbersome, and hence subject to obstruction by skilful lawyers, while at the same time they exposed the initial complainants to retaliation by the combine or the interests connected to it.

13 Reynolds, *Control of Competition*, 21-2, 26-7. For a discussion of the department stores, see Richard Wilbur, *H.H. Stevens* (Toronto 1977), chap. 4.
14 A survey of Canadian anti-trust policy can be found in J.A. Ball, *Canadian Anti-Trust Legislation* (Baltimore 1934); Maxwell Cohen, 'The Canadian Anti-Trust Laws – Doctrinal and Legislative Beginnings,' *Canadian Bar Review*, 16 (1938); Bliss, 'Another Anti-Trust Tradition,' and Reynolds, *ibid*.
15 Bliss, *ibid*.

The appointment of the Board of Commerce under the Combines and Fair Prices Act marked a major change in both the legal power and administrative procedures provided for the government's anti-trust agency. In contrast to the 1910 legislation, the new act allowed the board to initiate investigations on its own initiative and to issue cease-and-desist orders where necessary. However, no presecutions could be initiated under either the new combines law or the relevant part of the criminal code, Section 498, without the written authority of the Board of Commerce. Thus anti-trust investigations were centralized under the board's authority and the board alone was empowered to decide whether criminal charges ought to be laid. This, of course, allowed the board to distinguish between 'bad' combines, which operated against the public interest, and 'good' ones, which could continue.

Despite its apparent powers, the board's impact on price-fixing associations was negligible. In part, this result was attributable to sharp differences among the board's members about their proper role in anti-trust cases. From the outset, Judge Robson, the board's chairman, was distinctly unenthusiastic about attacking this issue. In October 1919 the board's secretary, W.T. White, wrote Robson several times urging that they begin to define an approach to combines policy. 'I do not see much prospect of there being a great deal of work unless we tackle the Combines. I for one am eager to get at it,' White declared. Robson, however, doubted the wisdom of such action: 'My recollection of the Combines part of the Act is that applications have to be made to the Board through one of the Commissioners. It seems to me that it would be very difficult to inaugurate general inquiries into combines on our own initiative.' Of course, the judge was mistaken, for the board's initiative was quite sufficient. As far as Robson was concerned, 'the proper course will be to let the public have the idea that we are a Board which can be approached to remedy grievances after they are, by a simple and formal application, laid before us.'[16] Obviously, Robson regarded the Board of Commerce as a judicial tribunal, similar in character to boards established under the old Combines Investigation Act, rather than as an active regulatory agency.

By January 1920, however, commissioners O'Connor and Murdock had successfully challenged Robson's view of the matter and the board agreed to undertake a more pronounced role in anti-trust issues. Its first step, though, was its last. After issuing an order that required all parties to existing or proposed trusts, mergers, price-fixing arrangements, and other combines to identify themselves and submit evidence to demonstrate that they were not operating against the

16 PAC, Board of Commerce Files (BCF), vol. 1, file 1-1, White to Robson, 30 Oct., Robson to White, 23 Oct. 1919

public interest, thirty-two companies and trade associations reported price-fixing arrangements covering nearly one hundred commodities. At this point, however, the board was stymied, for it lacked the manpower to investigate the impact of these arrangements, while the government, for its part, refused to assist them by appointing qualified personnel at the board's request.[17]

When the Judicial Committee of the Privy Council ruled that the Combines and Fair Prices Act was *ultra vires,* Mackenzie King introduced a revised version of the Combines Investigation Act in 1923. The principal difference between the new legislation and its 1910 predecessor was a provision for the appointment of a permanent official who was empowered to investigate combines on his own initiative or at the behest of either six concerned citizens or the minister of labour. Like its predecessor, the new legislation provided no penalties for efforts to restrict competition. For one thing, the prime minister did not believe that restraint of trade was in and of itself a mean-spirited act. As King observed during the debate over this issue: 'The legislation does not seek in any way to restrict just combinations or agreements between business and industrial houses and firms, but it does seek to protect the public against the possible ill effects of these combinations.' Secondly, the prime minister fervently believed that investigation and 'the power of a well-informed public opinion' was a much more powerful check to such behaviour than mere criminal prosecution. 'What is the power of the criminal code to prosecute some particular person or group of persons,' he asked, 'in comparison with the power of spreading broadcast throughout the land accurate and true information with regard to the public interest, and which the people themselves are certain to be concerned in remedying?' Unfortunately, the people had little chance to act on such broadcasts, for in the period up to the end of the decade only seven complaints were formally investigated, of which only one, breadbaking in Montreal, concerned a manufacturer.[18]

The Combines Investigation Act of 1923 was drafted primarily to control the detrimental consequences of price-fixing arrangements between separate firms, but the act also provided a basis for the investigation and prohibition of formal mergers that consolidated two or more firms into a single unit for the same purpose. Although it commonly was understood that the term 'combine' covered mergers as well under the meaning of the 1910 legislation and its successors, in 1927 the government tidied up this point by amending the Combines

17 For a more detailed discussion of this issue, see Traves, 'Some Problems,' 90.
18 King quoted in D. Gordon Blair, 'Combines, Controls or Competition?' *Canadian Bar Review*, 31 (1953), 1094, and in F.A. McGregor, 'Preventing Monopoly – Canadian Techniques,' in E.H. Chamberlain, ed., *Monopoly, Competition and Regulation* (London 1954), 371; Reynolds, *Control of Competition*, 155, n 30

Investigation Act so that 'combines' formally included, *inter alia,* mergers, trusts or monopolies.[19] However, since the first case under this legislation was not heard until 1940, the initial legislation and the amendment offered no obstacles to the progress of the greatest merger movement in Canadian history, which took place between 1925 and 1930.

In theory, monopoly provides the greatest guarantee of price and production control within any industry, and hence it provides the greatest flexibility in responding to market changes and political disruptions. Usually, the formation of price-fixing organizations provided the only means to approximate such control, but the history of such organizations was littered with broken promises and numerous failures. Under these circumstances it is hardly surprising that producers in many industries preferred to consolidate production under a single management rather than depend on the haphazard, and often less efficient, arrangements provided by trade associations and the like. While the consolidation of competing firms only occasionally produced monopoly conditions in Canadian industry, even the creation of oligopolies through mergers enhanced the prospects of continuing success for informal cartel agreements. Of course, not all Canadian mergers were forged to this end alone, or even primarily for this purpose, but the cumulative consequence of such mergers was to increase industrial concentration and decrease the likelihood of competition.

In the decade following the First World War the number and size of Canadian mergers increased markedly. As Figure 5.1 indicates, following the country's first great merger movement between 1909 and 1913, activity declined sharply, but it began to increase again following the war. The 1920 recession apparently restricted further consolidations, but with the revival of the economy around 1924 a remarkable upsurge in merger activity dominated the remainder of the decade. Indeed, one study reveals that during the five years from 1925 to 1929 the number of mergers and volume of assets consolidated account for roughly 40 per cent of all such activities from the turn of the century until 1948.[20]

The origins and consequences of this merger movement have not yet been analysed in detail, but financial considerations and the restriction of competition stand out as its most important features. Promoters' profits, of course, surface as a regular feature of any merger movement, and the late twenties proved no exception. Indeed, J.C. Weldon found, as did Ralph Nelson in a similar study of

---

19 J. Edgar Sexton, 'Mergers under Canadian Combines Law,' *Western Ontario Law Review*, 2 (1963), and W.G. Phillips, 'Canadian Combines Policy – The Matter of Mergers,' *Canadian Bar Review*, 42 (1964)

20 J.C. Weldon, 'Consolidations in Canadian Industry, 1900-1948,' in L.A. Skeoch, ed., *Restrictive Trade Practices in Canada* (Toronto 1966), 233, table 1

Figure 5.1
Number of mergers in Canada and assets consolidated, 1900-48

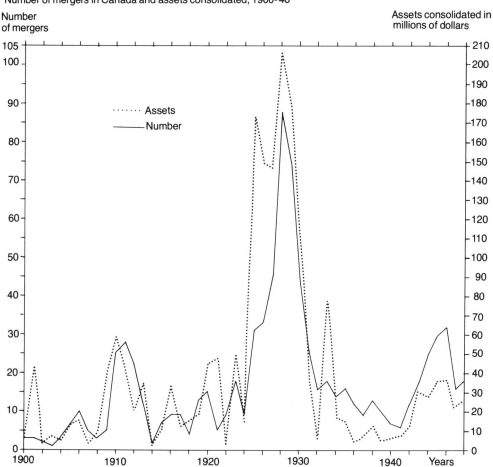

Source: compiled from Weldon, 'Consolidation in Canadian Industry, 1900-1948', 233, table 1

American mergers, that the common stock price index was the only economic variable that correlated with measures of merger activity. Commodity price series, gross national product, and national income data showed no correlation whatsoever with consolidation data.[21] Since the disposal of securities was normally required to finance major amalgamations, this finding is not surprising.

The degree to which numerous consolidations increased the prospects of restricted competition stands out as both a cause and a consequence of the merger movement. Nearly three-quarters of all consolidations in the twenties were horizontal mergers.[22] Such amalgamations generally point to a desire to reduce competition. The formation of Canada Power and Paper in 1928 by the Holt-Gundy interests was a spectacular example of this process. After the merger of the St Maurice, Belgo-Canada, Canada Paper, Anticosti, Laurentide, and Port Alfred paper companies into the largest paper producer in the world, the president of Canada Power and Paper explained that 'The underlying reasons were principally the idea of keeping the industry from flying into a thousand parts. We felt that if the paper industry could be organized into three groups – a Quebec group, an Ontario group, and the International Paper Co. – the thing would be run in an intelligent, economical manner.'[23] The consequences of such reasoning were clearly indicated by the early 1930s, when, as Table 5.1 reveals, significant parts of the Canadian industrial economy operated under near monopoly or oligopoly conditions.

In conclusion, it seems quite clear that Canadian manufacturers had private means to control competition in the event that government regulation failed to protect them from the vicissitudes of the market-place. Gentlemen's agreements to fix prices, trade association agreements to fix price and production quotas, and formal mergers all provided an alternative, or after 1920, a substitute for public regulation. However, such private solutions were not always effective. The history of Canadian Canners Limited, for example, demonstrates this point in a dramatic way. In 1893 nine canning companies formed a trade association, the Canada Packers Association, to carry out joint promotional campaigns, but a few years later they extended their co-operation to establish a Dominion Syndicate, which acted as their common marketing agent. By 1903, however, competition from independent canners proved so strong that Canadian Canners Consolidated

21 For a detailed discussion of the 1909-13 merger movement, see A.E. Epp, 'Cooperation among Capitalists: The Canadian Merger Movement, 1909-1913,' unpublished PH D thesis, Johns Hopkins University, 1973. Nelson, *Merger Movements in American Industry, 1895-1956* (Princeton 1959); Weldon, *ibid.*, 236-7, table 2

22 Weldon, *ibid.*, 263, table 13

23 Quoted in Reynolds, *Control of Competition*, 174, n 3 (see also Bladen, *Introduction*, 189-90)

TABLE 5.1
Control of output in selected manufacturing industries

	Cumulative percentage of output controlled by				
	1 firm	2 firms	3 firms	4 firms	5 firms
Automobiles	40	65	89		
Ammunition, explosives, ammonia, chlorine	100				
Agricultural implements				75	
Brewing (Ontario and Quebec)		60			
Cement	90				
Copper	53		93		
Canning (fruit and vegetables)	67	83			
Cotton yarn and cloth	48		79		
Electrical equipment (heavy)			100		
Fertilizer			70		
Lead	91				
Meat packing	59	85			
Milling					73
Nickel	71				
Oil	55				
Pulp and paper					90
Rubber footwear	39	50	61	72	
Silk (real)	23	42	61		
Silk (artificial)	66	100			
Sugar					100
Tires					65
Tobacco	70	90			
Zinc	74				

Source: Reynolds, *The Control of Competition in Canada*, 5, table 1

was organized to amalgamate the Dominion Syndicate and most of the independents, about thirty firms in all. During the first great merger movement seventeen more independents were absorbed and the new consolidation was christened Dominion Canners. Entry into the industry was fairly easy, however, because capital costs were low, and independent competition continued to pester Dominion so that in 1915 it became necessary to form yet another joint marketing agency, Canadian Canners Limited, which was controlled by Dominion Canners. In 1923 this arrangement was formalized and Canadian Canners was incorporated to purchase the assets of Dominion Canners and twenty-nine other independent firms.[24]

24 *Ibid.*, 174-5, n 3

It is notable that during this period the federal government passed several amendments to strengthen the anti-trust sections of the criminal code, and appointed no less than three agencies to monitor private efforts to control competition against the public interest. Despite these bows to the virtues of free enterprise, however, no action was ever taken to limit these successive attempts at price and production control in the canning industry. One report prepared for the Board of Commerce noted that 'if a combination is allowed to swallow up its rivals by fair means or foul and unfairly keep all competition out of the field, it is almost certain to become uneconomic, careless and inefficient and will charge too much for its services, whether its profits be large or whether they be small.' 'The canning business,' the report concluded, 'offers a most tempting field for such unfair throttling of competition.'[25] So it did, but Canadian anti-trust laws provided scant protection for consumers, other producers, or any of the other elements of the 'powerful public opinion' to which Mackenzie King regularly appealed.

THE CONTROL OF LABOUR COSTS

Labour costs reflected the influence of many factors including the general level of economic activity, the size of the labour market, labour productivity rates, the impact of unionization, and the cost of lost production due to strikes, lockouts, or individual absenteeism. Manufacturers could not hope to control macroeconomic variables, but they did possess both the capacity and the desire to limit the labour unrest that cost them many anxious moments and a good deal of money in the postwar decade. In retrospect, the union movement's decline in size, militancy, and effectiveness during these years prompted one historian, Stuart Jamieson, to describe the period as 'the torpid twenties,' but during the reconstruction era manufacturers neither anticipated such results nor felt free to leave labour issues to chance. All the indicators at the time pointed to very different conclusions. During the war, union membership had increased from a low of 143,000 in 1915 to 378,000 in 1919, and labour unrest increased at least as fast as union activity. In 1919, uprisings in Winnipeg and Vancouver, accompanied by smaller clashes in other important labour centres such as Calgary, Edmonton, Victoria, Prince Rupert, Regina, Toronto, Kirkland Lake, Montreal, and Cape Breton, produced social chaos and political hysteria. As Jamieson pointed out, '1919 was a peak period of labour unrest, with numbers of strikes, workers involved and man-days lost far exceeding any previous year in Canada's

25 BCF, vol. 12, file 2-33, Report on the Canadian Industry, prepared by W.T. Jackman
26 Stuart M. Jamieson, *Times of Trouble: Labour Unrest and Industrial Conflict in Canada, 1900-66* (Ottawa 1968), chap. 4: 'The Torpid Twenties'; 158, 185, 186

history. And, in proportion to the country's total paid labour and to total union membership, it has never been reached since ... ' The next year was much the same. Although strikes generally were smaller in size and shorter in duration, there were nearly as many walkouts as the year before, 310 compared to 322 in 1919.[26] Under these conditions it is hardly surprising that producers, alone in their own factories or together at Canadian Manufacturers' Association meetings, gave long and hard thought to their employees' attitudes, working and living conditions, and their politics.[27]

Changes in technology and the emergence of large corporations produced an urgent need for major reforms in industrial relations policies after the turn of the century. Although Gregory S. Kealey has argued that during the 1880s and 1890s 'craftsmen employed their monopoly on skill and experience to dictate terms to their employers in an amazing array of areas which in modern parlance gave to these late nineteenth century craftsmen a high degree of workers control of production,'[28] the subsequent development of the assembly line and mass production techniques destroyed this pattern in all but a few industries. As production functions became routine and were hived off from entrepreneurial functions in the main office, the social distance between employer and employee increased dramatically,[29] and industrial conflict intensified as manufacturers tried to force their workmen to adjust their production patterns to the rhythm of the assembly line. Manufacturers' attitudes towards their workmen hardened with each conflict. 'Under the factory system,' complained the *Monetary Times*, 'many employers fail to recognize an essential difference between machines and the human labor by which they are operated; kindly interest and consistent devotion have been replaced by indifference and distrust. The outcome has been strikes, lockouts and riots.'[30]

These attitudes, however, were counter-productive. The new production schedules required industrial labourers to perform assembly line work with in-

27 Throughout this period, the CMA's Industrial Relations Committee was composed of representatives of some of the biggest companies in the country. In 1919, for example, the committee was composed of spokesmen for Goodyear Tire and Rubber, the Steel Company of Canada, Massey-Harris, Vulcan Iron Works, the British American Oil Company, and Canadian General Electric.
28 Kealey, 'The Honest Workingman and Workers' Control: The Experience of Toronto Skilled Workers, 1860-1892,' *Labour/Le Travailleur*, 1 (1976), 32
29 T.W. Acheson, 'Changing Social Origins of the Canadian Industrial Elite, 1880-1910,' in Glenn Porter and Robert Cuff, eds., *Enterprise and National Development* (Toronto 1973), 78
30 Cited in Michael Bliss, *A Living Profit* (Toronto 1974), 75. See also Craig Heron and Bryan D. Palmer, 'Through the Prism of the Strike: Industrial Conflict in Southern Ontario, 1901-14,' *Canadian Historical Review*, 58 (1977)

creased intensity and attention to detail, but such changes in work habits by skilled and unskilled workers alike demanded more sophisticated managerial techniques and attitudes than had prevailed in the past.[31] During the 1920s the CMA tried to encourage these attitudes by promoting the spread of new ideas about industrial relations. As one reformer, CMA president S.R. Parsons of British American Oil, indicated, these policies might help 'to regain an attitude akin to that which prevailed in the seventeenth century when there was a glory and a pride in trade and craft which has been largely lost out of our industrial life.' However romantic, these sentiments reflected an attempt by Canadian manufacturers to confront the problem of industrial alienation. As a Massey-Harris official observed, perhaps somewhat hopefully: '... it is not too much to say that in Canadian industry the old point of view that labor was simply a commodity is a thing of the past. The employees are thought of and treated not as cogs in the industrial machine but as human beings; and it is becoming recognized more and more by the best type of manufacturer that the proper function of industry is to produce men no less than goods.'

The CMA leaders believed that the formation of co-operative works councils and improvements in working conditions and benefits were the best ways to achieve this goal. The association's Industrial Relations Committee argued 'that the real solution and the only solution of the so-called problem of industrial relations is the development of a spirit of mutual good-will and cooperation instead of antagonism.'[32] The committee recommended that manufacturers establish works councils, based on Mackenzie King's Colorado plan in the United States and the Whitley plan in Great Britain, as joint management-labour forums to discuss subjects such as 'wages, production, hours of labor, conditions of the plant, and suggestions to improve processes of manufacture.' Ultimately, the CMA hoped that 'such councils [would] awaken the interests of employees and make them feel that the prosperity of the individual plant adds to their own welfare.'[33]

Such councils, of course, were little more than company unions.[34] To make the idea more attractive to workmen and to increase their stake in the success of

31 Reinhard Bendix, *Work and Authority in Industry* (New York 1963), 204
32 *Industrial Canada*, July 1918, p. 151 (Parsons); Jan. 1927, p. 112 (Massey-Harris); July 1922, pp. 156-7 (IRC)
33 *Ibid.*, July 1920, p. 173, Report of the Industrial Relations Committee. For a discussion of King's work and ideas, see W.L.M. King, *Industry and Humanity* (Toronto 1973), with an introduction by David Jay Bercuson, and Paul Craven, 'The Invention of the Public: Mackenzie King and the Problem of Order,' unpublished paper read to Sociology Department Colloquium, University of Toronto, 26 Jan. 1977
34 For a revealing case study, see Bruce Scott, 'A Place in the Sun: The Industrial Council at Massey-Harris, 1919-1929,' *Labour/Le Travailleur*, 1 (1976).

the scheme, the CMA recommended that employers introduce many 'factory welfare' measures in conjunction with the co-operative councils. At this time, factory welfare measures included 'workingmen's clubs, physical culture, education, industrial training, religious work, music, social gatherings, profit sharing, stock purchase plans, domestic education, health (bathing facilities and lunch rooms), insurance and beneficial organizations, savings plans, financial aid, and the general promotion of close relations between employer and employee.'[35] In order to justify these improvements among themselves, some manufacturers pointed out that they had 'been brought to a realization that, in order to obtain 100 cents on the dollar paid to the employee, consideration had to be given to the mental and physical condition of the human unit of organization ... To say the [improvements] are costly is to falsify. The results that accrue more than equalize and justify the cost of upkeep.'[36]

The impact of these proposals on industrial circles is indicated by a survey conducted for the Ontario Department of Labour in 1928. From a sample of three hundred firms, employing 185,000 workers, it was found that 61 per cent of the firms had pension schemes of various kinds; 35 per cent had group insurance plans; 26 per cent of the firms, covering half of the employees, had insurance schemes other than group insurance; 25 per cent had bonus systems of some kind; 15 per cent had employee stock purchase plans; and 21 per cent of the firms surveyed, employing 48 per cent of the workers, had works councils and shop committee schemes in operation.[37]

H.C. Pentland regards the spread of these tactics as a consequence of the separation between ownership and management functions within the modern corporation. The new professional managers were more detached, and could 'more readily appreciate the advantages of good communication in an on-going concern divorced from the life-cycle of any particular individual.' As a result, they were 'better equipped for the work of getting joint-councils established and making them operate.' This view seems well founded. As noted, the CMA Industrial Relations Committee, which promoted these ideas so vigorously, was always dominated by representatives from bigger companies, which often employed specialized industrial relations officers.[38] This point is also borne out by the results of the Labour Department survey which indicated clearly that larger firms, employing a disproportionately large number of industrial workers, tended to establish works councils more frequently.

35 Stephen J. Scheinberg, 'Progressivism in Industry: The Welfare Movement in the American Factory,' Canadian Historical Association, *Historical Papers*, 1967, pp. 184-5
36 *Industrial Canada*, June 1918, pp. 65-6
37 *Ibid.*, June 1929, p. 147
38 Pentland, *A Study of the Changing Social, Economic and Political Background of the Canadian System of Industrial Relations* (Ottawa 1968) 100

The spread of factory welfare schemes reflected an important change in manufacturers' ideas about motivating their work force. At one time, employers generally had agreed with the view that 'It was flaws in the character of working-men – unwillingness to work or save or educate themselves – which held them back, not any failure of the system.'[39] The growth of the American industrial engineer F.W. Taylor's scientific management movement, however, and the development of the 'science' of industrial psychology, began to undermine this image of the industrial worker. As more and more manufacturers confronted the problem of industrial alienation, managers struggled to come to terms with the need to broaden their interpretation of the worker's conception of self-interest. The human engineering techniques associated with the scientific management and factory welfare movements represented a serious effort to provide social as well as economic incentives for increased production. As the Massey-Harris official observed, 'employees are thought of and treated not as cogs in the industrial machine but as human beings.'[40]

The spread of such reformist views encompassed an increased toleration, and sometimes even a demand, for more comprehensive social welfare policies from all levels of government. Factory welfare schemes alone could not ensure greater social cohesion or increased productivity. Obviously, the worker had a life beyond the factory walls. Sooner or later, general social problems became industrial problems. The housing crisis, for example, was typical of such concerns. *Industrial Canada,* the CMA journal, reported a study which 'after painting the picture of slum conditions prevailing in our cities in lurid hues, declares that even revolution in its full physical significance would be justified in the light of such revelations.'[41] Although the Toronto branch of the CMA had actively supported the first sizeable low-cost housing project in Canada in 1913,[42] the lack of adequate housing remained obvious. By the end of the war the situation had become alarming. 'In Toronto we have over 40,000 houses that have been condemned,' declared Thomas Roden, a senior CMA executive member, 'and yet [they] have been reinhabited, and similar conditions exist in other parts of Canada. That is a condition that we should not allow to exist. It was that condition that brought about the downfall of Russia, the indifference of the guiding classes to these conditions.' The solution to this persistent problem, however, seemed beyond the capacity of the private sector. Therefore the CMA

39 Bliss, *A Living Profit*, 63. Bliss (pp. 69-71) also provides a description of earlier factory welfare schemes which began around the turn of the century.
40 Bendix, *Work and Authority*, 204
41 Nov. 1920, p. 59
42 Bliss, *A Living Profit*, 70

proposed another approach: 'Private enterprise seems unable if not unwilling to shoulder the risk and expense of erecting enough houses to fill the present need and, in the emergency, the Government itself should do something to solve the problem.'[43]

This proposal, along with the CMA's generally favourable view of a state health insurance system and an old age pension plan, indicate clearly the CMA's growing realization that state-sponsored social welfare reforms were desirable. *Industrial Canada* put the issue bluntly: The whole system of state insurance must be grafted onto society in order to buttress the capitalist state. This includes more than securing compensation for accidents; it means out-of-work benefits, care for the health of the family, old age pensions, and even something in the way of death benefits and funeral expenses. To obstruct, as a class, the enactment of these ameliorative measures, is short-sighted ...'[44]

The development of such views, however, never completely displaced traditional attitudes which characterized the work force as selfish and short-sighted. Nor were all manufacturers swept away with enthusiasm at the birth of the social welfare state. As Reinhard Bendix has noted, reformist arguments were sufficiently ambiguous that it was 'easy for employers to feel with equal sincerity either that the old symbols of the struggle for survival were as valid as ever or that the new emphasis upon the attitudes of workers constituted a major change which redeemed the attitudes of the past.'[45] For every defence of social reform it was easy to find a contrary opinion. 'Our statute books are clogged now with hundreds of acts that are not only useless but mischievous,' complained Arthur Hatch, a Stelco executive who once served as the CMA's president. 'They make it harder and more expensive for people to live and to do their work without bestowing any benefits or furnishing any really necessary safeguards. They add immensely to the cost of Government. Many of the laws are designed to dissipate capital and distribute it in socialist schemes that will do more harm than good. Instead of this mass of legislation we need a few good and simple laws, severely, but justly, administered.[46] Hatch and similar-minded manufacturers objected most vociferously to workman's compensation, unemployment insurance, minimum wage and compulsory arbitration measures.

These manufacturers objected to workman's compensation benefits and proposals for unemployment insurance plans on much the same grounds. The work-

---

43 *Industrial Canada*, July 1918, pp. 196-7, June 1918, p. 40
44 *Ibid.*, July 1930, p. 152, July 1929, pp. 145-6, April 1919, p. 130: Judson Gennel,
  'State Insurance as a Means to Contentment,' reprinted from the *Michigan Manufacturer.*
45 *Work and Authority*, 296
46 *Industrial Canada*, July 1924, p. 146

man's compensation plan, they argued, failed to tax the workers who benefited from the scheme, and it was subject to the escalating demands of labour unions which persistently argued for higher rates of compensation. Furthermore, the plan often encouraged malingering, they claimed.[47] Unemployment benefits would also provide 'an invitation to stop work.' Such schemes, the manufacturers declared, obscured the real solution to the distress of the unemployed, which was more jobs through increased economic development. Moreover, experience in other countries, such as England, revealed that 'the principle of insurance is lost sight of, and under political exigencies the schemes degenerate into the mere distribution of public monies among the unemployed regardless of whether they have contributed or not.'[48]

Although they rejected proposals for a minimum wage law for adult males, the CMA did accept the principle of such regulations for women and minors. However, this legislation was appealing because it protected fair-minded employers from unscrupulous competitors who heartlessly exploited the most vulnerable segment of the work force. Such legislation, manufacturers pointed out, was social, not economic, and was justifiable on humanitarian grounds alone. The principle could not be applied across the whole labour market, however. In all but exceptional cases competitive values had to prevail over sentiment. Moreover, the CMA objected that once minimum wages were imposed for all workers, the government which initiated them would be most unlikely to lower them, even if economic conditions deteriorated, for fear of defeat by hostile voters.[49]

The CMA lodged a similar objection against proposed compulsory arbitration laws. 'Employers have learned by bitter experience,' *Industrial Canada* claimed, 'how unreliable is the third, or presumably disinterested party, in a commission. Instead of being a non-partisan, fair-minded judge, he is too often a political appointee who promptly sides with the employees and becomes their advocate rather than their judge.' The heart of the CMA's objection in this case, however, was that 'the application of the compulsory arbitration principle to general industry constituted an unwarranted interference with an employer's management of his own business.'[50]

These objections suggest two levels of analysis concerning manufacturers' attitudes towards the social welfare state. First, despite objections by some of

47 *Ibid.*, July 1924, p. 108, June 1917, p. 203. For the history of this dispute, see Michael Piva, 'The Workmen's Compensation Movement in Ontario,' *Ontario History*, 1975
48 *Ibid.*, Dec. 1919, p. 45, July 1930, pp. 152-3
49 *Ibid.*, April 1922, p. 50
50 *Ibid.*, Nov. 1919, p. 44, July 1929, p. 146

their contemporaries that social reforms buttressed rather than weakened the capitalist order, many manufacturers feared that successive governments would side with their employees at the employers' expense. Ultimately, such costs might become antithetical to the long-run interests of capital. This points to questions about the nature of the capitalist state itself, which will be discussed in detail in the conclusion to this study. Second, it is important to note that the difference between acceptable social welfare measures and unacceptable reforms lay in the fact that the former did not interfere with the traditional prerogatives of the employer to run his own shop as he saw fit and did not tax manufacturers as a special occupational group. This distinction suggests the basis of a psychological interpretation of the manufacturers' attitudes. For factory legislation of the kind described clearly struck at the heart of a code of ethics, long formalized in a series of popular myths and symbols, which manufacturers were prepared to defend fiercely. Whatever the economic costs, workman's compensation, unemployment insurance, minimum wage and compulsory arbitration laws all tampered with the manufacturer's traditional right to deal with his employees as the market or his conscience dictated. Robert E. Lane has argued that such tampering was psychologically intolerable:

While regulation came to businessmen with a relatively low price tag, it nevertheless was burdensome and exacted a toll of anxiety, frustration, and dejection beyond all relation to the economic cost. The reason for this, of course, is that men respond to a variety of motives and are moved by needs and desires not measured along economic parameters ... [Regulation], the events which prompted it, and the rationale which supported it, impinged on such motives and thwarted such needs. First, the regulation challenged the businessman's belief system, profaned his idols, and depreciated his myths. As the literature of anthropology testifies, such an attack is painful and disruptive to any community. Second, it denigrated the businessman himself, lowered his status in the community, and allocated to him a role subordinate to the one he had enjoyed. In this way it attacked what might be termed the business ego, psychologically a most traumatic experience. Third, it frustrated men by depriving them of choices to which they had become accustomed, choices associated with dealing with unions, paying for overtime, and advertising and pricing their products. Finally, it aroused new anxieties and developed uncertainties in a time already tense with doubt and foreboding. It exacerbated one of the defects of a mobile, free, and indeed, 'contract society.'[51]

51 Lane, *The Regulation of Businessmen* (Hamden, Conn. 1966), 19-20

To what extent, then, did manufacturers believe that a few factory and social welfare reforms could constitute an effective response to industrial alienation? One is tempted to dismiss such measures as blatant hypocrisy. After all, companies with the worst industrial relations records in the country often claimed the most enlightened views regarding the need for reforms.[52] Yet as Reinhard Bendix has noted, 'when ideologies are formulated to defend a set of economic interests, it is more illuminating to examine the strategy of argument than to insist that the argument is selfish.'[53] In this case, the strategy of argument is quite revealing. By the end of the war spokesmen in the CMA, the CRA, and even in the prime minister's office, accepted the apparently undeniable fact that large-scale enterprise and capitalist social relations created a profound sense of alienation from work and from the prevailing social system among the industrial working class. Given their unwillingness to reject economies of scale or change property relations, manufacturers opted to support the factory welfare movement. Problems that derived from systemic contradictions were thus transformed into 'industrial relations problems' amenable to managerial solutions. Questions of power and wealth gave way to answers stressing human engineering and communication techniques. While H.C. Pentland once noted that 'feudal employers understood better than capitalist ones that human motivation is a complex thing in which economic motives may play a minor part,'[54] the ideology, if not always the practice, of labour relations had begun to change. Together with stable prices, wage changes, declining unemployment, and apathetic union activity, this change helped produce 'the torpid twenties' after the seething reconstruction period.

THE CONTROL OF TARIFF POLICY

Manufacturers tried to draw upon their own resources to regulate competition and stablize labour relations, but their efforts to refashion the tariff system to protect the domestic market from foreign competition compelled them back into the political arena. During the twenties the control of tariff policy required action at two levels. First, manufacturers joined together in organizations like the CMA to defend the historic National Policy from the fierce attacks of anti-protectionist interests which for a time threatened to destroy the tariff system

52 See *Industrial Canada*, Oct. 1922, p. 47, for a discussion of the British Empire Steel Corporation's views.
53 *Work and Authority*, 199
54 Pentland, 'The Development of a Capitalistic Labour Market in Canada,' *Canadian Journal of Economics and Political Science*, 25 (1959), 454

altogether. As a first line of defence against this radical surge industrialists urged the appointment of a tariff board, which they hoped would depoliticize tariff questions. Secondly, once the board finally was appointed in 1926, manufacturers in numerous industries petitioned the government for a host of changes they needed to better their lot. At this stage, however, self-interest often fractured group solidarity as individual firms sought to rewrite the tariff schedule so as to better their market position against other domestic producers as well as foreign competitors.

The campaign to secure the appointment of a tariff board revealed many different aspects of Canadian manufacturers' attitudes about protection. Above all, they believed that the tariff was an essential element of their attempt to achieve economic stability, even predictability, by controlling competition, in this case from abroad. 'One of the chief requisites for national prosperity is to secure national stability,' the CMA declared, 'and this cannot be maintained for any period of time when there are frequent periods of uncertainty in regard to what sort of tariff will be in effect ... [Canadians] want a stable tariff which will keep business steady, and allow businessmen to make their plans several years ahead. They want, also, to get rid of the endless discussion and vague controversies which have been raging about the Canadian tariff for the last fifty years. They appear to believe that a Tariff Board would do much to attain these desirable results.'[55] To achieve this goal, manufacturers spent a great deal of money on public relations campaigns and secret schemes like the one promoted by the CRA. Obviously they expected a return on their investment. But the CMA's policies reflected more than just crude self-interest. Canadian industralists regarded the tariff issue as a moral question shaped by the dictates of nationalistic idealism. As a result, moral outrage, as well as economic self-interest, informed their response to tariff reductions and low-tariff political parties.

During the thirty years following the erection of protectionist barriers in Canada, manufacturers campaigned successfully to identify their own economic interests with more widespread concerns for national development. Industrialization, they declared, brought economic diversification, which in turn led to greater investment and employment opportunities, as well as increased national wealth. As Michael Bliss has argued: 'the nationalist appeal of the National Policy ... rested on a view of the kind of society that constituted a nation, a view of the process of economic development that was necessary, indeed ordained, if Canada were to become a nation in the full sense of the word. By equating industrial development with national development it established an image of the

55 *Industrial Canada*, Aug. 1919, p. 48

manufacturer as nation-builder and bound together his interests and the interests of the Dominion.'[56]

Following the Great War manufacturers lost none of their facility for manipulating images of patriotism and economic development in defence of the tariff. CMA president W.J. Bulman's remarks illustrate both the substance and rhetorical technique of the nationalist argument:

We want to retain in Canada our own citizens, to provide them with employment at fair wages, to build up a diversified nation, to develop our raw materials and our natural resources through the efforts of Canadians, and to secure the rewards of industrial enterprise for Canadians. Canada is one of the few countries of the world possessing vast natural resources in a largely undeveloped state, and consequently, the eyes of the world are turning enviously to this country, and if we do not take proper precautions, we shall lose the added value which would be created by completing manufacturing processes in this country. We do not wish our heritage to pass into alien hands.[57]

Although manufactuers and politicians were slow to recognize and articulate the links between its diverse elements,[58] post-Confederation development policy depended on the expansion of the country's railway system, its western agricultural frontier, and its industrial base. After the turn of the century, however, industrialists integrated these elements into a national development strategy at the centre of which they placed the tariff. For example, the CMA tied its view of railway policy to the notion 'that transportation is inseparably linked with the Customs tariff. A scrutiny of the articles carried by the transportation companies shows that a very large percentage of the high paid tonnage consists either of products moving to factories or to factory populations and those dependent on them, or of goods moving from factories to other factories in a partly finished condition, or to consumers in a finished condition.' Similarly, western farmers had to learn to appreciate that 'without the industrial expansion which provides return loads for the trains that carry farm products from the Prairies ... the freight rates on agricultural products from the Prairies would have been so high that the Western farmers could not ship their produce to the sea.'[59]

The CMA argued that the need for protection arose as a result of the size of the tiny Canadian market, not from a conspiracy to raise prices unnecessarily.

56 Bliss, *A Living Profit*, 102-4
57 *Industrial Canada*, July 1919, p. 170
58 Bliss, *A Living Profit*, 102
59 *Industrial Canada*, July 1922, p. 145

'By reason of Canada's more limited market,' *Industrial Canada* explained, 'diversification of product is often absolutely necessary to success. Whereas the United States manufacturer with his enormous home market is able to specialize and get all the benefits accruing from that competition on a limited number of products, his Canadian competition must spread his efforts to keep his plant occupied.' Since this argument did not apply to all producers, other manufacturers simply substituted another kind of 'limited market' justification for the tariff:

Do not many of you find that your greatest problem is reaching the domestic market with your wares at a reasonable cost, whereas your actual factory cost will compare favourably with the actual factory cost of your American competitors? In other words, I think that with our progressive factory methods, and on the whole, efficient and contented labor, we are well able in most lines to hold our own against our American friends. But when it comes to marketing and distribution we are faced with a condition entirely different from that prevailing south of the line, and find handicaps which it is very difficult, if not impossible, to offset by mere efficiency or economy. It becomes, of course, a question of population.[60]

In addition to joining the tariff issue to the question of national survival, manufacturers further exploited nationalist sentiment by encouraging Canadian consumers to give preference to 'made-in-Canada' goods. During the 1920s, as before the war, the CMA and the CRA spent thousands of dollars on newspaper advertisements, display signs, movies, and pay envelope cards urging support for Canadian producers. Even American branch plants took up the cry. General Motors' ads, for example, all contained a maple leaf with the slogan 'It's Better Because It's Canadian' written in the middle.[61]

The nationalist logic of the made-in-Canada campaign surfaced in cultural as well as industrial debates. In 1922, for example, *Industrial Canada* championed the cause of a disgruntled Canadian artist who complained that the new Manitoba legislative building did not contain any Canadian art. The new chambers were described as 'an impressive and gigantic monument to the glory of foreign art.' 'The question at issue,' the CMA explained, 'is not one as to the relative merits of Canadian and foreign art. It is as to whether the efforts of our Canadian artists to develop art in this country should receive encouragement or not. On this point, we feel that there can be but one opinion among Canadian

60 *Ibid.*, Sept. 1927, p. 53, June 1925, pp. 49-50
61 *Ibid.*, Oct. 1927, p. 97

manufacturers, and that the same consideration should be given to the work of the Canadian artist as is asked for the work of the Canadian artisan.' The CMA's support of Canadian periodicals stemmed from more practical motives: 'American magazines inculcate in the mind of Canadian buyers not certainly a Canadian national spirit, but an American spirit, and the advertising they carry creates a demand for American goods,' said C. Howard Smith, 'I can see no reason why the magazine publishers should not have protective duties put on these magazines to enable them to publish Canadian magazines to foster the National Spirit and to build up this country.'[62]

Although nationalism and protectionism undoubtedly were bound together by self-interest, manufacturers felt compelled to establish their political economy on a solid moral basis too. The businessman's right to 'a living profit' and the country's right to national self-development formed the core of this morality. During the 1890s manufacturers apparently took their philosophy from scripture: 'he that provideth not for his own household denieth the faith and is worse than an infidel.'[63] In the 1920s this consideration continued as an integral part of the manufacturers' rhetoric. 'Naturally, traders wish to purchase in the lowest price market,' remarked the chairman of the CMA's Montreal Branch, 'and we, as manufacturers, can find no fault with that custom if through inefficient practice or poor management our costs are too high. But it is not *right* that an industry should be asked to accomplish impossibilities, nor is it economically sound that it should perish when, through reasonable protective laws, it might be made an asset to the country.' The moral argument for national development obviously extended to the regional level too, since one spokesman for the Maritime Rights Movement claimed' 'we should always remember that it is not economically sound or *morally right* that one region of the country should suffer for the profit of another and more powerful region.'[64] Clearly, when morality, nationalism, and rational calculations of economic self-interest all converged around the issue of tariff protection manufacturers felt impelled, emotionally and rationally, to stand behind the established order and defend it as fiercely as they could.

In spite of their intensive propaganda efforts and their consistent record of political success, however, manufacturers distrusted public opinion and politicians who seemed too easily persuaded by alternative strategies of economic development. The history of the National Policy was littered with bitter conflicts between producers and consumers, and although industrial interests had

62 *Ibid.*, Oct. 1922, p. 45, Dec. 1923, p. 45; speech by Smith
63 Bliss, *A Living Profit*, chap. 2, 100
64 *Industrial Canada*, June 1926, p. 46, Nov. 1927, p. 55, emphasis added

won each major battle since 1878 the CMA feared that the forces of change grew stronger with each contest. During the reconstruction period anxiety about the postwar recession was exacerbated by the emergence of powerful farmers' associations committed to a New National Policy of lower tariffs. The CMA responded to this new threat by calling once again for the creation of a tariff board. The plot, jointly sponsored by the CMA and the CRA, to purchase labour support for this policy reflects the anxiety which manufacturers felt on this score. When the Meighen administration rejected the CMA's demand, and then went down to defeat at the hands of the Liberals and the Progressives, the road ahead looked extremely rocky.

With Mackenzie King in office after 1921 many manufacturers believed their worst fears had been realized. As the Liberal-Progressive alliance continued to introduce one minor tariff reduction after another, leading manufacturers became desperate to defeat the government, or, failing that, to force it to establish a tariff commission.[65] In 1924 the prime minister finally tried to defuse this opposition by committing his government to the eventual establishment of a tariff board (although it was not appointed until 1926). Mackenzie King, however, had a slightly different view of the tariff board than held by most manufacturers. 'We have become unanimous on agreeing to it,' he wrote in his diary, 'as necessary for purposes of information – permanent informed trained officials – not a tariff commission "to take the tariff out of politics." '[66]

The government established the Advisory Board on Tariff and Taxation on 7 April 1926. Initially G.P. Graham, a senior Liberal cabinet member, was appointed to chair the board, and Alfred Lambert, a Montreal manufacturer, and D.G. McKenzie, a Manitoba farmer, were also appointed to serve with Graham. Within a few months, however, these Liberal faithfuls passed on to a better reward (Graham went to the Senate), and the board was reorganized under the chairmanship of W.H. Moore, a one-time lawyer, professor, publicist, and utility promoter, who was assisted by Hector Racine, a Montreal wholesaler, and F.S. Jacobs, an Alberta farmer. In practice, the Advisory Board on Tariff and Taxation functioned as a branch of the Department of Finance, acting upon references made to it by the minister. The board had no legislative or administrative power. Its purpose was to collect information by investigation and public hearing, and to report its findings to the minister of finance. In the period from 1926 to 1930, after which R.B. Bennett abolished it, the board considered a

65 The views of the Montreal industrial community about these changes are reported in
   PAC, J.W. Dafoe Papers, MG30D17, vol. 3, Grant Dexter to Dafoe, 4 May 1926.
66 PAC, W.L.M. King Papers, Transcript Diaries, vol. 20, 18 April 1924, p. G3983

total of 178 references, all of which dealt with tariff, excise, or sales tax questions.[67]

Not all manufacturers agreed that the tariff board was a step forward. S.R. Parsons, former CMA president, denounced the government's policy and argued that 'as the Government of the day was pledged to a reduction of the tariff and as those who had much to do with controlling the policies of the Government were also pledged to free trade, it appeared to him that the Tariff Board was only going to work in the interests of free trade and not of protection.'[68] Other manufacturers disagreed, however, and they argued that the board offered more hope than the government. Perhaps they should have listened to Mr Parsons. For in 1927, when King appointed Moore to chair the Advisory Board on Tariff and Taxation, he privately noted that Moore was 'likely to be with low tariff forces.'[69]

Despite the prime minister's private musings, most manufacturers hoped that the tariff board would bring a measure of stability to their affairs, for during the 1920s many Canadian industries faced increased foreign competition at home. Traditionally, of course, the Canadian response to such competition had been to raise the tariff. But during the twenties political conditions practically ruled out any resort to increased protection. Indeed, for a time, tariff reductions seemed more the order of the day as the King government manoeuvred to secure the support of Progressive voters. The CMA's leaders hoped that the tariff board would reverse this trend and provide them with increased protection. As excess capacity ratios mounted towards the end of the decade tariff reforms became imperative and pressure on both the government and the tariff board intensified. The revision of tariff schedules, however, was no simple matter. Broad political considerations had to be meshed with the complex market relations that prevailed in each industry. And at the beginning of the decade, the Board of Commerce had foundered precisely because it failed to achieve this delicate balance among conflicting forces.

67 PAC, King Papers, Memoranda and Notes, vol. 135, file 1083, C98143 and C98310-6
68 *Industrial Canada*, July 1926, p. 134
69 King Diaries, vol. 23, 4 Jan. 1927, p. G4757

6

The political economy of
the automobile tariff

By the 1920s the automobile industry was a creature of the tariff. All the leading Canadian auto companies were subsidiaries of American producers; most had established operations in Canada in order to exploit the price differential created by the tariff on American imports. Although the Canadian industry was in many ways a replica of its American counterpart, it did differ in one important respect: by and large the Canadian branches operated simple assembly plants where American parts were 'manufactured' into Canadian cars; these vehicles were then sold for prices far in excess of those prevailing south of the border. In 1926, however, the Canadian government introduced tariff changes designed to force substantial price reductions and encourage a greater degree of indigenous auto production. Naturally these changes severely disrupted the economic environment within which the Canadian auto companies operated. Over the next five years the auto producers struggled to adjust their operations to these changed conditions; when market forces turned against them at the end of the decade they demanded another reform of the tariff schedule.

The 1920s in North America are remembered popularly as the age of the flapper and the flivver. In 1920 one out of every twenty-two Canadians owned a car; by the end of the decade the motor-bound population increased to one in 8.5 Canadians (see Table 6.1). Most people drove cars produced by either the Ford Motor Company of Canada or the General Motors of Canada Corporation. Between them these two firms supplied 61.7 per cent of all Canadian consumption from 1920 to 1930, and their combined output during this period accounted for 77.6 per cent of all Canadian production.[1] Although other firms

---

1 Dominion Bureau of Statistics, *Automobile Statistics for Canada, 1932* (DBS did not distinguish between automobile and truck registration so the ratios given are somewhat distorted). Mira Wilkins and Frank E. Hill, *American Business Abroad: Ford on Six Continents*

TABLE 6.1
The Canadian automobile industry, 1917–31

	Production	Imports	Exports	Re-exports	Apparent consumption	Registrations
1917	93,810	16,656	9492	567	100,407	197,799
1918	82,408	10,812	10,361	322	82,537	275,746
1919	87,835	11,750	22,949	305	76,331	341,316
1920	94,144	9145	23,012	542	79,735	407,064
1921	66,246	7270	10,726	254	62,536	465,378
1922	101,007	11,591	37,958	268	74,372	513,821
1923	147,202	11,822	69,920	438	88,666	585,050
1924	132,580	9301	56,655	326	84,900	652,121
1925	161,970	14,632	74,151	341	102,110	728,005
1926	204,727	28,630	74,324	370	158,577	836,794
1927	179,054	36,630	57,414	438	157,832	945,672
1928	242,054	47,408	79,388	467	209,607	1,010,664
1929	262,625	44,724	101,711	671	204,967	1,888,929
1930	153,372	23,233	44,553	818	131,234	1,232,486
1931	82,559	8738	13,813	726	76,759	1,200,907

Data on production, imports, exports, and consumption include passenger vehicles and
trucks; data on registrations include motor cycles, road tractors, and government vehicles
as well as automobiles and trucks.
Source: DBS, *Automobile Statistics for Canada, 1932*

such as the Willys-Overland Company, the Chrysler Corporation, Durant Motors
of Canada, the Studebaker Corporation, and the Dodge Brothers Motor Company of Canada also sold popular cars, they had little choice but to follow the
price leadership and sales strategies established by General Motors and Ford.

The auto industry developed in Canada at a time when the protective tariff
on completed cars and chassis was 35 per cent. Since the duty on most parts was
lower than on the completed automobile, several Canadian carriage makers,
including Gordon M. McGregor and R.S. McLaughlin, who founded respectively
Ford and General Motors of Canada, were inspired to secure arrangements with

(Detroit 1964), 442; General Motors of Canada Limited, Domestic and Export Production, 1908- 31 Dec. 1972 (provided courtesy of General Motors of Canada Ltd.) It should
be noted that the first figure cited here (61.7) was obtained by adjusting GM's data to
take account of exports. I used the industry average of exports to total production
(31.1 per cent) as a correction factor. In the case of both the figures cited here, it was
necessary to count trucks as automobiles. Trucks averaged 16.8 per cent of total production for the period 1920-30.

some of the newly established American producers to import most of their parts and assemble them in Canada. In other instances, the American producers themselves established subsidiary branch plants in Canada to serve Canadian and imperial markets. The president of the Studebaker Corporation testified in 1920: 'We are merely a subsidiary of the Studebaker Corporation of South Bend, Indiana. We are in Walkerville purely because of the tariff on the completed automobile and because we could assemble the parts in Walkerville, make some purchases in Canada and reduce the cost slightly. If it were not for the present tariff on the completed automobile it would simply be a case of there being no advantage in being over here. That is all there would be to it. We have our plant at South Bend and we would simply ship from there.' [2] In time, some parts were manufactured by domestic producers, especially for the Ford company, but progress was slow and in 1926 most of the companies still operated what were little more than assembly plants.

Even the simple assembly of more than 200,000 vehicles a year, however, had a substantial impact on the Canadian economy. In 1926 eleven auto plants were capitalized at $82.8 million and about 12,000 men and women were directly employed by the auto companies. Another 2750 workers were engaged by the parts producers. Moreover, it was clear that the auto industry exerted a considerable impact on other parts of the economy. *Industrial Canada* noted that 'If the production value of the plants producing automobile supplies, tires and refined petroleum be added to that of the automobile industry proper, the total considerably exceeds that of any other industry.' The article went on to point out that substantial amounts of iron and steel, brass and bronze, tubes and piping, lead, glass, fasteners, lumber, and upholstery materials were consumed by the auto producers. Even the railroads, which suffered so much from the development of motor transportation, benefited to the extent of over $10 million in freight revenues from automotive products.[3]

Such figures were impressive, but most people outside of the Oshawa to Windsor region cared only about the price they had to pay for a Canadian-built car. Everyone knew that automobile prices were much higher in Canada than in

2 PAC, Tariff Commission, 1920 Papers, vol. 8, file 23, pp. 4288-9, testimony by W.P. Shillington, Studebaker Corp., 30 Nov. 1920
3 DBS, *Canada Year Book, 1929* (Ottawa 1929), 416-17; *Industrial Canada*, Oct. 1925, pp. 59 and 75. The development of the auto industry also had a significant impact on the sources of provincial government revenues. Whereas in 1921 revenues from motor vehicle licences and gasoline taxes accounted for only $3.4 million of total provincial revenues in Canada of $90.4 million (3.7 per cent), by 1930 these sources accounted for for $43.4 million of total tax revenues of $173.8 million (25.0 per cent). J.H. Perry, *Taxes, Tariffs and Subsidies* (Toronto 1955), 238, table 18

the United States. Part of this sacrifice could be rationalized as the cost of supporting a domestic automobile industry. But why was the cost so high? Most industry spokesmen replied with an 'economies of scale' argument. A Ford official, for example, contrasted the unit costs of making 55,000 cars in Canada with those arising from the production of a million units in the United States. He concluded that lower American prices were 'due entirely to uniform quantity production and merchandising made possible by the more favourable geographical location of the territory served by the American company.'[4] While few doubted the obvious advantages of mass production, the question still remained why Canadian prices were so uncomfortably close to the sum of the American price plus the tariff. Canadian prices ranged between 29 and 54 per cent above those prevailing a few hundred miles to the south; the tariff stood at 35 per cent.[5] Were the Canadian producers simply taking advantage of the tariff to secure higher prices and extra profits?

Apparently the government thought they were. On 15 April 1926 the minister of finance, James Robb, announced a sharp reduction in the industry's rate of protection. The general tariff, which covered American imports, was slashed from 35 to 20 per cent for all cars valued at not more than $1,200; fully 75 per cent of the Canadian market was covered by this change. More expensive vehicles were reduced from 35 to 27.5 per cent. The general rate on most parts remained fixed between 27.5 and 35 per cent, but a significant new feature appeared in respect to these duties. In order to increase the rate of indigenous production the government announced that those companies that purchased or produced 50 per cent of the value of their finished automobile in Canada henceforth would be eligible for a 25 per cent drawback on all duties paid on parts and materials.[6] These regulations marked the first time that made-in-Canada content requirements had been attached to the tariff schedule, although they were a common feature of the imperial tariff system within which Canada received preferential treatment.

4 Tariff Commission, 1920 Papers, pp. 4321-2, testimony by W.R. Campbell, Ford Motor Co. of Canada, 30 Nov. 1920
5 Advisory Board on Tariff and Taxation (ABTT), *Record of Public Sittings, Iron and Steel*, Hearing of 12 Dec. 1929 and 22, 23 Jan. 1930, vol. 3, Automobiles and Parts, testimony of T.A. Russell, Willys-Overland Co., p. 44
6 *Financial Post*, 25 Nov. 1921. The complete tariff for all classes of imports prior to 1926 was 22½ per cent, 30 per cent, 35 per cent. After the change the complete tariff was 12½, 17½, 20 on cars valued at retail at not more than $1200 and 15, 25, 27½, on cars valued at retail at more than $1200. The duty, however, was charged against the wholesale price, not the retail value.

The government's new policy clearly reflected the exigencies of its political position. In April 1926 the Mackenzie King Liberal administration had two objectives that stood above all others. It had to keep the support of the agrarian Progressive party in Parliament, and it had to regain an increased measure of public support from an electorate that had only recently voted a plurality to the opposition Conservative party.[7]

The reduction of the duty on automobiles served both these ends. The Liberals had considered such tariff revisions in 1924 and again in 1925, but were reluctant to proceed. By 1926 these changes became imperative. King's canvass of his supporters following the disastrous 1925 campaign revealed that auto prices were a serious cause of complaint among voters. One defeated MP urged: 'Get the support of the Progressives, by a substantial reduction in the Tariff on Automobiles, and some other lines; which will appeal to the rural voter.' The mayor of Calgary complained 'that the whole of the West are grumbling (and have been for years now) at the prices the motor car manufacturers, with the aid of high protection, have been making them pay.'[8]

The made-in-Canada provisions of the new tariff schedule also reflected the temper of the times. During the twenties nationalist sentiment rose sharply. Organizations such as the Canadian Manufacturers' Association supported and encouraged this tendency by massive advertising campaigns urging consumers to purchase Canadian-built products in order to build up the country's manufacturing base. The drawback provision of the new schedule finally provided a mechanism whereby nationalist sentiments could be translated into action. As one manufacturer noted following the announcement of the new budget provisions: 'It is a question whether exploitation of Canada by American manufacturers who have no interest in the country except profits for themselves will be of ultimate value.'[9] Obviously the government hoped to appeal to these

---

7 In the 1925 federal election the Liberals won 101 seats, the Conservatives 116, the Progressives 26, and Others 2. At the same time the Conservatives won 46 per cent of the national popular vote while the Liberals captured only 40 per cent. M.C. Urquhart and K.A.H. Buckley, *Historical Statistics of Canada* (Toronto 1965), 618 and 620. The Liberals, however, decided to retain office and to meet Parliament, and for a short period this tactic was successful.

8 PAC, W.L.M. King Papers, Transcript Diaries, vol. 20, p. G4085, 17 Nov. 1924, and pp. G4185-6, 16 March 1925; Correspondence, MG26J1, vol. 113, 96263, J.W. Carruthers to King, 13 Nov. 1925, vol. 133, 133428, Hon. P.C. Larkin, High Commissioner to London, to King, 17 April 1926

9 PAC, Arthur Meighen Papers, vol. 134, file 168 (1), 80774, Chas. T. Todd, director, J.H. Todd & Sons, Ltd., Victoria, BC, to Dr S.F. Tolmie, MP, 26 April 1926

sympathies by promoting what appeared to be a more nationalistic industrial development strategy. Shortly after the 1926 budget debate Mackenzie King observed: 'It was evident to me in the Border Cities [Windsor] that the working men had come to see that our budget is a real boon to them in the matter alike of employment and savings.'[10] Later, a contemporary student of the auto industry noted that 'Mr. Robb, in one of the few comments which he has subsequently made upon his tariff revisions, when approached in connection with this very subject, stated that it was frankly the intention of the government to force plants to produce at least half of the value of their products in Canada or purchase an equivalent amount from other Canadian firms.'[11] As we have already seen, even the auto companies responded to the nationalist surge, General Motors adopting the slogan 'It's Better Because It's Canadian' in its advertisements.[12]

The automobile producers naturally reacted fiercely to the government's initiatives. Reduced protection and increased pressure to expand the degree of Canadian content in their output threatened to alter the terms under which they had traditionally conducted their affairs. Within days of the new budget the auto companies began a massive campaign to preserve their position. On 21 April over two hundred manufacturers representing thirty-four cities, towns, and villages in Ontario and Quebec assembled in Toronto to demonstrate their allegiance to the auto producers' cause. Five days later a similar meeting in Montreal attracted another hundred manufacturers. The most massive demonstration against the new tariff, however, occurred in Ottawa on 23 April when some three thousand auto workers from Oshawa jammed Keith's Theatre to cheer on a series of anti-government speakers. General Motors encouraged its employees' support by publicizing an American head office directive not to release inventory orders beyond 1 August, an unsubtle hint that the Oshawa plant might soon be shut down if the new tariff remained unchanged.[13] W.R. Campbell, the president of Ford of Canada, protested that it was now cheaper to import a finished car at a duty rate of 20 per cent than to assemble or manufacture in Canada, since the tariff on parts still ranged from 27.5 to 35 per cent.[14] Such threats naturally

10 King Papers, Correspondence, vol. 139, 118211, King to W.E.N. Sinclair, MPP, 1 Aug. 1926
11 C.H. Aikman, *The Automobile Industry of Canada*, McGill University Economic Studies, no 8 (Toronto 1926), 39. Though Robb himself was not very sympathetic to this position it is suggestive that he adopted this line of response.
12 See, for example, *Industrial Canada*, Oct. 1927, p. 97
13 *Ibid.*, May 1926, p. 39; King Diaries, vol. 21, 1926, p. G4503, 23 April 1926; Correspondence, vol. 128, 108992, C.M. Bowman to King, 2 June 1926
14 Quoted in Wilkins and Hill, *American Business Abroad*, 132

received extensive coverage in the nation's press, whose attention was guaranteed by a series of belligerent advertisements paid for by the automobile companies.[15]

In spite of their intensive campaign, the auto manufacturers' power to move the government was limited. For their part, the Liberals were trapped by broader political considerations and consequently had little room to manœuvre. Sharply focused consumer agitation represented a potent political force. Adept politicians could exploit the mass market just as effectively as businessmen. In this instance the auto makers possessed very little countervailing power. They could shut down their plants, of course, but this involved the potential loss of substantial fixed capital. Moreover, their US parent companies could ill afford to export cars since freight rates were much higher for assembled automobiles than automobile parts. What is more, despite their enormous fortunes, the principal auto manufacturers were isolated from the country's major centres of political power. In Canada the auto industry developed on reinvested profits, not bank loans or stock flotations, and politically powerful financiers, brokers, and bankers had no significant political stake in its fortunes.[16] Thus, excluding the support of some interested manufacturers the car makers were unable to find allies with sufficient political clout with the King government to forestall completely the administration's intended reforms. For example, in February, when the government drafted its new budget, a parade of powerful businessmen trooped in to advise the prime minister to sacrifice the auto industry for the good of the party. J.H. Gundy of Wood, Gundy and Company,[17] and later W.E. Rundle of National Trust, Sir Clifford Sifton, and Leighton McCarthy, all urged that the auto tariff must be reduced. At the same time they recommended that the government raise the duties on woollens, glass, boots, and shoes. Such increases served to prevent a general uprising by the manufacturers, and protected the Liberals' flank if the Progressives decided to desert the government.[18]

15 See, for example, ads in the *London Free Press*, 28 April 1926, and the *Globe*, Toronto 24 April 1926

16 In the case of Ford, 'the record of the company shows that 72% of its earnings since incorporation has been reinvested in the business.' PAC, Advisory Board on Tariff and Taxation (ABTT) Papers, vol. 49, file 134-6, Supplementary memorandum to be presented to the ABTT, 22 Jan. 1930. A study of the intercorporate directorship links between the auto companies and other business interests revealed that only Willys-Overland, a small company, had significant ties to leaders of the Toronto business community. The boards of the other companies were made up of local management and US parent company representatives.

17 King Diaries, vol. 21, p. G4444, 18 Feb. 1926. Gundy was one of the leading financiers of the 1920s. For biographical data and a list of his business activities, see B.M. Greene, ed., *Who's Who in Canada, 1928-29* (Toronto 1929), 369-70.

18 King, *Ibid.*, p. G4450, 23 Feb. 1926

Above all, Mackenzie King's personal influence was decisively deployed against the auto industry. The prime minister had a very low regard for Canadian car makers. Once, he described them as 'the hardest looking lot of manu-facturers' promoters I have seen, a genuinely brute force gang from Fords and other concerns.'[19] Moreover, it seems clear that the auto tariff revisions greatly appealed to King's imagination; in one stroke he increased jobs and reduced prices for the working man, he strengthened the Liberals' popular political base, and he furthered the Liberal-Progressive party alliance.

Henry Ford did not help matters for the Canadian manufacturers. A com-mitted free-trader, Ford upstaged his Canadian associates' dramatic protests in a devastating interview carried in newspapers across the country. 'You people are just waking up,' he said. 'You ought to rub the other eye, now, too, and clean out the tariff.' Ford claimed that it was now possible to produce cars in Canada as cheaply as in Detroit: 'Give me that plant at Ford City [Windsor], and I'll compete with the plant here at Highland Park any day. Why should't I? Our unit in Canada can buy as cheaply as we can here. We make every part of the car in the Canadian plant, and 95 per cent, over 85 per cent anyway is supplied right in Canada. We get our steel from Algoma, lumber, everything we need.' Economies of scale seemed no longer an issue. Canadian producers would just have to become more efficient. 'Free competition brings healthy business,' concluded Ford. 'I can tell you that those fellows over in our Canadian unit are going to manufacture more efficiently now. They'll have to; it's going to be a better plant over here, better organization. That's another reason why it's a good thing for the manufacturer.'[20]

Setting their sails against this ill wind the auto producers launched into a series of negotiations aimed at mitigating the impact of the new tariff schedule. On 1 May, the manufacturers and the independent parts producers lobbied the minister of customs and excise, Georges Boivin. The parts makers opposed the government's reforms too: they believed that the auto companies would pass the tariff cuts along to them, and they were already hard pressed to compete with American exporters. The Canadian content quota offered little promise either, since the auto companies could play off the parts producers against each other

19 *Ibid.*, vol. 17, p. G3861, 13 April 1923
20 Quoted in Aikman, *Automobile Industry*, 41. Ford's position on the tariff was unique among American automobile manufacturers. It reflected both his business strategy and his ideological commitment to free trade. Given his place in the popular imagination of the twenties, however, despite his isolation, Ford's comments had a tremendous impact. By 1931, the executives of Ford Canada had prevailed upon Henry Ford to the point where he agreed to refrain from commenting on Canadian tariff policy against their wishes. Wilkins and Hill, *American Business Abroad*, 132

by demanding price reductions on parts which apparently were not necessary for the auto producers' qualification for duty drawbacks. Ultimately all parts producers would suffer since only the auto companies really knew the true state of their Canadian content levels. Accordingly the parts producers preferred that the government lower the maximum duty on parts from 35 to 25 percent, and drop the drawback provisions and content regulations.[21]

The auto producers merely repeated their previous claims. Naturally they did not object to a reduction on parts duties. However, since imported parts were still subjected to higher duties than fully assembled automobiles, ultimately, they claimed, manufacturing must cease. An article in *Canadian Machinery and Manufacturing News,* however, pointed out that this view was 'entirely erroneous, as it would take the parts of two or three cars to equal in value for duty purposes the value of one finished car.' In addition the manufacturers neglected to discuss freight rate differentials on parts and fully assembled frames, which also affected locational decisions in the auto industry.[22]

The Canadian industry's export position also weakened the force of threats to withdraw. As Table 6.1 indicated, export sales amounted to 36.8 per cent of total Canadian production during the twenties. Under preferential imperial tariff arrangements Canadian exports to imperial markets soared.[23] Apart from increased economies of scale and huge revenues, exports were particularly important to Canadian producers since sales in southern markets such as Australia, New Zealand, and South Africa peaked at precisely the period when the Canadian market sunk into the winter doldrums. Accordingly, export sales made it possible for Canadian producers to smooth out their annual production schedules and to provide year-round employment for both their men and machinery. The Canadian government had long recognized the obvious benefits of exports to both the industry and the country and had sought to encourage such sales. Canadian producers who imported parts for subsequent re-export, either in completed chassis or in pieces, received a 99 per cent drawback on all duties and sales tax paid. The far-reaching 1926 amendments to the tariff schedule did not disrupt this important feature. Canada's preferred access to imperial markets still provided an important locational advantage for American automobile corporations.

21 King Papers, Correspondence, vol. 128, 108843-6, Hon. G.H. Boivin to King, 1 May 1926
22 *News*, 25 (22 April 1926), 12; Aikman, *Automobile Industry*, 26
23 By the early 1920s over 80 per cent of all Canadian automobile exports went to imperial markets. See T.C. Byrnes, 'The Automotive Industry in Ontario,' unpublished MA thesis, University of Toronto, 1951, pp. 68-9, and Sun Life Assurance Company, *The Canadian Automotive Industry*, study prepared for the Royal Commission on Canada's Economic Prospects (Ottawa 1956), 11

Mackenzie King was ill-disposed to accept the industry's prophecies of doom and gloom. When General Motors dramatically shut down its Oshawa plant, turning out three thousand employees, the prime minister calmly noted: 'All a bluff and result of threat – good for us, however, as showing tariff changes meant something, also as something to point to later when industry continues to prosper, as was the case with agricultural implements.' Four weeks later, on 14 May, King still felt that 'full consideration is showing that agitation did not have very much ground,' but by then he was prepared to admit that 'we may consider some minor adjustments in committee.'[24]

Several elements combined to force the prime minister into a more flexible position. First, although the business community was far from united behind the industry,[25] opposition to the new tariff had spread beyond the auto manu-facturs' narrow circle. C.M. Bowman, an insurance company executive, im-pressed upon King that he was 'fully convinced beyond all doubt that unless some solution is found, that the Mutual Life Assurance Company of Canada has very substantial mortgage investments in Oshawa which will not be worth 50 cents on the dollar.' Bowman was a life-long Liberal. Other prominent members of the party also opposed the government's position. The Liberal leader of the opposition in Ontario, Oshawa MPP William E.N. Sinclair, wrote: 'I think that even yet your government can give certain concessions in the way of certain drawbacks or further relieving of sales tax, or excise, in such a way as not to injure the country. But at the same time to make it possible for the companies to carry on without hardship.'[26]

These external pressures reinforced opposition to tariff reforms from within the cabinet. At least two ministers, Robb and Boivin, were reluctant to proceed with drastic changes. Boivin had 'become convinced that several firms now man-ufacturing cars in Canada cannot carry on unless they are given some relief.'

24 King Diaries, vol. 21, p. G4498, 16 April 1926. The tariff on agricultural implements had been cut by more than half in 1924 to nominal rates of 5 per cent, 7½ per cent, 10 per cent: see O.J. McDiarmid, *Commercial Policy in the Canadian Economy* (Cambridge, Mass. 1946), 264. King Papers, Correspondence, vol. 133, 113469, King to Larkin, 14 May 1926

25 For an example of business hostility to the industry, see Public Archives of Ontario, G.H. Ferguson Papers, RG3, General Correspondence, file 1926 (automobile industry), memo to Ferguson from Hon. William H. Price, provincial treasurer, 14 May 1926. 'In discussing this important question with a number of life long Conservatives, businessmen, I find a total lack of sympathy with the auto manufacturers ...'

26 King Papers, Correspondence, vol. 128, 108983, Bowman to King, 30 April 1926 (it should be noted that Bowman's son was an auto parts manufacturer in Owen Sound, (Ont.); vol. 139, 118201-2, Sinclair to King, 24 April 1926

Robb, the finance minister, who was closely connected with St James Street financial interests, opposed tariff reductions from the start and even went so far as to carry his opposition to the caucus. Later, King noted privately: 'I confess I have little confidence in the Finance department so far as tariff changes go. They make little real investigation.'[27]

Ultimstely these pressures enabled Robb to press his case for relief for the industry to a successful close. Under Schedule 1 of the revised (1926) War Revenue Act, Robb proposed that the government repeal the excise tax of 5 per cent on the retail price up to $1,200, and 10 per cent of the excess over that, on all cars that met the Canadian content regulations. The tax continued to apply to imported vehicles. King and the Progressives finally accepted this amendment when the auto producers publicly promised that consumers would receive the full benefits of this tax cut.[28]

Although the auto producers were not entirely satisfied with this arrangement, they had to accept it. Customs minister Boivin reported that

... it is bitterly opposed by the Durant people, Dodge Bros., the Studebaker Corporation and the Chrysler automobile manufacturers. They all employ several hundred hands in Canadian assembly plants but the fact that their cars are not 50% Canadian would place them at a disadvantage as compared with Ford, Overland and Chevrolet cars which are slightly more than 50% Canadian made. It appears that Mr. McLaughlin stated before his departure last night, that he had no objection to the plan proposed by Mr. Robb because it would give him some relief in connection with his Chevrolet car, but that it would be no advantage in inducing the General Motors to continue the manufacture and assembling of their higher priced cars in Canada. Mr. Campbell of the Ford Company would welcome the removal of the 5% excise tax ... [29]

Since the two largest producers supported the Robb plan, the smaller companies had little choice but to concede agreement. The government subsequently mollified these dissident firms by agreeing to reduce the content regulations to 40 per

27 *Ibid.,* vol. 128, 108846-7, Boivin to King, 1 May 1926; Diaries, vol. 21, p. G4513, 8 May 1926
28 O.J. McDiarmid, 'Some Aspects of the Canadian Automobile Industry,' *Canadian Journal of Economics and Political Science*, 6 (1940), 262. Automobiles entering under the British preference were automatically granted the exemption from the excise tax as well, but such imports were a negligible factor in the industry. King Papers, Correspondence, vol. 137, 116649, T.A. Russell, president, Automotive Industries of Canada, to Robb, 5 June 1926
29 King, *ibid.*, vol. 128, 108843-6, Boivin to King, 1 May 1926

cent Canadian labour and materials until 1 April 1927, when the 50 per cent content condition became effective. Furthermore, the government also agreed to base drawback qualifications upon total factory output rather than individual models.[30]

These amendments, introduced on 7 June 1926, made the Tory leadership almost apoplectic at what they considered King's duplicity. Arthur Meighen described the events from April through June as 'nothing but sham and fraud.' The excise tax repeal effectively increased protection to 26 per cent. By this step, Meighen wrote: 'the government has put the automobile people back practically where they were so far as protection is concerned, and whatever reduction in price there is already made or yet to be made, is at the expense of the treasury of Canada.' It especially irked the Conservative leader that these changes occurred only 'after getting many weeks of publicity for what they have done.'[31]

The 1926 tariff reforms had a significant impact upon the development of the auto industry over the next four years. First, the tariff cuts did produce price reductions. Estimates vary, but one auto official indicated that the range of Canadian prices, which were 29 to 54 per cent above American levels, declined to a range of 23 to 30 per cent higher. A Dominion Bureau of Statistics memorandum in 1928 reported an estimated reduction of 10 per cent from 1926 price levels.[32]

The repeal of the excise tax produced less noticeable results. Ford's new 1928 Model A cost roughly 30 per cent more in Canada than a similar model south of the border. General Motors maintained a 25 per cent price spread, while Willys-Overland's Canadian touring cars were 25.9 per cent and its sedan cars were 28.3 per cent above the price of their American equivalents. Canadian auto manufacturers, however, denied that they were exploiting the extra protection afforded by the excise tax on imports. The general manager of General Motors, for example, explained that 'the markup has no relation as far as we are concerned, to duty or excise tax.' Cynics scoffed at these claims, however. 'The Ford Company seems, on the face of it,' noted one journalist, R.J. Deachman, 'to be

30 ABTT Papers, vol. 48, file 134-3, Circular no 565C, file no 126453, Department of Customs and Excise, 26 Jan. 1927
31 Meighen Papers, vol. 134, file 168(1), 80822-3, Meighen to F. Tolputt, 21 June 1926. Since the excise tax applied only to imports, Meighen contended that it had become a duty. Though only 5 per cent, the tax was taken on the duty value plus the duty so that it amounted effectively to an extra 6 per cent protection for domestic producers.
32 ABTT, *Iron and Steel Hearings* (n 5 above), Russell, p. 44; King Papers, Memoranda and Notes, vol. 135, file 1086, C98509. There is no author cited but internal evidence indicates fairly clearly that this memo was prepared by the DBS.

charging American prices plus an allowance for the inconvenience of going over and buying a car in the United States, plus another sum which by strange coincidence, works out at almost exactly five per cent and represents or appears to represent the luxury or excise tax a car would have to pay if it were brought in from the United States.'[33]

In contrast to their expectations, the parts makers did not suffer under the new regulations. Total sales by the parts industry climbed from $52.9 million in 1925 to $104.9 million in 1929, an increase of almost 100 per cent.[34] By 1928 all the Canadian auto companies had qualified for duty drawbacks, which meant they all contained at least 50 per cent Canadian content according to Customs Department regulations. At the end of the decade, one parts producer confessed: 'we knew one thing [in 1926], that we were out 25% duty protection, and I think the average parts man felt worse about that than he did about the thought of additional business. But after three years of operation I think every parts man is a unit in feeling that this brought a great deal of business to Canada, and, speaking for our own point of view, we would be loath to see that taken out of the present Act.'[35]

Even the auto companies prospered initially under the new tariff. Canadian sales rose steadily between 1926 and 1929 as consumption increased from 102,000 vehicles per annum to 205,000 vehicles. However, imports also increased dramatically. Total imports rose from 14,632 vehicles in 1925 to 44,724 units in 1929;[36] the imports' market share also jumped from 14.3 to 21.8 per cent over the same period.[37] Since the Canadian industry utilized only 66 per

---

33 PAC, R.J. Dachman Papers, MG30D104, vol. 2, file 1, 45. 'Auto Price Comparison,' 3 Jan. 1928; ABTT, *Iron and Steel Hearings*, testimony of H.A. Brown, General Motors of Canada, pp. 22, 31, Russell, pp. 44, 47
34 Sun Life, *Automotive Industry*, 173. 16, table 7
35 ABTT, *Iron and Steel Hearings*, testimony by R.T. Herdegen, Galt Art Metal Co. Ltd., p. 146
36 DBS, *Automobile Statistics*. Of course the government's tariff policy did not 'cause' increased automobile consumption. One could argue that the industry would have sold more cars and provided more jobs during the boom period if the tariff had not been reduced, but such counter-factual hypotheses, while interesting, are historically irrelevant since they completely ignore the socio-political context of the industry's development.
37 There appear to have been two causes for these increased imports. First, the number of low-priced cars had increased and many smaller American producers were now more competitive with the industry leaders. The second reason is related to the first in that the reduced tariff allowed these American exporters to sell their vehicles at a lower price in Canada than heretofore. For the extent of increased low-price competition, see James Dalton, 'What Will Ford Do Next?' *Motor*, May 1926, collected in A.D. Chandler, Jr., *Giant Enterprise: Ford, General Motors and the Automobile Industry* (New York

cent of its total capacity at this time,[38] these imports represented a serious check on its prosperity.

Ford of Canada was the first company to react to these developments. Although Ford was the leader of the Canadian industry at the start of the decade, in the period following the 1926 tariff reforms its position deteriorated badly. Ford's market share declined from 43.4 per cent over the period 1920-26 to 23.2 per cent during the remaining years of the decade; over the same period, General Motors became the industry leader by increasing its market share from 25.1 to 32.1 per cent.[39] Of course the 1926 tariff reforms did not cause this dramatic shift in market shares. Rather, Canadian developments merely reflected the transformation of the continental industry.[40] Henry Ford's Model T had swept all competition before it during the first two decades of the century when the mass market in automobiles first developed. As early as 1921, however, it became evident that the low-price market, which Ford dominated, was becoming saturated. Many consumers now preferred to trade in their old black Model T and interest in different or better products mounted.[41] Under these circumstances commercial strategy and organization requirements in the industry changed. Production techniques, at which Ford excelled, became relatively less important, and marketing and management skills soon became the key to industrial success. While Ford resisted change, General Motors' executives took up the challenge of devising an organizational structure necessary to run a corporation dedicated to the market strategy of 'a car for every purse and purpose.'[42] By 1927 these strategic and structural changes produced a market revolution. The Model T was vanquished and Ford plants throughout the world shut down operations in order to facilitate the costly shift to production of Henry's new Model A. Despite the subsequent success of the Model A, General Motors

1964), 104-11. On the face of it these increased imports suggest that prices under the new tariff were no longer artificially high, but changing consumption patterns that stressed style as well as price might also account for part of this increase.

38 ABTT Papers, vol. 48, file 134-3, data prepared by Professor H.R. Kemp, University of Toronto. These figures for capacity include both truck and auto production, as do the utilization figures.

39 Wilkins and Hill, *American Business Abroad*, 442; GM Domestic and Export Production (see note 1 above for additional comments)

40 See A.D. Chandler, Jr., *Strategy and Structure* (Cambridge, Mass. 1962); *Giant Enterprise* (New York, 1964); with Stephen Salsbury, *Pierre S. Du Pont and the Making of the Modern Corporation* (New York 1971)

41 William T. Hogan, *Economic History of the Iron and Steel Industry in the United States*, III (Lexington, Mass. 1971), p. 1019, table 29-16

42 Chandler, *Giant Enterprise*, 16

managed to maintain its new position as market leader in both the United States and Canada.[43]

Ford of Canada attempted to halt the decline of its share of the market by seeking favourable tariff reforms. When the Advisory Board on Tariff and Taxation met to review the auto tariff, Ford of Canada demanded three major amendments to the existing schedule.[44] The first was designed to hamper its foreign competition. Ford proposed that the Customs Department consider retail prices in an import's country of origin rather than wholesale rates when they established the value for duty. Since American auto companies usually granted their distributors a 30 per cent discount on the list price of their cars, Ford's proposal meant that the effective rate of protection in Canada would increase by 6 per cent (30 per cent discount times 20 per cent duty rate).

Ford's other proposals struck directly at its domestic competition. 'The Drawback and Excise Tax exemption,' the company argued, 'should operate as an inducement to promote ... manufacturing in Canada.'[45] Since 1927 Canadian producers had qualified for this exemption on the degree of Canadian content in their entire factory output. Diversified producers thus maintained high-volume production runs by assembling some models and manufacturing others. Ford, however, was basically a one-model company. Accordingly, Ford lost little when it proposed that individual models rather than the total factory output qualify for drawbacks and tax exemptions. Moreover, since Ford had long managed to achieve a Canadian content level of about 75 per cent, it had no hesitations in proposing that required content levels must henceforth increase from 50 to 60 per cent. Naturally, some of Ford's more diversified competitors would have had problems complying with either proposed regulation.[46] These companies also

43 It has been argued that the American low-price market became saturated before the Canadian market, and that the continental application of a commercial strategy which aimed to minimize price competition and substitute product differentiation as the basis of competition in the auto industry had the effect of limiting the potential size of the Canadian market. The evidence cited for this view is the higher ration of population to autos in Canada than in the United States, a ratio which income differentials between the two countries alone does not explain. See J.C.S. Grimshaw, 'Problems and Policies of Labour and Management in the Automobile Industry in Relation to Prices, Competitive Conditions and Industrial Structure,' unpublished MA thesis, University of Toronto, 1946, pp. 241-3

44 ABTT, *Iron and Steel Hearings:* the directions from the minister of finance are printed in full on p. 15; ABTT Papers, vol. 49, file 134-6, memo presented to the ABTT, 12 Dec. 1929, and supplementary memo to be presented, to the ABTT, 22 Jan. 1930.

45 *Ibid.*, 22 Jan. memo, p. 8

46 Tariff Commission, 1920 Papers, p. 4320, Campbell. In 1927 the Canadian content of Ford cars was: touring, 72.3 per cent; runabout, 71.5; coupe, 63.3; tudor, 64.2; fordor

objected to Ford's final proposal to abolish duty drawbacks for their more expensive models, which to now had been protected at a general rate of 27½ per cent.

The entire industry was united in support of Ford's plan to restrict imports. General Motors pointed out that customs valuations based on retail prices would force the Essex, which sold 16,000 units in 1929, out of the Canadian market since its dealers would no longer receive a profit margin sufficient to permit further marketing of this car in Canada. The parts makers also supported Ford's plan, but naturally import dealers and consumer groups opposed it.[47]

Yet the industry could not close ranks against this opposition because Ford's proposals for Canadian content regulation reforms obviously divided them. In 1926 the industry's opposition to content regulations had collapsed when the dominant producers conceded that they could live with the government's proposals. By 1929, the industry was split again because the most 'Canadian' of all the producers sought to capitalize on its position by pushing the government to an even tougher stand on content regulations. The chairman of the tariff board probed this split when he noted that Ford was not a member of the industry's Canadian Auto Manufacturers and Exporters Association. W.R. Campbell, Ford's president, reluctantly explained: 'Well, if you must have reasons, I think it is because there is not a common interest between ourselves and the others in the industry.' A spokesman for the Studebaker Corporation explained the basis of this divergence of interest very clearly:

Our position differs slightly from other Canadian automobile manufacturers in that we offer a larger variety of models through one dealer organization than does any other manufacturer. The same volume included in fewer types of cars would entail less difficulty in meeting the present qualifications requirements for duty refunds, which refunds are essential to our continued manufacturing operation; however, we find in actual experience that we must offer to the Canadian buyer the same advantages and the same choice of models as if the cars were imported ... Obviously, any increase in content requirements for duty refunds or

---

61.6; chassis, 78.7; truck chassis, 78.1 per cent. ABTT Papers, vol. 49, file 134-6, E.R. Musselman, Ford Motor Co., to W.H. Moore, board chairman, 11 June 1929, file 134-7, Professor J.A. Coote to Moore, 20 Aug. 1929

47 ABTT Papers, vol. 49, file 134-6, memo, Musselman, undated but clearly post 22 Jan. 1930: see also file 134-8, memo, General Motors of Canada, Ltd., 12 Dec. 1929; ABTT, *Iron and Steel Hearings:* letters from parts manufacturers supporting the anti-import plan are reprinted on pp. 94-5; letters and telegrams from import dealers are reprinted on p. 90; consumer opposition is recorded on p. 53.

any reduction in the duty refund itself, would seem to preclude the possibility of our continuing a manufacturing operation in Canada.[48]

The Great Depression heightened the auto industry's desire to procure tariff reforms at the same time that it produced political circumstances that made such changes possible. On 28 July 1930 the King government fell from power and an avowed protectionist succeeded to the prime minister's office.[49] Along with its ideological sympathy, the Bennett government had other reasons for responding to auto industry pressures. First, economic collapse added a bite to the industry's complaints which had been missing in the record years from 1926 to 1929. By 1931, output had fallen by 68 per cent from 1929, and excess capacity in the industry reached 45 per cent. The auto producers also had better political connections to the Bennett government than to King's Liberals. For example, T.A. Russell, the president of the Willys-Overland Company, was a close adviser to Bennett. Also, E.B. Ryckman, the new minister of national revenue, who supervised the department responsible for customs valuations, had previously served as president of the Dunlop Rubber and Tire Company and as a director of the Russell Motor Car Company.[50]

None the less, the new government did not move immediately to limit imported automobiles. Dealers in imported and higher-priced cars also had to be considered. By February 1931, however, the pressure for increased protection via changes in valuation practices became overwhelming. The auto producers organized a campaign of telegrams and petitions from their salesmen across the country, while Conservative MP s from Windsor badgered the prime minister with letters on behalf of their leading constituents.[51] A Windsor paper, *the Border Cities Star,* reported on 20 February that 'Assurance was given last September that action was to be taken, but consideration for the dealers in high priced cars and other factors intervened to prevent anything being done while the prime minister was in England.' At the beginning of February 1931, 'intimation was privately given that the order-in-council was to be passed then. Again the case of

48 *Ibid., Iron and Steel*, p. 55 (Campbell), p. 54 (Studebaker)
49 Prior to the election the King government was on the edge of announcing favourable tariff changes, but the political manœuvrings around this issue fell apart at the last moment. See King Diaries, vol. 26, p. G5670, 12 March; p. G5740, 2 June; and p. G5742, 3 June 1930
50 DBS, *Automobile Statistics*; Russell's influence on Conservative leaders is apparent in both the Meighen Papers and the Bennett Papers. Greene, *Who's Who in Canada, 1930-31* (Toronto 1932), 1592 (re Ryckman).
51 PAC, R.B. Bennett Papers, MG26K, vol. 734, file T-100-A, 449077-341 (see also vol. 735, file T-100-A); 449067, R.D. Morand, MP, to Sir George Perley, acting prime minister, 23 Oct. 1930

the dealers in high priced cars came under review.' These dealers, particularly those who carried Packards, argued that if the government forced a reduction in their dealer discount they could not continue their sales operations in Canada at current price levels.

The new minister of national revenue attempted to promote a compromise solution to these conflicting interests. Ryckman suggested that the government fix dealer discounts at 20 per cent only on cars priced below $1,200. 'It will well take care of the low priced field − Essex, Hudson, Nash, Graham-Paige, etc.,' he wrote Bennett, 'and will not draw general attention to an increased tariff on the poor man's car.' Thus, high-priced dealers would be exempt from the proposed changes. This proposal did not upset the Canadian manufacturers since they concentrated their efforts on the production of low- and medium-priced automobiles.[52]

The prime minister was more sensitive to the political implications of this proposal than his advisers. 'My difficulty, I am sure you appreciate ...' he wrote his friend T.A. Russell, 'is the difficulty of favouring the high priced car against the low priced car. In other words, the city dweller with large means against the rural citizen with limited resources.' At the same time, though, Bennett also was convinced that 'it is now quite apparent that unless the industry is to be wiped out, something must be done and action will be taken in that direction without delay.'[53]

The government finally took action on 19 February 1931. By order-in-council the cabinet fixed a maximum discount for valuation purposes on imported cars of 20 per cent off the list price in the country of origin. The *Border Cities Star* on 20 February estimated this change 'to mean increased tariff protection of from 10 to 15 per cent, as wholesale prices on which the customs duties have been levied have been between 25 to 35 per cent below list prices.' In return for this arrangement the auto companies delivered their familiar solemn pledge not to take advantage of their increased protection in order to raise prices.

The government's policy seemed vindicated only a few days after it was announced. A General Motors vice-president wrote the prime minister: 'I am very pleased to advise you that I have just received permission from New York to immediately start operations in our Regina plant which had previously been closed down due to lack of business. This is a direct result of the favourable

52 *Ibid.*, vol. 736, file T-100-A, 450787-8, Ryckman to Bennett, 9 Feb. 1931; vol. 735, file T-100-A, 449999, T.A. Russell to Bennett, 20 Feb. 1931
53 *Ibid.*, vol. 735, 450791, Bennett to Russell, 449961, Bennett to J.H. Fortier, both 18 Feb. 1931

consideration given by you to our request for increase in value for duty purposes on imported completed automobiles entering Canada.'[54]

The long-run impact of the tariff changes is reflected in subsequent import statistics and industry policies. Completely finished imports, which averaged roughly 20 per cent in 1929 and 1930, dropped to a mere 8.1 per cent of Canadian consumption in 1931 and 1932. Moreover, four of the leading American exporters during the 1920s, the Nash Company, the Hudson Motors, Graham-Paige and Packard companies, all established manufacturing and assembly operations in Canada during the first two years of the depression.[55] The 'Canadianization' programme begun in 1926 thus achieved a significant success within just a few years of its adoption.

Government policy alone did not determine the auto industry's development; nor did market forces operate exclusively. Rather, the history of the Canadian industry and the changes in its rate of protection reveal the complexity of the interplay between industrial structure, institutional forces, and the process of economic development. More directly, the history of the automobile tariff casts an interesting light on an important aspect of government industrial development policy during this period, as well as on the complex and often hostile environment within which corporate investment strategies were formulated to deal with specific uncertainties.

The tariff policies adopted by the King and Bennett governments reflect their attitudes towards industrial development in Canda. King's administration appeared to oppose the auto producers while Bennett's seemed to favour them, but such differences do not necessarily reveal different development policies. The circumstances that each government confronted were dissimilar, but the thrust of their policies was much the same. In 1926 the Liberals discerned a need for a greater Canadian manufacturing component in the auto industry's output. Since the majority of firms operated assembly plants rather than manufacturing concerns, the auto companies opposed this policy. By 1929-30, however, the industry had become 'Canadianized,' at least within the terms laid down in the tariff regulations, and the Bennett government agreed to protect it against American competition. In both cases, then, the government of the day agreed to develop and protect domestic production facilities and jobs against foreign competition. Neither government sought to influence or disrupt the pattern of ownership in the industry. The National Policy of 1879, in short, served as the basis

---

54 *Ibid.*, 450035, H.A. Brown to Bennett, 28 Feb. 1931
55 DBS, *Automobile Statistics*; Motor Vehicle Manufacturers' Association, 'Background on the Canada-U.S. Automobile Products Agreement' (mimeo.), p. 8

of the policy decisions of both governments.[56] In Bennett's case, this is the accepted view of his administration. King's efforts have not been so widely appreciated.[57]

Government policy certainly disrupted the environment within which auto industry planning proceeded. It is clear that after 1926 political and institutional imperatives affected the course of structural change in the Canadian industry at least as much as the changing nature of the market. The Canadian industry owed its existence in large part to Canadian tariff policies. Historic political decisions to differentiate and isolate Canadian demand from American suppliers sustained the domestic market, not any combination of distinctly 'Canadian' demographic or geographic factors. However, once automobile prices became the focus of class and sectional politics in Canada the industry was especially vulnerable to pressures to change the terms of the tariff schedule under which it operated. After 1926 these forces, together with changing market conditions and altered entrepreneurial capacities, decisively reshaped the environment within which auto producers made their investment decisions.

Ultimately the auto industry adapted to changed circumstances, but adaptation was slow and hesitant The industry's response to uncertainty took the form of revised product policies, temporary price cuts, and a long-term campaign to persuade the government to modify its tariff regulations. In Canada the tariff campaign was critical, yet auto producers disagreed on the goals and the methods of tariff reform. Radical changes in market shares produced sharp conflicts of interest among the different automobile companies; unity emerged only in the face of disaster.

Tariff decisions in the automobile industry reflected the delicate balance of political and economic power in Canada. Forced to act by the critical deterioration of its political base, one government struck out against the auto industry and lowered the protective barrier against foreign competition. Another government, forced into action by the critical deterioration of the country's economic base, raised the barrier once again. Throughout, auto manufacturers struggled to gain a new sense of equilibrium, a new sense of stability in the wake of the winds of change. Industrialists alone did not and could not shape their own destiny. The impact of political decisions rebounded throughout their industry and manufacturers had little choice but to throw themselves headlong into the politics of the tariff.

---

56 Michael Bliss, 'Canadianizing American Business: The Roots of the Branch Plant,' in I. Lumsden, ed., *Close the 49th Parallel* (Toronto 1970)
57 See, for example, D.G. Creighton, 'The Decline and Fall of the Empire of the St. Lawrence,' Canadian Historical Association, *Historical Papers*, 1969, p. 21

7
The political economy of
the steel tariff

The primary iron and steel industry developed relatively late in Canada. Demand for primary steel arose from two major sources, railway construction and highly manufactured goods geared to the expanding urban industrial economy. But the gradually expanding Canadian market was unable to support primary production on a reasonable scale until the turn of the century. The slow development of the primary industry greatly concerned Canadian politicians who held the common nineteenth-century view that a successful industrial revolution depended upon the creation of viable coal and steel industries. Accordingly, after 1879 Canadian leaders stood ready to encourage the development of iron and steel mills by bonuses and protection. Born under the paternalistic eye of the state, the industry matured only slowly, and in subsequent decades its growth prospects remained tightly bound to the direction of public policy. Time and again leading producers trooped off to Ottawa or to provincial capitals in search of tax concessions, increased tariff protection, or extended bonus programmes. During the 1920s, as excess capacity in the industry mounted, the country's two largest primary producers initiated an extensive campaign aimed at securing increased government assistance. During this campaign private interests fused with broader regional problems, and by the end of the decade the politics of the steel industry became a matter of national concern.

After the First World War three major steel companies accounted for Canada's entire primary production capacity. The British Empire Steel Corporation (Besco), located at Sydney, Nova Scotia, and the Algoma Steel Corporation at Sault Ste Marie, Ontario, concentrated their efforts on primary production and steel rail rolling mills. The Steel Company of Canada (Stelco) in Hamilton, Ontario, initially focused its attention on secondary manufacturing finishing mills, but by the 1920s Stelco became a large primary producer as well.[1]

1 William Kilbourn *The Elements Combined: A History of the Steel Company of Canada* (Toronto 1960), 83-4, 211

The development of the Canadian industry proceeded in stages marked by shifting patterns of demand. Despite generous public support,[2] the industry grew very slowly during the 1880s and 1890s. In 1894 Canadian pig iron and steel ingot production stood at only 44,613 and 28,767 short tons respectively. The wheat boom, increased railway construction, and munitions orders during the war, however, prompted a tremendous expansion of Canadian output, and by 1918 primary production climbed to over one million tons of pig iron and just under 1.9 million tons of steel.[3] As Table 7.1 indicates, the rapid expansion of the Canadian railway system was the vital link between broad national developments and the industry's growth.[4] Following the war, however, new forms of motor transportation provided serious competition for the railroads, and steel rail sales declined markedly. During the 1920s the locus of Canadian steel demand shifted from the railways to the automobile companies and the mass production consumer goods industries. Highway construction and automobiles absorbed increasing amounts of steel as did the tin cans and the multi-storey buildings that began to dot the Canadian landscape.[5]

2 Iron and steel producers were included in the first National Policy budget of 1879, but the finishing industry received the greatest attention. In 1883 the primary industry received a bonus of $1.50 per ton for pig iron made from Canadian iron ore and a specific duty of $5.00 a ton was applied to steel ingots. Subsequently the government extended bonuses and protection to cover pig iron, puddled iron bars, steel ingots, billets, and wire rods irrespective of the source of the raw materials used in their production. The bonusing of the industry lasted until 1912. Between 1884 and 1912, $17,596,434 was paid out in iron and steel bounties. For the early history of public policy towards the industry, see W.J.A. Donald, *The Canadian Iron and Steel Industry* (Boston 1915); W.D.R. Eldon, 'American Influence in the Canadian Iron and Steel Industry,' unpublished PhD thesis, Harvard University, 1952; and PAC, Advisory Board on Tariff and Taxation (ABTT) Papers, vol. 1, file 2-3, Memorandum on Bounties on Ores of Iron, Pig Iron and Steel, Mineral Resources Division, 18 Oct. 1927.
3 Edward J. McCracken, 'The Steel Industry of Nova Scotia,' unpublished MA thesis, McGill University, 1932, p. 19, and Eldon, 'American Influence,' p. 3. Canada's share of world pig iron output rose from .22 per cent in 1900 to 1.33 per cent in 1911, Donald, *ibid.*, 192-3. By the end of the First World War Canada's steel production capacity accounted for 2.25 per cent of world tonnage. Gordon P. Hayes, 'Canadian Iron and Steel Industry,' unpublished MA thesis, Acadia University, 1949, p. 45
4 Between 1870 and 1890 the iron and steel industry grew at an annual average rate of 4.1 per cent and the transportation equipment industry grew at a rate of 3.8 per cent. From 1900 to 1910, both grew at a rate of 12.4 per cent. G.W. Bertram, 'Economic Growth and Canadian Industry, 1870-1915: The Staple Model and the Take-Off Hypothesis,' in W.T. Easterbrook and M.H. Watkins, *Approaches to Canadian Economic History* (Toronto 1967), 94-5.
5 W.T. Hogan, *Economic History of the Iron and Steel Industry in the United States*, III (Lexington, Mass. 1971), 993-4, 878-80, and Hayes, 'Canadian Iron, and Steel, 50-1

TABLE 7.1
Canadian iron and steel production, 1900-30 (short tons)

	Pig iron (long tons)	Steel ingots and steel castings	Hot rolled iron and steel bars	Structural steel shapes made in primary mills	Steel rails	Steel pipes and tubing	Plain steel wire
1900	86,228	26,406			784		
1901	244,979	29,214			998		
1902	319,555	203,880			38,024		
1903	265,969	203,296			1392		
1904	270,941	166,380			40,562		
1905	469,023	451,863			200,351		
1906	534,295	639,407			350,422		
1907	582,110	706,982			348,836		
1908	563,245	588,763			300,935		
1909	676,037	754,719			386,210		
1910	714,997	822,284			410,441		
1911	819,228	882,396			403,813		
1912	905,881	957,680			474,751		
1913	1,008,006	1,169,034			567,514		
1914	699,254	828,641			428,225		
1915	815,871	1,020,784			234,922		
1916	1,043,979	1,428,269			91,277		
1917	1,045,071	1,745,744			46,311		
1918	1,067,456	1,873,749			162,746		
1919	819,447	1,030,342			316,305		
1920	973,568	1,232,717	386,740		255,323		107,129
1921	593,829	747,582	134,079		298,110		72,722
1922	382,967	537,742	152,768		140,970		136,900
1923	879,822	987,306	239,468		231,684		123,148
1924	593,049	738,939	191,055		224,795		84,731
1925	570,766	842,803	244,029		216,695		94,018
1926	757,317	869,413	218,344		186,838	72,300	123,542
1927	709,697	1,016,898	220,866		263,965	79,300	118,784
1928	1,037,727	1,382,976	302,923		391,092	118,000	148,815
1929	1,080,160	1,543,427	273,944	35,060	428,962	140,100	155,680
1930	747,178	1,130,808	184,286	35,997	261,444	110,800	148,505

Source: M.C. Urquhart and K.A.H. Buckley, *Historical Statistics of Canada* (Toronto 1965), 484 and 486

The shift from the railway age to the automobile era had a marked impact upon the fortunes of the different steel companies. New forms of heavy structural steel for construction purposes and light rolled steel for consumer goods industries became an important component of domestic steel demand. However, unlike Stelco, neither Algoma Steel nor Besco were equipped with the finishing capacity to meet these needs. Moreover, these two firms were poorly situated to serve the growing markets of urban central Canada. Accordingly, during the 1920s Stelco surged ahead as the Canadian industry leader.[6]

The changing structure and composition of the Canadian steel market required the leading primary producers to adapt their corporate strategies to altered conditions. Algoma and Besco found the challenge extremely trying. Ultimately both had no choice but to look to the state to support their cause. Algoma was initially established to cater to western Canadian needs, while Besco sought to serve Europe. Over time both suffered major disappointments in these markets, so that by the 1920s they looked to the growing central Canadian market as their principal source of business. A number of impediments blocked the successful prosecution of this new strategy, however, especially organizational and financial difficulties, and tariff and transportation problems. In order to appreciate fully the impact of these problems and the limits they imposed upon the range of available corporate strategies it is necessary to review briefly the development of both Algoma and Besco to 1926.

A dazzling Philadelphia promoter, Francis H. Clergue, had established the Algoma Steel Company in 1901 as one of a series of integrated enterprises which included a power company, pulp mill, sulphite mill, nickel mines, the Algoma Central Railway, and a number of railway works (see Figure 7.1). Clergue spread his efforts too broadly and his capital too thinly, however, so that by 1903 his barely finished empire at the Sault collapsed in a heap of unpaid debts. Another group of Philadelphia investors moved in to salvage Clergue's wreck in 1904, and in the years that followed the new masters of the Sault concentrated their efforts on expanding the capacity of the recently built steel plant. Clergue's ramshackle organization was rationalized (Figure 7.1), and the pulp and paper and power companies were sold to other interests. When the federal government imposed a $7 per ton duty on steel rails, new funds were secured on the London bond market, and the Algoma Steel Company expanded to grasp the opportunities inherent in the recent Canadian railway boom. These efforts produced a

6 For a discussion of the components of the old and new industrialism in Canada, see
W.T. Easterbrook and H.G.J. Aitken, *Canadian Economic History* (Toronto 1963),
515-20; Walter Isard, 'Some Locational Factors in the Iron and Steel Industry since the
Early Nineteenth Century,' *Journal of Political Economy*, 61, 3 (1948) 212-17

Figure 7.1
The corporate structure of Algoma Steel Corporation and its predecessors, 1897-1930

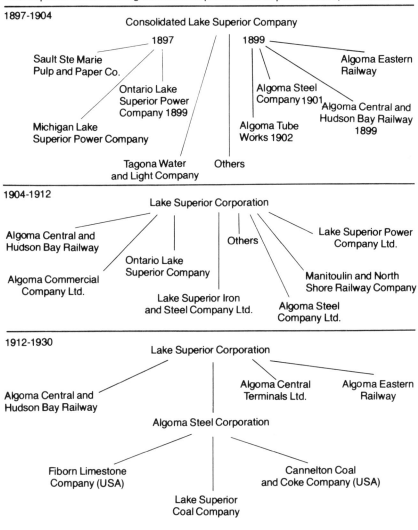

Source: Eldon, 'American Influence in the Canadian Iron and Steel Industry,' 558-9

measure of success, but success in this case led to an excessive concentration on a very narrow range of railway products.[7]

During the war Algoma made extraordinary profits filling munitions orders, but failed to diversify its output in any significant fashion. For a time, Algoma executives negotiated with Imperial Munitions Board officials about a proposal to build a structural steel mill capable of producing the steel beams necessary to support a Canadian shipbuilding industry, but ultimately nothing came of these talks. Although such a structural mill appeared to be excellently suited to absorb Algoma's primary capacity, the company hesitated to finance an expansion programme without a guarantee of government loans and contracts. As the haggling proceeded the war ended, and the government subsequently balked at peacetime commitments to stockpiling contracts. The 1920 recession halted all efforts at further diversification.[8]

Algoma's failure to diversify its output during the war cost the company dearly during the 1920s. Railway supplies accounted for 98½ per cent of Algoma's output in 1913; in 1921 they still accounted for 71 per cent of the company's tonnage. As rail sales plummeted during the twenties Algoma consistently operated well below its capacity. Between 1921 and 1928 the company's excess capacity averaged 61 per cent. Operations in 1921-22 were typical. Steel ingot production totalled 230,237 tons, against a capacity of 660,000 tons. To produce this tonnage the mill operated at full capacity for only 104 days, at 50 per cent capacity for 194 days, and it remained completely closed for the rest of the year. This under-utilization of capacity was very costly. One consultant reported that between 1922 and 1926 the cost of shutting down the mill and starting it up again annually averaged $450,00, while gross earnings each year amounted to less than $600,000.[9]

7 The early history of the Algoma Steel Corporation is covered in Eldon, 'American, Influence,' 83-94, and Leonard L. Prior, 'Sault Ste. Marie and Algoma Steel Corporation,' unpublished MA thesis, University of Toronto, 1956, 34
8 Net operating profits rose from $914,711 in 1915 to $6,001,891 in 1918. PAC, Sir James Dunn Papers, MG30B38, vol. 313, file 8, Algoma Steel Corporation, Net Operating Profits from Fiscal Year Ending 30 June 1915 to 30 June 1934. Details of the plans to build a mill may be found in PAC, Sir Joseph Flavelle Papers, Imperial Munitions Board Correspondence (IMB), MG30B4, vol. 10, file 97, see especially J.F. Taylor to Flavelle, 22 Oct. 1917; Taylor to Hon. C.C. Ballantyne, minister of marine and fisheries, 24 Nov. 1917. Dunn Papers, vol. 80, telegram, Dunn to F.P. Jones, 9 Jan. 1919; PAC, Tariff Commission, 1920 Papers, vol. 6, file 11, p. 1793, testimony by W.C. Franz, 18 Oct. 1920
9 ABTT Papers, vol. 1, file 2-4; Sault Daily Star, 23 Aug. 1928; Eldon, 'American Influence,' 152; Advisory Board on Tariff and Taxation, Record of Public Sittings, Reference 2, Iron and Steel, Resumed Hearing, 27-9 Nov. 1928 (Ottawa 1929), 41; Financial Post, 1 Sept. 1922; Dunn Papers, vol. 387, file 7, Algoma Steel Corporation, Ltd., memo

TABLE 7.2
Algoma Steel Corporation net profits and losses, 1919-30

1919	+$ 669,836.87	1925	−$1,069,549.33[a]
1920	+ 1,359,568.74	1926	− 638,759.66[a]
1921	− 2,133,360.97	1927	− 251,248.76[a]
1922	− 831,896.00[a]	1928	+ 3,555.76[b]
1923	− 581,639.71[a]	1929	+ 1,188,083.46[c]
1924	− 23,954.12[a]	1930	+ 751,559.61[d]

a Without any provision for depreciation, which in 1921 was recorded as $500,000.
b Depreciation of $670,000 is recorded here.
c Depreciation of $1 million is recorded here; almost all these net profits were set aside to
  provide for depreciation accrued in previous years.
d Subject to income tax.
Source: compiled from the annual statements of the Algoma Steel Corporation, Limited

TABLE 7.3
Algoma Steel Corporation earnings record, 1922-26

	1922	1923	1924	1925	1926
Rails	$206,164,.85	303,431.25	1,098,361.80	732,259.20	889,285.08
Merchant bars	− 30,483.14	3,505.34	52,840.42	−117,881.89	−223,650.03
Tie plates	76,959.83	−8,695.69	100,877.97	18,944.64	32,669.61
Pig iron	−172,152.10	360,421.48	38,750.15	−61,324.99	19,762.29
Coke	−5,738.69	77,571.90	20,243.27	32,999.29	80,257.86
Other	−6,816.84	−8,987.56	136,115.63	21,756.00	25,767.45
Net earnings	$ 67,933.91	727,246.72	1,447,189.24	626,752.25	824,092.26

Source: Dunn Papers, FKS–JMY memo, p. 2

The loss of economies of scale was reflected in Algoma's pitiful earnings
record during the 1920s (see Table 7.2). A more detailed examination of this
record clearly reveals the company's dependence on the rail market and high-
lights its need for increased diversification. As Table 7.3 indicates, profits and
losses from pig iron, coke, merchant bars, and tie plates usually cancelled each
other out. Rail sales provided almost all of the company's net earnings.
    A consulting firm that analysed Algoma's operations neatly summarized the
company's problem and pointed to its only solution:

dealing with suggested changes in capital structure, FKS, JMY, Chicago, 22 Sept. 1926
(hereafter cited as FKS-JMY memo), FKS, p. 2

We repeat ... the absolute necessity of continuous operation of the plant. This cannot be assured unless the product is diversified. We place great reliance upon DIVERSIFICATION, rather than upon large tonnage of a limited range of product. We also emphasize that unless steps are taken to diversify the product, thereby securing continuous operation, it is hopeless to look for relief to economies and betterment in mill practice, since present practice is exceptionally good under existing conditions ... In fact, the only correct and the really significant deduction that stands out as a contrast between the average plant in the United States – not to mention the highly successful plants – and the plant of the Algoma Steel Corporation, is that the average successful plants in the United States enjoy considerable periods of uninterrupted operation. The percentages of operation may vary from 60% to 100%, but it is impossible to find any plant in the United States of the capacity of the plant of the Algoma Steel Corporation that suffers such regular yearly interruption of rolled steel output as is the case of Algoma ... The fundamental cause for the repeated interruptions to operations at Algoma, and the consequent poor earnings, is to be found in the lack of diversified rolled steel product to meet the requirements of the Canadian trade.[10]

The consultants recommended that Algoma construct a structural steel mill capable of producing the frames required in the urban construction industry.

Algoma's location severely restricted its search for a product suitable to 'the requirements of the Canadian trade.' Sault Ste Marie was 439 miles from Toronto, which in the 1920s was the centre of the largest iron and steel market in Canada. Stelco, in Hamilton, was only 39 miles from the market. Contemporary American experience indicated that the zone for economical distribution of pig iron was about 300 miles. Moreover, besides Stelco, Algoma also had to compete with American steel plants in Buffalo which had a distinct advantage over the Canadian company in so far as freight rates to the Toronto-Montreal market were concerned.[11] Adequate tariff protection might restrict its American competition, but in order to compete with Stelco, Algoma had to market a distinctive product which it alone produced in Canada. A structural steel mill fit these purposes exactly.

Two factors, finances and tariffs, checked Algoma's plans to build a combination rail and structural mill during the 1920s. The story of Algoma's finances is a tangled yarn but their impact was crucial. 'During the 1920s,' wrote W.D.R. Eldon, 'diversification was only possible to a limited extent on account of financial difficulties, and yet the only possible solution of financial difficulties

10 Public Archives of Ontario, G.H. Ferguson Papers, RG3, General Correspondence, file 1924 (Algoma Steel Corporation Ltd.), Condensed Summary of Freyn Brassert and Company's Report, 10 May 1924, pp. 6-7
11 Eldon, 'American Influence,' 160-1; *Iron and Steel Hearings*, 27-9 Nov. 1928, pp. 32-3

was diversification.'[12] For our purposes Algoma's financial circumstances can be put quite briefly.

The Algoma Steel Corporation was a wholly owned subsidiary of the Lake Superior Corporation, a Philadelphia concern. The Lake Superior Corporation had guaranteed the interest payments on a series of Algoma first mortgage bonds which were mainly held in England, and after 1927 controlled by Sir James Dunn, a Canadian expatriate. In addition, the Lake Superior Corporation had also guaranteed interest payments on the bonds of two of its other subsidiaries, the Algoma Central and Hudson Bay Railway and the Algoma Central Terminals Limited, upon which payments it had defaulted after 1914. The railway and terminal company bondholders could have sued Lake Superior on their guarantee and put it into liquidation, but since their property and their bonds were largely worthless without a properly functioning steel industry the committee for the bondholders elected to give the Lake Superior Corporation time to establish Algoma Steel on a more solid footing before pressing their claims. While this decision served the interests of the Lake Superior shareholders who controlled Algoma, it did not help the steel company much since Lake Superior was hardly in a position, given its poor credit rating, to raise further funds for a new structural steel mill. The Lake Superior shareholders, moreover, were anxious not to lose control of their steel plant to Sir James Dunn who waited on the sidelines for Algoma to default on its interest payments. During the twenties the Lake Superior interests ensured that Dunn's claims were regularly met, but as time wore on Dunn became most anxious that the common shareholders either finance the necessary diversification or allow him to take over the steel property for that purpose. As Dunn complained to an associate: 'Our Philadelphia friends seem to be able to keep themselves cheered up by a good month now and then but the position has not really improved and sooner or later Algoma will go to pieces unless before it is too late the Company extends its operations into other branches of the industry for which there is a demand in the country. This means new money which can only be had after reorganization on lines which the Philadelphia people so far have refused to face.' Needless to say, while control of their enterprise was at stake, Algoma's directors were hardly in a position to turn their full attention to the necessary strategic decisions needed to save the steel company, even if they had been able and willing to do so.[13]

---

12 *Ibid.*, 150
13 The story of Algoma's financial position can be pieced together from letters and documents in the Dunn Papers. In particular, see vol. 299, letterbook, p. 436, Dunn to Taylor, 21 July 1927. The attitude of the Philadelphia interests is summed up best in a story that Frank Common, president, Lake Superior Corp., told to Sir James Dunn. He re-

Algoma needed to diversify, but diversification alone would not solve all its problems. New products would generate new business only if low cost foreign producers were squeezed out of the market. European and American producers sold structural steel shapes in Canada at relatively low prices. Tariff protection clearly was required if Algoma hoped to corner the Canadian market. On 3 April 1926 the Algoma Steel Corporation petitioned the minister of finance to revise the iron and steel schedule of the tariff to that end.[14]

The British Empire Steel Corporation also petitioned the minister for increased protection.[15] Besco's desire for tariff reforms stemmed from similar concerns to those prompting Algoma's action. Locational, financial, and management problems, as well as lack of markets, hampered Besco's operations. The Nova Scotia company hoped to alleviate these difficulties through a broad public programme of subsidies and tariff protection.

From its inception financial problems plagued the Nova Scotia steel industry. The formation of Besco in 1921 once again revealed the extent to which industrial enterprise had become the subject of financial manipulations by promoters and stock jobbers. The men associated with the Besco amalgamation had little experience in the steel business and perhaps even less interest in it. T.W. Acheson's description of the prewar industry holds true for the twenties as well: 'The increasing reliance on the stock market as a technique for promoting and securing the necessary financial support to develop the massive Nova Scotia steel corporations emphasized the growing shift from industrial to financial capitalism. Centred on the Montreal stock market, the new movement brought to the control of industrial corporations men who had neither a communal nor a vocational interest in the concern.'[16]

During the closing days of the war the potential of the Nova Scotia steel industry excited interest in many quarters. An English group of promoters and steel men, led by the Canadian-born British MP Grant Morden, wanted 'to weld

minded him of 'The inscription put on an Arch over the Appian way by one of the wiser Roman Emperors who reading a former inscription "Be bold, be bold, and evermore be bold" caused it to be changed to read "Be bold, be bold, but not too bold." ' 'This in my opinion,' concluded Common, 'should be the spirit of our policy.' *Ibid.*, vol. 387, file 2, Common to Dunn, 6 Nov. 1930

14 ABTT Papers, vol. 1, file 2-1, W.C. Franz, Algoma Steel Corp., to Hon. J.A. Robb, minister of finance, 3 April 1926 (hereafter cited as Algoma brief)

15 *Ibid.*, Memorandum for Presentation to the Tariff Advisory Board on Behalf of the Nova Scotia Steel and Coal Co., Ltd., and the Dominion Iron and Steel Co., Ltd., Roy M. Wolvin, president, 26 May 1926 (hereafter cited as Besco brief)

16 Acheson, 'The National Policy and the Industrialization of the Maritimes, 1880-1910,' *Acadiensis*, 1, 2 (1972), 23-4

together the primary steel plants of Nova Scotia, other eastern Canadian fabricated steel producers and important shipping interests into a vast enterprise which would supply the British steel producers with great quantities of semi-finished steel, and which would prove to be a fitting rival and counterpart of the United States Steel Corporation.'[17] Roy M. Wolvin and J.W. Norcross of the Montreal-based Canada Steamship Lines Limited (CSL) also took an interest in the possible amalgamation of the Nova Scotia industry.

Wolvin and Norcross had little background in the primary steel industry. Their interest in Nova Scotian enterprises had been provoked by the Imperial Munitions Board's efforts to promote a steel shipbuilding industry in Canada. The board's chairman, Sir Joseph Flavelle, believed 'that the steel corporations in Canada will make a mistake if, in addition to securing important profits which betters their financial position, they fail to establish additional capacity to serve the country after the war as will lend added character to their enterprise when the immediate war business has passed.'[18] Since both the British and Canadian merchant marines needed ships, Flavelle encouraged the Algoma Steel Corporation to build a structural mill and the Dominion Iron and Steel Company (Disco) of Sydney, Nova Scotia, to build a steel plate mill, thus securing diversification and a shipbuilding industry in one stroke. While Flavelle's efforts on behalf of Algoma came to nought, he managed to convince the federal government to guarantee Disco's plant by placing an order for 50,000 tons of steel plate per annum for five years. Flavelle then brought Wolvin and Norcross into the project by encouraging their interest in the government's plan to upgrade Halifax's shipbuilding and repair facilities, which had been devastated in the great explosion of 1917. Wolvin and Norcross subsequently agreed to establish a new concern, the Halifax Shipyards Limited.[19]

17 *The Iron Age*, 4 March 1920, cited by McCracken, 'Nova Scotia,' 139. The London group was composed of Morden, Viscount Furness, chairman of the United Steel Companies of Great Britain, Sir Trevor Dawson, managing director of Vickers, Ltd., Sir Newton Moore, an important figure in the Australian steel industry, Sir William Bradmore, Henry Steel, and Benjamin Talbot. In November 1919 this group purchased 50,000 shares of Dosco stock from J.K.L. Ross for $3.5 million. At the time 185,001 shares were required for absolute control. *Financial Post*, 29 Nov. 1919 and 17 Jan. 1920; also Eldon, 'American Influence,' 140

18 Flavelle Papers, IMB, vol. 10, file 97, Flavelle to Mark Workman, president, Disco, 5 Jan. 1917. Concern with the need for a balanced steel industry arose, in part, as a result of shortages caused by US controls on exports which were first applied in 1917. See R.D. Cuff and J.L. Granatstein, *Canadian-American Relations in Wartime* (Toronto 1975), 60-3

19 *Ibid.*, memo from Flavelle, 6 Nov. 1917. The government also granted Disco a drawback on duties paid for necessary machinery which was estimated to be worth $750,000,

Since the new Disco plate mill supplied Wolvin's shipyards, the basis of a merger was readily apparent. By 1920 the Wolvin group had allied itself with the Morden syndicate, and together they quickly assumed control of the entire Nova Scotia steel industry. Initially the new partners promoted a scheme to amalgamate a ragtag collection of moribund shipbuilding concerns, the Canada Steamship Lines, and the two leading Nova Scotia steel mills, but concerted opposition from suspicious minority shareholders in the steel companies ultimately checked this scheme. Undaunted, Wolvin successfully promoted a smaller version of his original plan.[20]

Wolvin's British Empire Steel Corporation, capitalized at $500 million, amalgamated three Nova Scotian concerns, the Dominion Steel Corporation (Dosco), the Nova Scotia Steel and Coal Company (Scotia Steel), and the Halifax Shipyards Limited. The two steel companies were themselves the product of a series of earlier mergers dating back to the late nineteenth century (see Figure 7.2). The only feature common to all these mergers was the steady expansion of promotion stock accompanying each amalgamation. By 1921 Dosco, Scotia Steel, and Halifax Shipyards carried a total of $38.5 million of

McCracken, 'Nova Scotia,' 154. The Halifax Shipyards Ltd. was capitalized at $8 million, of which the $5 million common stock was for promotional considerations. For details of the company's background, see *ibid.*, 185, and Province of Nova Scotia, *Report of the Royal Commission on the Coal Mining Industry* (Halifax 1926), 53.

20 *Financial Post*, 17 Jan., 1 and 8 May 1920, 25 March 1921; Eldon, 'American Influence,' Dissident shareholders and directors objected that the distribution of securities to the minor companies in the merger was out of all proportion to their value, and that the British syndicate had received a prior claim on Besco's earnings ahead of all other shareholders. See Forsey, Eugene *Economic and Social Aspects of the Nova Scotia Coal Industry* (Toronto 1925), 38; *Financial Post*, 19 June 1920; and PAC, Robert L. Borden Papers, vol. 117, file OC597, 64894-7, Fred R. Taylor to Sir George Foster, 10 May 1920. The terms of Besco's proposed agreement with Canada Steamship Lines appear to lend credence to these criticism. CSL agreed to operate its business for the next twenty-five years for the profit and loss of Besco which would be entitled to any earnings after all expenses of operation were met. In return Besco agreed to guarantee to the holders of CSL common and preferred stock an annual 7 per cent dividend, which, if not earned would be paid by the steel company. CSL debenture stock, bond, and mortgage holders were also similarly guaranteed payment of their claims. Moreover, Besco agreed to finance any needed CSL expansions. In short, though Taylor observed that 'Steamship Lines in the near future will have a very checkered existance,' Wolvin and Norcross were arranging that CSL, which they controlled, should be established as a 'sure thing' with a prior claim on Besco's earnings ranking ahead of even Besco's bondholders and first preferred shareholders. It is interesting to note that in 1921, after the Besco deal fell through, CSL ceased to pay dividends on either its preferred or common stock, and that this state of affairs continued for several years afterwards. For details, see the *Financial Post*, 23 and 30 July 1920, and the annual report of Canada Steamships Ltd., for year ending 31 Dec. 1921.

Figure 7.2
The corporate structure of British Empire Steel Corporation and its predecessors, 1872-1921

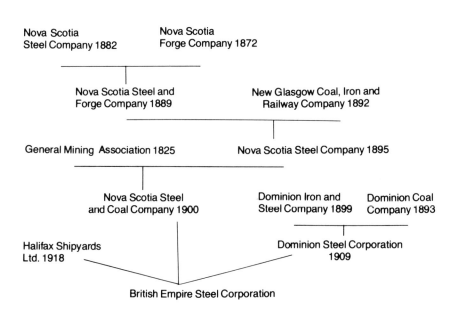

Source: Eldon, 'American Influence,' 557

watered stock. With the Besco merger, Wolvin added another $19 million to the capitalization of the constituent companies.[21]

Following the merger Roy Wolvin attempted to defend Besco against the common gossip that the corporation's stock was 'watered.' His explanation revealed clearly that financiers rather than industrialists dominated Besco's management. 'The outstanding capital stock of the British Empire Steel Corporation is considerably in excess of the outstanding stock of the three companies at the time they were acquired,' he admitted, 'but this increase is only a [portion?] of the earned and undistributed profits of the three companies at the time of their acquisition ...'[22] Wolvin's explanation turned on the argument that the promoters had merely capitalized the corporation's consolidated surplus of $21 million, which had been earned by Scotia Steel and Dosco during the war, and which was well in excess of the $19 million increase in Besco's capital stock. Technically this point was valid, but it ignored the fact that this money was sorely needed to rehabilitate Besco's existing plant. During the war, work on the coal mines and the steel mills had been neglected in order to allow the plant to operate continuously at full capacity. The company's general manager subsequently testified that the rehabilitation of this property would cost at least $15 million.[23] Besco's $21 million surplus, then, should not have been capitalized but used instead as a reserve for depreciation.

Besco possessed neither the locational advantages nor the exceptional management needed to overcome the accumulated handicaps imposed by years of successive financial manipulations. Investors in the Nova Scotia industry were initially 'attracted by the proximity of Nova Scotian coal, Newfoundland ore, and the shipping lanes that they hoped would carry their steel to markets all over the world.'[24] Actual operating experience, however, failed to confirm these expectations. Cape Breton coal, for example, although near at hand, proved to be less than ideal for steel-making purposes because of its high sulphur content and the highly volatile gases it produced. During the 1920s Besco officials esti-

21 The financial details of the merger are found in ABTT Papers, vol. 4, file 2-34, Documents Prepared by Price, Waterhouse and Co. for the committee appointed on 12 April 1927 to represent the Holders of the 7 per cent First Preference Stock of the British Empire Steel Corporation Ltd., 26 April 1927; and Roberta N. McEachran, 'Corporate Reorganizations,' unpublished MA thesis, University of Toronto, 1934, p. 100
22 PAC, Arthur Meighen Papers, vol. 63, file 24 (2), 35744, Wolvin to Meighen, 31 March 1922
23 For an example of the way the property was run down, see Flavelle Papers, IMB, vol. 39, file: F.P. Jones, 1918-21, Jones to Hon. J.D. Rein, minister of railway and canals, 1 Aug. 1918; also see McEachran, 'Corporate Reorganizations,' 100-1; general manager quoted in Forsey, *Nova Scotia Coal Industry*, 41
24 Kilbourn, *Elements Combined*, 54

mated that the use of their own coal cost them a dollar a ton more than coal purchased elsewhere. Although less of a problem, the Wabana ores were found to be somewhat refractory and to contain more silica and phosphorous than was ideally desirable.[25] One consulting firm concluded that 'these deficiencies in the quality of raw materials have, in the past, resulted in high coke rates, low production and an irregular quality of iron that has been difficult and costly to convert into steel.'[26]

Besco's location, like Algoma's, severely restricted its access to potentially profitable markets. Although Wolvin once characterized the company's position as strategic, 'half way between the two continents, just where they could supply Canada, take care of Europe, look after the rejuvenation of the British steel industry, and ultimately ship ore and basic products into Pittsburgh itself,' this vision was but a pipe-dream. In reality, Besco was equally far away from all its potential markets. As a rule, Besco's production costs were just too high to allow competition with European producers. In 1928, for example, the company exported only 12 per cent of its iron and steel output; the rest was sold in Canada. Yet as W.A. Mackintosh, who investigated the company for the tariff board, pointed out, 'the location which is advantageous for the export trade, is distinctly disadvantageous from the point of view of domestic trade.'[27] Besco's freight costs reflected this disadvantage. Prior to 1927 Besco paid $5.10 per ton to ship pig iron to Montreal and $6.60 on shipments to Toronto. During the same period Stelco paid $3.50 on shipments to Montreal and only $1.50 to Toronto. After 1927 the three primary producers faced the following rate structure for pig iron shipments:[28]

Stelco to		Besco to		Algoma to	
Montreal	Toronto	Montreal	Toronto	Montreal	Toronto
$3.50	$1.50	$4.30	$5.80	$5.60	$4.00

25 Eldon, 'American Influence,' 370, Arthur G. McKee & Co., *Report on Steel Industry*, Nova Scotia, Royal Commission on Provincial Development and Rehabilitation, XI (Halifax 1944), 47; Queen's University Archives, Sir Joseph Flavelle Papers, vol. 49, file National Trust Company, Correspondence, 1917-29, F., M. Brocklebank to F.R. MacKelcan, KC, National Trust, 10 April 1929

26 McKee, *ibid.*, 47

27 Wolvin quoted in Forsey, *Nova Scotia Coal Industry*, 34. McCracken, 'Nova Scotia,' 111, 275. Indeed in 1928 Mackintosh reported that 'Disco has found it profitable during the past few years to purchase bar iron both in Belgium and in Germany for use in its finishing mills. This, perhaps, more than any other fact, makes clear the unsatisfactory conditions under which the Sydney plant is operating.' ABTT Papers, vol. 9, file 3-15, Confidential memo to chairman, ABTT: visit to Sydney, Cape Breton, by Dr W.A. Mackintosh, 15 Sept. 1928

28 Eldon, 'American Influence,' 390, table 34; 399, table 37; and 405, table 42

Perhaps competent, aggressive management might have overcome these disabilities. The Wolvin group, however, did not possess such capacities. As Sir Joseph Flavelle complained:

From the first these companies have been cursed with control by shareholders who hold their shares primarily for the purpose of making a profit out of shares, either through manipulation in the stock market, or in some other way. Certain of the subsidiary companies originated in a healthy manner, through a sincere desire to operate a successful business, with the primary purpose of carrying on a successful business, and without thinking of the stock market. All of them have been drawn into the whirlpool of stock market profits, and I suppose the result has been very disturbing stock market losses.[29]

These gloomy views fairly reflected Besco's fortunes. Between 1921 and 1923, while the steel plant operated at 18 to 47 per cent of capacity, Besco earned only enough to cover its depreciation costs, bond interest, and first preferred dividends. In 1923, the concern that had aspired to be 'the largest corporation in the British Empire' was able to forward $6833 to surplus account, and the following year was worse. The steel works lost $1,574,862, and for the first time since its formation Besco failed to pay the dividend on its first preferred stock. In 1925 Disco once again failed to earn interest charges or depreciation costs, and Besco recorded a $4.4 million deficit for the year.[30] For the first time it seemed as though the parent holding company might be unable to guarantee the interest payments on its steel company's bonds.

In 1926 Besco's sorry tale came to an end. The corporation's steel property, the Dominion Iron and Steel Company, faced an annual fixed charge on its bonded debt of almost $900,000. A portion of this debt had been guaranteed and paid in the past by the Dominion Steel Corporation, itself a holding company. At Besco's annual meeting in 1926 the directors announced that they would allow Disco to default on its interest payments. On 2 July 1926 the Nova Scotia Supreme Court appointed Sir Joseph Flavelle's National Trust Company, trustee for the bondholders, to serve as receiver and general manager of Disco.[31] In his findings in the case Mr. Justice Mellish adequately summed up Disco's history and condition to this point:

29 PAC, Sir John Willison Papers, vol. 29, file 114, 10594, Flavelle to Willison, 8 April 1925
30 McCracken, 'Nova Scotia,' 200-3; *Financial Post*, 23 Feb., 19 and 23 May 1923, 29 Feb. 1924; ABTT Papers, vol. 4, file 2-34, Auditors' statement for year ending 31 Dec. 1924 (see also annual report of Besco, 1924) and same for 1925
31 Price, Waterhouse report (n 21 above)

The properties of the Dominion Iron and Steel company shew cost (after depreciation) of some $47,000,000, of which approximately $22,000,000 are not considered of value at the present time. Spreading this increased depreciation, or obsolescence, over the life of the enterprise, the Dominion Iron and Steel Company, on a proper accounting basis, shewed no earning capacity from its inception in 1899 to the war period, shewed a large earning capacity during the war (due, however, solely to conditions created by the war) and has shewn no earning capacity since the war. To provide such modern improvements as are necessary to supply existing finishing mills with semi-finished steel and to improve its working capital, would involve an additional capital investment of $8,000,000.[32]

Both Besco and Algoma hoped that favourable tariff revisions would put them on the path to prosperity. While they struggled with the burden of crushing excess capacity ratios (see Figure 7.3), Canadian primary steel imports mounted steadily. During the 1920s these imports averaged 55.5 per cent of total Canadian consumption (see Figure 7.4). However, studies revealed that Canadian producers already possessed the facilities to manufacture almost 40 per cent of the wire, iron, and rolled steel products being imported. Import subsitution alone would produce another $20 million in sales.[33] Expansion and diversification would produce more revenues. But import substitution and diversification could not proceed without increased protection. Public policy held the key to industrial success.

The creation of the Advisory Board on Tariff and Taxation in 1926 established a forum where the steel companies could present what they regarded as legitimate grievances about the existing tariff schedule. On 30 April 1926 the minister of finance, under pressure from the steel companies, recommended that the board hold hearings to investigate the entire iron and steel schedule.[34] These hearings lasted four years.

The tenor of the arguments advanced by both Besco and Algoma at the board's 1926 hearings were much the same. So were their recommendations. Algoma's statement put its principal problem most clearly:

32 In Re Dominion Steel Corporation, *Nova Scotia Reports*, LIX, 407
33 ABTT Papers, vol. 1, file 2-3, List of iron and steel imports showing those items which could be produced from present facilities and those items which would require installation of new facilities, 10 Oct. 1927, MJA/IA; vol. 4, file 2-34, Canadian Imports, Iron and Steel Products, 1911-28, prepared by MJMcK/LE, 15 Dec. 1928
34 Algoma brief (n 14 above), Robb to G.P. Graham, 30 April 1926

Figure 7.3
Canadian steel ingot production and capacity, 1905-35

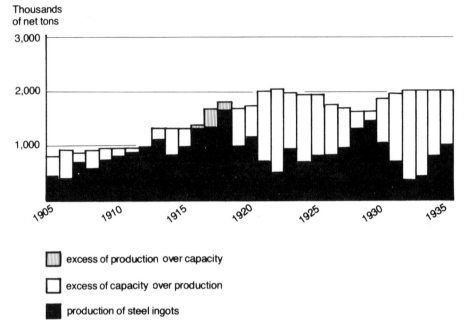

Thousands
of net tons

■ excess of production over capacity

□ excess of capacity over production

■ production of steel ingots

Source: Compiled from Lucy Morgan, *The Canadian Primary Iron and Steel Industry,* Study prepared for the
Royal Commission on Canada's Economic Prospects (Ottawa 1956), 98

Canadian iron and steel producers are faced with either relatively higher costs of
raw materials, labor, or transportation to consuming markets than are their
foreign competitors; we ourselves are compelled to pay higher prices for ore,
fuel, alloys, supplies and equipment than are the leading foreign competitive
plants. The cost of labor in Canada is practically the same as in the United
States, but is very much higher than in Great Britain, France, Belgium and Germany. Freight on iron and steel from Europe to Montreal is approximately the
same as from Hamilton to Montreal, and from $2.00 to $4.00 per ton less than
from Sault Ste. Marie to Montreal. On the other hand, freight rates from leading
producing centres in the United States to Central Ontario consuming markets are
much lower than from Sault Ste. Marie. We wish to stress this point particularly,
as it has a distinct bearing on the question of tariffs inasmuch as in many cases
the higher rates of freight we have to pay to reach the important consuming

Figure 7.4
Primary steel in Canada, 1900-34, showing production, exports, imports, and imports as percentage of consumption

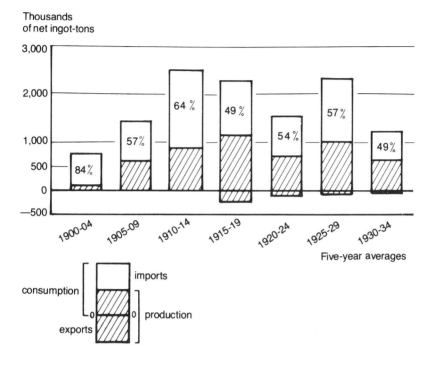

Source: Compiled from Morgan, *Canadian Primary Iron and Steel Industry,* 99

markets for our products in Canada offset to a very considerable extent whatever protection is afforded by the present tariff.

To support this contention, Algoma provided figures that revealed that Buffalo pig iron producers had a $2.60 a ton freight cost advantage over Algoma on shipments to St Catharines, Ontario, 'one of the large pig iron consuming centres in Canada,' while the duty on pig iron was only $2.80 a ton.[35]

The steel companies also complained that the impact of specific duties, such as the $2.80 tax on pig iron, had declined markedly over the past decade as

35 *Ibid.*, 1-2, 3

general iron and steel price levels had increased and the percentage of protection, the *ad valorem* rate, had decreased. Besco produced a summary of the changes in the *ad valorem* rate of protection on their principal products covered by specific duties (see Table 7.4). These duties had been imposed at the time of the last general revision of the tariff in 1907.[36]

In order to moderate their difficulties, both Besco and Algoma suggested a series of increases on the specific duties attached to their major products. Besco also advanced the principle that the *ad valorem* effect of specific rates should never be allowed to fall below 20 per cent. Both companies agreed that the duties on pig iron, currently $1.50, 2.00, 2.50, were too low. Pig iron imports had averaged 40,048 tons a year since 1920, and Besco suggested that they could keep this business in Canada with a new duty of $3.50, 4.00, 4.50. Algoma did not think this was possible without a $5.00 duty in all categories. Over 10,000 tons a year of billets, blooms, and slabs had been imported since the beginning of the decade but Algoma felt that this demand for foreign steel could be reduced if Parliament increased the tariff on this item to $7.00 from the current rate of $1.50, 2.25, 2.50. Besco, which was closer to the Montreal market where most of this steel was rolled, felt that it could manage if the duty was only $4.00, 4.50, 5.00.[37]

In addition to these increases, Besco also suggested new rates for angles and tees, steel plates, rails, and wire rods. They wanted all to be dutiable at $6.00, 7.00, 8.00, whereas the current rate was $4.25, 6.00, 7.00 on angles and tees, $2.00, 2.75, 3.00 on plates, $4.50, 6.00, 7.00 on rails, and $2.25, 3.50, 3.50 on wire rods. Besco further suggested that Parliament cancel the drawback of duty on steel used in the manufacture of a host of items including agricultural implements, machine tools, bedsteads, and some iron and steel tubes.[38]

For its part Algoma wanted a greater measure of protection accorded to structural steel. Imports averaged 73,103 tons per annum and Algoma desperately needed this business. If the government raised the tariff from $2.00, 2.50, 3.00 to $4.25, 6.00, 7.00 Algoma might then build a structural steel mill. Algoma also wanted to increase its share of the auto steel business so it suggested that different types of alloy steel, which it alone produced in Canada and which had been, to this point, imported duty free, henceforth should be dutiable at a

---

36 By 1927 this problem was no longer as important since iron and steel prices declined slightly. See Lucy Morgan, *The Canadian Primary Iron and Steel Industry*, Study prepared for the Royal Commission on Canada's Economic Prospects (Ottawa 1956), 101
37 Besco brief (n 15 above), 22-4, 18; Algoma brief, 12-15
38 Besco brief, 18-21, and ABTT Papers, vol. 1, file 2-3, Canadian Duties on Steel Products, 7 Oct. 1927, MJM/IA

TABLE 7.4
Ad valorem effect of specific duties, 1908-25 (percentages)

	1908 British	General	1915 British	General	1925 British	General
Pig iron	11.1	15.4	12.1	20.3	7.5	12.7
Steel billets, 60 pounds and over	6.0	10.4		13.2	3.0	4.9
Steel billets, other	10.3	28.4	17.1	30.0	10.3	10.7
Rails	16.4	26.0	8.7	27.4	14.7	18.2
Wire rods				16.2	8.3	8.5
Bars	13.2	22.6	11.1	25.2	9.7	15.2
Angles and beams, 35 inches or less	16.7	23.5	13.9	26.4	9.9	15.1
Angles and beams, over 35 inches	8.7	10.4	7.0	11.7	5.5	7.2

Source: Besco brief (n 15), 17

35 per cent *ad valorem* rate. Finally, Algoma, too, attacked the drawback of duties on flat spring steel, steel billets, and steel axle bars used in the automobile industry, and on the special spring steel used by the railway companies.

Besco concluded its appeal with two important points. First, it recommended an amendment to the dumping clause in the Customs Act to deal with imports from countries with very depreciated currencies. Because of the relatively low value of their currencies, Belgium, Luxembourg, France, and, to a lesser extent, Germany, were all able to sell steel in Canada at prices which neither Canadian nor American producers could hope to match. Belgium and Luxembourg, for example, quoted wire rods, f.o.b. Channel ports, at $24.02 a ton, while the best that North American producers could manage was $45.00, f.o.b. Pittsburgh. In such cases Besco recommended that the Customs Department impose an additional duty in order to bring the depreciated quotation up to a level not less than the British domestic price.

Besco also sought a bonus for its use of domestic coal. The other steel companies used imported American coal and received a 99 per cent drawback of the fifty cents a ton duty they paid. Besco claimed that this drawback was an implicit subsidy which it alone did not receive since Disco used Nova Scotian coal. As compensation for this inequity, Besco demanded that the Dominion pay it a subsidy on its coal equal to the amount rebated to the steel companies that imported American fuel.[39]

It took four years for the federal government to respond to these claims. Over that period Algoma and Besco returned to Ottawa six times to appear before the

39 Algoma brief, 4-11; Besco brief, 10-14

tariff board. Each new presentation they made basically reworked the arguments advanced in 1926. New trade figures were cited — Algoma noted that structural steel imports were up from their five-year average of 73,103 tons to 118,552 tons in 1926 — and a few new demands were advanced. In February 1927 Disco declared that if the government declined to grant its requests regarding steel and coal tariff changes 'it will be necessary ... to receive assistance by way of bounty on steel ingots produced. This bounty should be not less than $2.50 per gross ton.' Nine months later Disco returned to request an increase in the rates of protection on skelp, tin plate bars and sheet bars, black sheets, galvanized sheets, and tin plate. Although the Nova Scotia producer did not yet manufacture any of these products, it claimed that it was discouraged from entry into these markets because of the high levels of American and European imports.[40]

Both steel companies stressed that increased protection was crucial to their future viability. Algoma officials explained their plans as follows:

The expansion plans contemplated, in the event greater tariff protection is achieved, include construction immediately of a combination rail and structural steel mill capable of handling up to 130-pound rails, and structural steel up to 24-inch beams. Algoma Steel would next build a new sheet mill capable of handling 40,000 to 50,000 tons of product, and diversified for stamping roofing. The next plan calls for the entire revamping of the present merchant mill so as to include a much wider range of product, and increase the present merchant capacity by 100%. Finally the company intends to build a combination skelp and strip mill.

Disco was even more precise about the impact of its tariff suggestions. Company officials estimated that if the coal bonus and tariff hikes on pig iron, blooms,

40 The verbatim report of these hearings are reprinted in *Iron and Steel Hearings*, 2 Oct. 27-9 Nov. 1928; 29-31 Jan., 26-9 Nov., 3-11 Dec. 1929; and 23-4 Jan. 1930. For new trade figures, see ABTT Papers, vol. 1, file 2-1, Franz to W.H. Moore, 15 Sept. 1928. For a more detailed version of Algoma's position, see vol. 67, file unmarked, Amplified Brief of the Algoma Steel Corp. Ltd., compiled by Professor B.K. Sandwell, FRSC, in support of Application for Alterations and Additions to the Canadian Customs Tariff, 1907, and Amendments submitted to the ABTT for Consideration at a hearing on 27 Nov. 1928. See also vol. 4, file 2-34, Brief presented by the Dominion Iron and Steel Co.Ltd., Sydney, Nova Scotia, National Trust Co. Ltd., receiver and manager, Montreal, 24 Feb. 1928, and *ibid.*, Brief relating to Reference no 2, Iron and Steel, presented to ABTT by Dominion Iron and Steel Co. Ltd., National Trust, receiver and manager, Nov. 1928 (this brief was prepared for the steel company by Dr W.A. Mackintosh)

billets, and wire rods went through, Disco's revenues would increase by $763,749.50.[41]

As the tariff board's hearings dragged on, it became clear that the federal government was reluctant to deal with Algoma's and Besco's claims. The lack of unanimity in the steel industry about the need for tariff changes caused the King government to hesitate. Opposition to these tariff revisions stemmed from several sources. Perhaps the most influential of these was the Steel Company of Canada.

Stelco, like Algoma and Besco, was an important primary producer. Unlike Algoma, however, Stelco produced a diversified output of finished and semi-finished products which were in great demand.[42] Unlike Besco, Stelco had no transportation problems since it marketed fully 70 per cent of its output within two hundred miles of its plant at Hamilton. Moreover, although Stelco was also formed during the first great Canadian merger movement and had to carry its share of promotion stock, the company was subsequently guided by a capable, conservative management to the premier position in the Canadian steel industry.[43] Blessed with a good location, a good product mix, and good manage-

---

41 ABTT Papers, vol. 1, file 2-1, article clipped from *Wall Street Journal*, 25 Sept. 1928; vol. 4, file 2-34, E. Fitzgerald, National Trust, to Moore, 11 Dec. 1928. It must be appreciated that at this point Disco was operating at near capacity and that it was already showing substantial profits on this output. Between 1927 and 1929 Disco had average net earnings of $1,959,183. In addition to this, a depreciation reserve of $1.5 million was established, and a $2 million reserve was established to meet the interest charges on the company's consolidated bond issue which had not been paid during the period of receivership. McCracken, 'Nova Scotia,' 216-23, and Queen's University, Flavelle Papers, memo for Mr McNaught regarding Managerial Services rendered by National Trust, 13 Dec. 1928, prepared by W.E. Rundle, gen. mgr., pp. 5-6

42 In 1927 the three companies had the following rated capacities (tons per annum):

Primary products	Pig iron	Ingots	Blooms and billets
Stelco	290,000	300,000	260,000
Algoma	500,000	600,000	520,000
Disco	550,000	400,000	375,000

Rolled products	Wire rods	Bars and shapes	Rails and structural	Sheet	Wire	Wire nails, etc.
Stelco	90,000	45,000		15,000	87,000	37,500
Algoma		55,000	445,000			
Disco	90,000	75,000	300,000		60,000	25,000

Source: ABTT Papers, vol. 1, file 2-3, Rated Annual Capacity of Canadian Steel Mills – Producing Pig Iron & Rolled Steel Products from Ore, 10 Oct. 1927, MJM/C

43 Eldon, 'American Influence,' 135. For details on Stelco's formation, see Kilbourn, *Elements Combined*; T.W. Acheson, 'The Social Origins of Canadian Industrialism: A

ment, Stelco recorded substantial profits in almost every year after its formation.[44] Therefore, during the 1920s Stelco did not feel menaced by the same forces that threatened to crush both Algoma and Besco. The Hamilton company did not need tariff revisions to set it on the road to prosperity. Indeed, quite the opposite was true since a substantial overhaul of the existing tariff schedule might threaten its position in the Canadian market. One analysis of Stelco's position revealed that

The Steel Company of Canada probably enjoyed a greater average protection on account of its large output of fabricated products carrying a high rate of duty. In 1915, nuts, rivets, washers and bolts were protected by a tariff of 75 cents plus 10 percent under the British preferential tariff, of 75 cents plus 25 percent, and 35 percent, and on screws 22½ percent and 35 percent. This degree of protection did not apply to all of the company's products, as large quantities of primary products were also marketed. But about 35 percent would mark the upper limit which the company received on its finished products. The Dominion Iron and Steel Company, which manufactured many of the same products, probably received a slightly lower degree of protection than the Steel Company of Canada, which produced a considerable output of fabricated products, while firms whose products were more limited to the primary sphere [like Algoma] were less fortunate.[45]

Stelco did not appear before the tariff board during the first hearings. This abstention clearly had its effect on the other companies' chances of favourable revisions. The trade magazine, *Hardware and Metal,* reported that 'the consensus

Study in The Structure of Entrepreneurship,' unpublished PhD thesis, University of Toronto, 1971; A.J.P. Taylor, *Beaverbrook: A Biography* (New York 1972). The character of Stelco's management is discussed in Kilbourn.
44 Steel Company of Canada, net profits and losses, 1910-30:

1910	$ 245,918	1921	$ - 442,448
1911	337,681	1922	356,145
1912	476,972	1923	627,875
1913	511,032	1924	264,769
1914	-313,173	1925	458,567
1915	1,756,211	1926	869,471
1916	1,632,856	1927	735,630
1917	1,550,357	1928	1,143,692
1918	1,125,017	1929	1,978,526
1919	872,430	1930	481,540
1920	545,663		

Source: compiled from annual reports of the company
45 Eldon, 'American Influence,' 470-1

of opinion ... from interviews with a number of firms engaged in the production and distribution of iron and steel products, is that the case presented to the Tariff Advisory Board on this industry lacked strength because of its lack of unanimity in representing the interests of the three chief mills in Canada ... ' [46]

In subsequent hearings Stelco opposed its competitors' programme. 'The steel companies,' reported *Hardware and Metal,* 'far from working in unanimity in the matter, are actually pulling against each other in putting forward their individual wants.' Between 1927 and 1929 Stelco's appearances before the tariff board were mainly for defensive purposes. In 1927 the Hamilton company objected to Besco's proposals for a bonus on coal. In 1929 the company appeared in Ottawa to oppose Algoma and Besco's proposal to increase the duty on skelp, which was the steel used in the production of seamless tubing. Finally, Stelco was adamant in its opposition to the proposal of the Dominion Foundries and Steel Company to eliminate the duty on pig iron, and to the proposal of the Canadian stove manufacturers who sought a reduction in the protection accorded sheet steel.[47] The Hamilton giant clearly saw no need and felt no sympathy for the changes apparently required by firms on the fringe of the central Canadian market.

Stelco supported tariff changes only when its own position was threatened. In January 1928 Stelco complained to the minister of trade and commerce that the US Steel Corporation was building a wire mill at Ojibway, Ontario, in order to circumvent the provisions of the dumping clause in the Customs Act. Stelco explained that US Steel could no longer export wire to Canada, where very low prices prevailed, since the spread between its domestic US price and the lower Canadian export price would put it in violation of the dumping clause. By building a wire mill in Canada, however, US Steel could sell its subsidiary wire rods at a cut-rate price and thus continue its dumping of surplus output. By 1930 Stelco complained that it was losing business to US Steel's subsidiary, the Canadian Steel Corporation, which sold galvanized wire fencing in central Ontario at prices which Stelco claimed involved a loss of fifty cents a hundred pounds.[48] These events prompted Stelco to advocate an increase in the tariff on

46 ABTT Papers, vol. 1, file 2-4, extract from *Hardware and Metal,* 'Claim Lack of Unanimity Weakened Steel Companies' Case,' 5 June 1926

47 *Ibid.,* vol. 9, file 3-18, Brief submitted on behalf of the Steel Company of Canada, Ltd., Hamilton, Ont., in respect to the application of the British Empire Steel Corporation, Ltd., 18 Jan. 1927, asking for the cancellation of Tariff Items nos 1019 and 1049, 24 Sept. 1928; vol. 2, file 2-11, H.M. Jaquays, vice-president, to R.H. McMaster, president, Stelco, 13 May 1930, H.T. Diplock, vice-president, Stelco, to W.H. Moore, 28 and 29 Jan. 1929; *Iron and Steel Hearings,* 26-9 Nov. 1929, pp. 85-2

48 *Ibid.,* Diplock to Moore, 3 Dec. 1929; R.H. McMaster to Hon. James Malcolm, minister of trade and commerce, 27 Jan. 1928; McMaster to Moore, 15 Jan. 1930; and memo, confidential, 12 Feb. 1930, from Stelco

wire rods. When pressed, then, it is clear that the Hamilton company responded similarly to the other steel firms. Only a favourable market position for most of its output insulated Stelco against the kind of pressures which impelled Algoma and Besco to seek political solutions to their market problems.

Stelco was not alone in its opposition to tariff changes. Over a hundred different companies and sixteen associations and councils appeared before the tariff board to register their views as well.[49] Many of them came simply to deny Besco's or Algoma's claims and to denounce their proposed revisions. The request to increase the tariff on pig iron provoked the opposition of the Dominion Foundries and Steel Limited, Canada Iron Foundries Limited, the National Iron Corporation, and the secretary of the Malleable Castings Manufacturers of Canada, who spoke for nine of the association's member firms. Algoma's position on alloy steel and spring steel drew the fire of the auto companies, a spokesman for the railways, the Dominion Forge and Stamping Company, Butterfield and Company (tool steel industry), the Guelph Spring and Axle Company, the Ontario Steel Products Company, and the Gananoque Spring and Axle Company. Similarly, Disco's proposals regarding wire rods, bars, and skelp were opposed by a host of steel users.[50] Finally, a spokesman for the Consumers' League of Canada appeared regularly at board hearings to oppose almost all requests for higher tariffs and higher prices.[51]

Such strong opposition prompted caution in government circles about proceeding too rapidly on steel tariff revisions. The welter of competing claims required careful sifting. As Mackenzie King observed in 1929: 'It seems clear to

49 PAC, W.L.M. King Papers, Memoranda and Notes, vol. 135, file 1083, C98143 and C98310-6

50 *Iron and Steel Hearings*, 2 Oct. 1928, pp. 23-5, 27, 33-5, 47-8; 29-31 Jan. 1929, pp. 22-3; 26-9 Nov. 1929, p. 33; ABTT Papers, vol. 2, file 2-4 J.J. Frame, secretary, Malleable Castings Manufacturers of Canada, to H.B. McKinnon, secretary, ABTT, 6 Oct. 1926; vol. 5, file 2-43, letters from Ford Motor Co., 28 Jan. 1929, Dominion Forge and Stamping Co., 24 Nov. 1928, Butterfield and Co., 26 Nov. 1928; vol. 5, file 2-45, W.W. Near, Page-Hersey Tubes, to Moore, 19 Nov. 1928 and 4 Dec. 1929; also vol. 3, file 2-22, memo to the Tariff Board from Frost Steel and Wire Co., B. Greening Co., Morrison Steel and Wire Co., Laidlaw Bolt and Tie Co., Northern Bolt and Screw Co., P.L. Robertson Manufacturing Co., Canadian Tube and Steel Co., Toronto Nail and Wire Co., Graham Nail Works, 18 Jan. 1929

51 The League was formed in 1926 by a group of members of Parliament, Charles Bothwell, Fred Totzke, and George Spence, for the purpose of defending consumers' interests before the Tariff Board. Robert J. Deachman, formerly editor of the *Westerner*, a Calgary journal, acted as the league's spokesman. In a sense, Deachman was the Ralph Nader of his era as he vigilantly pursued the smallest misrepresentation of the business community at one Tariff Board hearing after another. Some of Deachman's journalistic writings are collected in PAC, R.J. Deachman Papers, MG30D104.

me that the tariff is a very technical and intricate matter and a tariff schedule as complicated as a railroad schedule of rates. It has to be managed in a business-like fashion and each change has to be tested to use [tariff board chairman] Moore's expression by the test 'does it work.'" '[52] Naturally, such testing, which involved political considerations as well as cost-benefit analyses, took time.

The King government had good reasons to oppose tariff changes altogether. First of all, Stelco was prosperous, so why should the government intervene to save two if its competitors? Moreover, after 1926, when Disco went into re-ceivership, the National Trust Company was able by careful management under booming conditions to revive the company's fortunes significantly. Finally, King believed that both Algoma's and Besco's managers were committed Tories who had actively worked for his defeat.[53] Despite these factors, however, in 1930 the King government tried to satisfy many of the steel companies' claims.

The rise of the Maritime Rights Movement propelled the government to action. On the same day that the cabinet appointed the Advisory Board on Tariff and Taxation, the prime minister announced that he had established a Royal Commission on Maritime Claims, headed by A.R. Duncan. King had once been quite hostile to any action designed to aid the Atlantic provinces. In 1922, for example, he observed: 'I find the BC group hard to satisfy, they are like wolves. Stewart remarked the same was true of province by Atlantic – both maritime. The conception of government is diff't. than that some of us hold to – I have no sympathy with govt. as an agency to supply a few with favours ...'[54] Later, as the political pressure from the east mounted, King was forced to discount his views.

In Nova Scotia the Maritime Rights Movement was a response to two sepa-rate, but related, impulses. At one level it represented increasing dissatisfaction with the continuous decline of the Maritime economy. The fortunes of the steel and coal industry, which employed about one-fifth of the entire male labour force in Nova Scotia, played a major role in these concerns. At another level, the movement represented an attempt by the Conservative party to boost its politi-cal prospects by promoting regional grievances and focusing them on the Liberal governments in Ottawa and Halifax.[55]

52 PAC, King Diaries, vol. 25, p. G5465, 24 July 1929

53 *Ibid.*, vol. 21, p. G4515, 12 May 1926; and vol. 26, pp. G5774-5, 17 July 1930. See note 41 above re revival of company.

54 *Ibid.*, vol. 17, p. G3760, 6 Nov. 1922; see also vol. 24, p. G5059, 3 Feb. 1928

55 This aspect is most fully covered in E.R. Forbes, 'The Rise and Fall of the Conservative Party in the Provincial Politics of Nova Scotia, 1922-33,' unpublished MA thesis, Dal-housie University, 1967. The best discussion of the rise of the Maritime Rights Movement is Forbes, 'The Origins of the Maritime Rights Movement,' *Acadiensis*, 5, 1 (1975).

Maritime grievances and the rise of political movements in support of provincial rights, of course, dated from Confederation. After the First World War, however, Nova Scotians increasingly identified the province's interests with the corporate interests of the coal and steel companies. As Premier G.H. Murray warned the 1920 Tariff Commission:

We sometimes think that perhaps the importance of these two great industries of the Province of Nova Scotia is not fully recognized in other parts of Canada ... Our population is only half a million and you have 120,000 of that population actually dependent on these two great industries of coal and steel. You can therefore see how serious a thing it would be if anything should happen to these industries. During the regime of other Governments in Canada there were times and occasions when it was necessary for us who live in Nova Scotia to use our full force in order to maintain a tariff which permitted these industries to grow and become great national industries.[56]

During the next three years, the provincial Conservative party, guided by the owner and editor of the Halifax *Herald*, W.H. Dennis, ceaselessly lobbied the Maritime Board of Trade and other interests in the province to promote yet another regional protest movement. These efforts culminated in April 1923 when the Nova Scotia Conservative leader, H.W. Corning, called for a referendum on secession from Confederation. In this speech, the historian of the movement wrote, 'the chief grievances of Nova Scotians in general and of Haligonians in particular – freight rates, tariffs, taxation and competition with American ports – were summed up and blamed on Confederation and the policies of the Liberal Federal Government.'[57]

The Nova Scotia Liberal government, headed by E.H. Armstrong, could not ignore these attacks, and it, too, tried to stand as the champion of Maritime rights. On 2 December 1924 Premier Armstrong led a delegation to Ottawa to present a 'Memorandum with Regard to the Conditions Presently Existing in the Coal and Steel Industries of the Province of Nova Scotia.'[58] This brief anticipated almost all the points contained in Besco's submission to the tariff

---

56 See G.A. Rawlyk, 'Nova Scotia Regional Protest, 1867-1967,' *Queen's Quarterly*, 75 (Spring 1968); Tariff Commission, 1920 Papers, vol. 6, file 14, pp. 2103-4, testimony by Hon. G.H. Murray, premier of Nova Scotia, 8 Nov. 1920
57 Forbes, 'Rise and Fall,' 4, 10-11, speech to the legislative assembly, 19 April 1923; and G.A. Rawlyk, 'The Farmer-Labour Movement and the Failure of Socialism in Nova Scotia,' in L. Lapierre, ed., *Essays on the Left* (Toronto 1971), 38-40
58 PAC, J.L. Ralston Papers, MG27IIIB11, vol. 6, file: Coal Data Re: 1935-37. I am grateful to Ms M.N. Ralston for granting me partial access to these restricted papers.

board in 1926. Prime Minister King, however, was not impressed. 'Today was taken up with Nova Scotia matters,' he wrote in his diary, '... a deputation of Premier Armstrong – mayors of towns and our members from N.S. asking for higher tariff on coal, increasing rates on slack [coal], and asking for more help to steel industry – also pressing for orders for coal and steel railways. They picture a serious condition re unemployment in mining and mffg. centres. The truth is the steel industry in N.S. has been over done, artificially started and needs continuous artificial bolstering.'[59]

In the months ahead the interests of the steel industry remained an important element of the Maritime Rights Movement. A local Conservative correspondent informed Arthur Meighen that 'In this district the movement can be confined practically to two items: (1) Freight rates, (2) Protection on Steel and Coal.' King received similar advice, but he refused to act on it.[60]

Mackenzie King's intransigence cost the Liberals dearly. In 1925 the Tories swept the Liberals out of office in Halifax and captured eleven of Nova Scotia's fourteen federal seats. The following year the Conservatives won twelve federal seats, a far cry from 1921 when the Liberals had swept the province.[61] W.H. Dennis eloquently expressed the sentiments that prompted these crushing rejections of the Liberals and their policies:

In discussing any question affecting Nova Scotia, it is always necessary to remember that ordinary political standards do not apply here. This Province is fighting for its existence. The exodus from Nova Scotia is as bad as it ever was, possibly more serious this Spring than before. The minds of Nova Scotians are agitated not by political but by economic considerations. Nova Scotians cannot be brought to worry about remote conditions; their concerns are too grave and immediate. They see many sections of their Province being depopulated; they see industry strangled by excessive freight rates and ruinous competition; and they may be excused if they remind their representatives in Parliament that 'Charity begins at home.' They take the position, and with very good reason, that Central Canada has done little for this part of the Dominion, and if they are 'sectional' in their demands, it is the sort of 'sectionalism' that asks for an even break and a fair deal. They have gone on year after year, decade after decade, voting for national policies, the advantages of which have been reaped largely by

59 King Diaries, vol. 20, p. G4098, 2 Dec. 1924
60 Meighen Papers, vol. 118, file 123(2), 69350, G.S. Harrington, KC, Sydney and Glace Bay, to Meighen, 6 March 1925; King Papers, vol. 133, 112733, Memorandum of Suggestions Regarding the Nova Scotia Situation, prepared by Peter R. Jack, 8 March 1926
61 Rawlyk, 'Farmer-Labour Movement,' 40; Forbes, 'Rise and Fall,' 43-5, 78-80; J.M. Beck, Pendulum of Power (Scarborough 1968), 160, 188

other provinces. Now the time has come when, threatened by virtual industrial and commercial extinction, they ask for a chance to live.[62]

The Royal Commission on Maritime Claims arrived at much the same conclusions as Dennis. Promises made to Nova Scotia at the time of Confederation had been either unfulfilled or broken. The province's current depression was, in part, a function of these betrayals. The Duncan Commission advanced twenty-nine proposals to redress grievances and revive the regional economy. Three of them directly affected the steel industry. First, the commission recommended a 20 per cent reduction of freight rates in and out of the Maritimes. Next, it agreed with the contention that Nova Scotian coal used in the steel industry ought to receive a subsidy equal to the drawback of duty attached to foreign coal imported for the same purpose. Finally, although the commissioners declined to interfere with the tariff board's concurrent investigation of the iron and steel tariff schedule, they did record their belief that 'prompt action' was required.[63]

King's response to the Duncan Report was frankly political. Although he felt 'a little afraid they have gone too far in the matter of subsidies to the Maritimes,' he concluded that 'knowing what is in the report, we should carry it out, having regard to what we can get Parliament to do. We must make every effort to get its recommendations fulfilled. I believe by so doing we can win the Maritime Provinces back.' Despite his initial impulse, however, King's government moved slowly. A 1930 memorandum revealed that only seven of the Duncan Commission's recommendations had been fully implemented; another ten were partially implemented, and the rest remained for action. The steel industry certainly had not yet received the full measure of government assistance it sought. No action had been taken on bonusing coal used in the steel industry and the steel tariff remained unchanged.[64] Of the Duncan Commission's three recommendations regarding the steel industry, only one had been implemented. On 14 April 1927 the federal government passed the Maritime Freight Rates Act which reduced rates by 20 per cent on all local traffic, on all westbound all-rail traffic, and on all traffic culminating in European exports.[65] This measure had a

62 Meighen Papers, vol. 69, file 42, 38937-40, Dennis to Meighen, 6 May 1926
63 Canada, *Report of the Royal Commission on Maritime Claims* (Ottawa 1926), 21-3, 37-8
64 King Diaries, vol. 22, p. G4666, 22 Sept. 1926; Papers, vol. 181, 154242-3, Memorandum Showing Present Standing of the Duncan Recommendations, Saint John Board of Trade, 10 April 1930, prepared by F. Maclure Sclanders, commissioner of Board of Trade
65 McCracken, 'Nova Scotia,' 168; A.W. Currie, 'The Maritime Freight Rates Act, 1927,' *Economics of Canadian Transportation* (Toronto 1954), 93-5

limited impact on the steel industry, however, since Disco relied on water transportation for most of its shipments to the Montreal area.

As the 1930 election approached, partisan considerations came more prominently to the fore in King's mind. The prime minister regarded the budget as his government's major policy statement, and at last the steel industry received the attention it had so long sought. A general revision of the iron and steel tariff formed a central part of the government's fiscal programme. The prime minister was exuberant. 'It will be a real bombshell in the Tory camp,' he crowed. 'They will certainly keep us here as long as they can and we will almost certainly by obliged to dissolve and go to the country on the budget.'

Although King noted that the budget 'really wipes out large slices of protection,'[66] the steel industry did not come away entirely empty-handed. The items in Table 7.5 received increased protection. In addition to these tariff changes, the government also agreed to grant a bounty on the coal used in the Nova Scotia steel industry. Despite King's initial opposition to this measure, pressure from Defence Minister J.L. Ralston and intensive lobbying by J.H. Gundy, who had recently reorganized the Nova Scotia industry as the Dominion Steel and Coal Corporation, finally won the prime minister over to the idea of the bonus.

These tariff changes and the coal bonus fractured Tory solidarity against Charles Dunning's budget. After three Conservatives from Cape Breton and Sault Ste Marie voted for the budget, King observed that 'it is amazing how the bonusing of industry swings votes to a govt. It seems to [be] the strongest factor to compel support in individual localities.'[67] Individual voters were not so moved, however, since the King government went down to defeat in the election that followed the presentation of the budget. The ungrateful voters in Hamilton, Sault Ste Marie, and most of Nova Scotia were content to re-elect Tories in their local ridings.[68]

Although Algoma and Besco had gained much from the Dunning budget, they did not grieve to see the King government defeated. After the election the president of Algoma Steel, W.C. Franz, noted: 'we are quite pleased with the result of the election. Mr. Bennett has visited our plant on several occasions and is fully familiar with our requirements in the way of tariff protection.' A few days later he expanded on his view of the new situation: 'I think we are in a

66 King Diaries, vol. 26, p. G5626, 20 Jan., p. G5685, 29 March, p. G5691, 5 April 1930
67 King Diaries, vol. 26, p. G5679, 22 March, p. G5687, 1 April, p. G5707, 25 April, p. G5722, 15 May 1930; Papers, vol. 180, 153405, Ralston to King, 14 March 1930. The formation of Dosco Corp. is discussed in McEachran, 'Corporate Reorganizations,' 89-90, and McCracken, 'Nova Scotia,' 226-30.
68 Beck, *Pendulum of Power*, 227. 202

TABLE 7.5
Steel tariff changes, 1930

	Pre-1930 rates	Dunning rates
Iron and steel ingots	$1.50, 2.25, 2.50	$1.50, 2.50, 3.00
Blooms, cogged ingots, slabs, and sheet bars	$1.50, 2.25, 2.50	$2.50, 4.00, 4.50
Billets, bars, and rods used to make wire	$2.25, 3.50, 3.50	$2.25, 4.50, 5.00
Steel plates (40 inches or less)	$2.00, 2.75, 3.00	$2.00, 4.00, 6.00
Steel plates (over 40 inches)	free, 3.00, 5.00	$2.00, 2.75, 3.00
Structural steel	$2.00, 2.75, 3.00	$4.00, 5.50, 6.00
Cast pipe	$6.00, 7.00, 8.00	$5.00, 9.00, 10.00
Skelp (pipes and tubes)	5%, 5%, 5%	5%, 10%, 12½%

Source: *Can. H. of C. Debates*, 1 May 1930, pp. 1643-53

good position now to get a fair protective tariff on a number of articles that we had to keep away from with the old government so as not to bring opposition from the west.'[69]

After the 1930 election all the major steel companies co-ordinated their campaigns for further tariff changes. The Dunning budget had dealt with many of the issues that once had divided them, and the depression united their common interests as never before. Together, Algoma, Besco, and Stelco hired the advertising agency of Cockfield, Brown and Company to direct the prime minister's attention to the continuing needs of the industry. The agency's research director assured Bennett that 'the proposals made are not only all below the conventional maxima of the Canadian tariff, but are strictly limited to those items which would divert the greatest tonnage of steel now imported to Canadian mills. It is conservatively estimated that between 150,000 and 200,000 tons of steel per annum can be so diverted if these proposals are implemented during the Emergency Session.'[70]

Bennett obviously agreed with such arguments. On 15 September 1930 his government passed another set of revisions of the iron and steel schedule. The intermediate duty rate, which applied to European producers, was raised by fifty

69 Dunn Papers, vol. 315, file 2, Franz to Dunn, 1 and 6 Aug. 1930. US Steel Corp. also supported the Conservatives. A letter from counsel to the Canadian Steel Corporation claims that the company supported the Tories in three Essex ridings. PAC, R.B. Bennett Papers, vol. 732, file T-100, 44713, O.E. Fleming to Bennett, 11 Sept. 1930
70 Bennett Papers, *ibid.*, 446986-7, W.W. Goforth to Bennett, 5 Sept. 1930

cents a ton on ingots of iron or steel, blooms, cogged ingots, slabs, sheet bars, billets, bars and rods used in the manufacture of wire, and on structural shapes weighing over thirty-five pounds per lineal yard. The intermediate tariff on bars and rods, and on unmanufactured angles, beams, and channels increased by $1.00. If these latter shapes were further manufactured by drilling, punching, or processing they faced an increased *ad valorem* duty of 25 per cent, 35, 40, up from 15 per cent, 30, 35. Finally, the government raised the duty on cast pipe of iron or steel from $5.00, 9.00, 10.00 to $7.00, 12.00, 14.00.[71]

Bennett's revisions of the steel tariff followed much the same pattern as those in the automobile industry. In both instances, tariff reforms provided a weapon for Canadian producers to blast their way into the Canadian market. However, the irony was that as the economy faltered and then collapsed, the steel men recognized that tariff tinkering would not save their companies. 'We have had our matters continually before the government,' Algoma's president wrote, 'but received nothing in this [1931] budget, although I feel that when the Prime Minister gives our case some consideration we will get further protection and just at this time it would not mean much to us as there is no further business we could secure with a higher tariff.'[72]

During the 1920s the Canadian primary iron and steel industry suffered badly from chronic excess capacity. Much of this excess, however, was concentrated in two firms, the Algoma Steel Corporation and the British Empire Steel Corporation. Alfred Chandler has noted that twentieth-century industrial corporations generally pursued three types of growth strategies: 'Growth came either from an expansion of the firm's existing lines to much the same type of customers, or it resulted from a quest for new markets and sources of supplies in distant lands, or finally, it came from the opening of new markets by developing a wider range of new products for different types of customers.'[73] The American steel industry followed the first pattern, and because of the size of their domestic market American producers gained all the benefits accruing from specialization and mass production. In Canada, neither Algoma nor Besco could easily pursue a similar policy because of their peripheral location and the smaller size of the Canadian market. While both of these firms attempted to deepen their penetration of existing markets, both also tried to follow Chandler's third option, the development of new products for new markets. Corporate organizational changes and new marketing techniques alone, however, could not produce the desired results. Internal structural change in this case was not

71 *Statutes of Canada*, 1930, Second Session, An Act to Amend the Customs Tariff, 21 Geo. V, c. 3, p. 6
72 Dunn Papers, vol. 315, file 2, Franz to Dunn, 17 July 1931
73 A.D. Chandler, Jr., *Strategy and Structure* (Cambridge, Mass. 1962), 42

sufficient to facilitate strategic goals. Both Algoma and Besco had to change the structure of the environment within which they operated if they hoped to be successful. To that end they sought tariff revisions, coal bonuses, and freight rate changes in order to increase their competitive advantage.

A substantial part of the Canadian steel industry required state support to ensure continued survival during the twenties and early thirties. Demands for such support, however, provoked considerable opposition both within and outside the steel industry. The federal government attempted to mediate this conflict between producers and consumers by means of a series of delays and piecemeal concessions. Under normal circumstances the powerful forces opposed to change possessed sufficient means to limit government concessions to a minimum. In the latter half of the twenties, however, events turned in favour of Algoma and Besco. When J.H. Gundy, in association with Sir Herbert Holt, wrested control of Besco from the Wolvin syndicate in 1927, the company gained powerful new advocates in Ottawa. Mackenzie King especially appreciated Gundy's efforts to reorganize the Nova Scotian concern and became reconciled to assisting what he once had scornfully regarded as an industry in need of 'continuous artificial bolstering.' Narrow private interests alone, however, were not decisive. The emergence of the Maritime Rights Movement raised the problems of the steel industry to a new level of importance in Ottawa, as local concerns finally became a matter of grave national interest. Although most Maritimers despised the outside interests that dominated their economy, their fortunes, for better or worse, were tied to those of the corporate interests that controlled the coal and steel industries. The hinterland's political resistance compensated for its economic weakness in the central Canadian market. Ultimately the government's concern for national unity and political stability prompted a series of concessions in favour of the steel industry. Ironically, however, just as Algoma and Besco achieved many of their political goals, the Great Depression wiped out the national steel market and the weak sisters of the industry limped onward to fresh disasters.

8
The state and enterprise

Freedom of enterprise in Canada does not mean 'laissez-faire.' Rather, the term expresses a broader conception of bourgeois freedom. But since the bourgeois ideal is founded upon the desire to establish a private realm within which the individual freely expresses and realizes his emotional and intellectual capacities for personal development and social aggrandizement, the ideal presumes a measure of personal power over environmental threats to life, liberty, and the enjoyment of property. From the individual perspective, therefore, the pursuit of freedom of enterprise is inextricably bound up with a quest for power. As Hannah Arendt once observed: 'Power, according to Hobbes, is the accumulated control that permits the individual to fix prices and regulate supply and demand in such a way that they contribute to his own advantage. The individual will consider his advantage in complete isolation, from the point of view of an absolute minority, so to speak; he will then realize that he can pursue and achieve his interest only with the help of some kind of majority.'[1] In Canada, as in other developing capitalist societies, the unlimited pursuit of private capital accumulation necessitated the development of a political structure that could protect growing property only by growing more powerful itself. As leading firms grew ever larger and their areas of enterprise widened, concomitant risks and uncertainties also grew. Ultimately, only the coercive power of the state could reduce the uncertainty of the market and restore the security necessary to the enjoyment of property. In other words, as capital became increasingly concentrated and economies of scale mounted, the pursuit of freedom of enterprise led to demands for the creation of a variant of state capitalism.[2]

1 Arendt, *Imperialism* (New York 1968), 19; see also C.B. Macpherson, *The Political Theory of Possessive Individualism* (Oxford 1962)
2 In this case, state capitalism does not refer to public ownership of the means of production. Rather, the term is used more loosely to describe the enormously expanded role of the state in twentieth-century capitalist societies. This phenomenon is often referred to

Yet, despite this tendency within the economic and political order, Canadian manufacturers confronted the vicissitudes of the Great Depression with little more state support than that accorded producers at the turn of the century. After half a decade of war and reconstruction plannning, and another half a decade of unparalleled prosperity, Canadian industrialists possessed neither the private economic resources nor the public institutional mechanisms needed to rationalize markets, productive facilities, or prices during the chaos of the early thirties. These means were not established until the 1940s and 1950s when war and phenomenal postwar prosperity brought the requisite political, economic, and ideological changes.[3] An assessment of these events raises several problems. To what extent do these cases of business-government relations reveal in microcosm the dynamics of the entire Canadian political economy? Why did these relations assume the specific character already described? And how do these cases enlarge our understanding of the role of the state in the Canadian political economy?

The dominant tendency within the Canadian political economy is conflict, both between and within classes. This study, of course, focuses upon conflict within the dominant class, between sectors, regions, and within industries. However, a sensitive reading of the significance of these events must ultimately encompass inter-class as well as intra-class conflict, for the Canadian state and the political economy are the product of both levels of struggle. Indeed, although no effort was made here to recover the mass of men and women of the past from their regrettable oblivion,[4] their palpable presence as both consumers and producers was a constant factor in the politics that determined relations between businessmen and the government. National policies nearly always represented a careful effort to minimize class divisions as well as to mediate and reconcile interest group conflicts.

The creation and elaboration of the state apparatus reflected the delicate balance of power between contending classes and interest groups. As James O'Connor observed, 'interest-group politics is inconsistent with the survival and expansion of capitalism,' for 'interest consciousness obviously leads to contradictory policies, making it difficult or impossible to plan the economy as a whole. Thus, a class-conscious political directorate is needed to coordinate the activities of nominally independent government agencies.' This distinction between interest groups and classes forms the basis of a more precise theory of the state:

by various terms such as the welfare state, pentagon capitalism, welfare-warfare capitalism, and so on.

3 See J.L. Granatstein, *Canada's War* (Toronto 1975); R. Warren James, *Wartime Economic Cooperation* (Toronto 1949); and Peter C. Newman, *The Canadian Establishment* (Toronto 1976)

4 See 'Bibliographic Essay,' in Gregory S. Kealey and Peter Warrian, eds., *Essays in Canadian Working Class History* (Toronto 1976)

... the [chief executive] and his key aides must remain independent; they must interpret class (as opposed to particular economic) corporate interests and translate these interests into action, not only in terms of immediate economic and political needs, but also in terms of the relations between monopoly capital and competitive sector labor and capital. Monopoly capitalist class interests (as a social force rather than as an abstraction) are not the aggregate of the particular interests of this class but rather emerge within the state administration 'unintentionally.' In this important sense, the capitalist state is not an 'instrument' but a 'structure.'[5]

Franz Schurmann makes much the same point with the observation that 'it is class war, not class, that produces the state.' Starting from the distinction between the use value and the exchange value of capital Schurmann argues that the capitalist class cannot rule directly or though its chosen instruments because it is pulled in opposite directions by an irresolvable contradiction in the nature of capitalism. 'As a system of free enterprise seeking ever broader avenues for expansion, it strives constantly to break down existing forms of property. It must destroy savings and turn them into investment. As conservative and classical economists have long recognized, the inherent tendency of capitalism is to break down interests wherever they exist, particularly in the state, which create ever more rigid and inelastic forms of property and interest.' At the same time, however, Schurmann contends that 'as a ruling class, the capitalist class strives with all its might to preserve its property, to make its savings inviolable, to build walls around its ownings to protect them against all agressors.' Thus the contradictory nature of capitalism is expressed by two competing political strategies, for 'while one tendency of the capitalist class is to create ever more freedom by eroding structures of interests, the other, equally inherent, is to create more unfreedom by generating structures of monopoly, power, prestige and wealth.'[6]

Schurmann contends that the capitalist state embodies this contradiction, and gains its *raison d'être* from its efforts to resolve it. However, the capitalist state also embodies the struggle of the propertyless class to assert its claims for a greater share of power and wealth. In order for capitalism to persist the state must ensure such minimal changes as are necessary to satisfy the propertyless class and bind their interests to those above them. Indeed, as C.B. Macpherson has noted: 'The central problem of liberal-democratic theory [has been] to reconcile the claims of the free market economy with the claims of the whole mass of individuals to some kind of equality. It cannot be too often recalled that liberal-democracy is strictly a capitalist phenomenon. Liberal-democratic institu-

5 O'Connor, *The Fiscal Crisis of the State* (New York 1973), 67-9
6 Schurmann, *The Logic of World Power* (New York 1974), 139

tions have appeared only in capitalist countries, and only after the free market and the liberal state have produced a working class conscious of its strength and insistent on a voice.'[7]

The capitalist state, then, internally replicates and ultimately seeks to resolve the primary contradictions inherent in the capitalist social order. Schurmann concludes that 'from the point of view of a capitalist class which contains both these warring [capitalist] elements, there is no alternative but to create a democratic state which somehow expresses the interests of freedom and property, but also the aspirations of the revolutionary classes. Through that state and its "regulative" functions, the capitalist class seeks "compromises" which must be made day after day to keep the entire system functioning.'[8] These compromises, however, are not the equivalent of brokerage functions in pluralist theories of the state. For while the capitalist state does not directly represent the instrument for domination by a single class, it does assume the burden of perpetuating capitalism itself. In this sense it is not a value-free broker, but rather the protector and promoter of a specific set of rules and social relationships founded upon capitalist property relationships and the transformation of all values into commodities through the operation of a market system of exchange.[9]

The 'compromises' between classes and interest groups adopted in Canada between the war and the depression constituted a process whereby government leaders not only continually revised national policies but also remade the state apparatus in order to facilitate the expression of contradictory tendencies within the political economy. Neither classes nor interest groups depended exclusively on continuous favours from political leaders. All sought to embed their interests within the state apparatus itself, to guarantee a measure of control over the state budget, and to ensure a voice in the process whereby new policies were formulated. At the same time, however, by virtue of their power to fashion the daily compromise through which the state guarantees the continued legitimacy of the capital accumulation process, government leaders achieved a measure of autonomy from the classes and interests among whom they mediated. The creation of new agencies of government, such as the war boards or the tariff board, not only enshrined particular private interests within the state, it also served to create mechanisms through which government leaders tried to regulate

7 Macpherson, 'Politics: Post-Liberal-Democracy?' in Robin Blackburn, ed., *Ideology in Social Science* (New York 1972), 19

8 *Logic of World Power*, 140

9 See N. Poulantzas, 'The Problem of the Capitalist State,' in Blackburn, *Ideology*; and Claus Offe and Volker Ronge, 'Theses on the Theory of the State,' *New German Critique* (Fall 1975)

and discipline conflicting elements of society. To the extent that group or class interests entered the state apparatus they were forced by the process of government to compete and collude with the other interests of society and thus they were co-opted into an accommodation with those interests. (Logically, in the absence of successful accommodation, new interests have no choice but to try to take over the state completely and utterly destroy all other interests and their manifestations within the state apparatus, that is, a revolution.[10])

The creation of the Board of Commerce, the paper controller, and the tariff board each entailed an effort to achieve harmony within the social order. In each case, neither the market nor the established political channels sufficed to resolve conflict and ensure accommodation. Under these circumstances government leaders created new agencies to localize conflict and restore order. As Rianne Mahon argues, 'a regulatory agency is created to provide a framework for facilitating an "exceptional" compromise in the face of a political challenge that can only be met by altering the juridical rights of capital ... Such an "exceptional" limitation may be general in scope (e.g., labour relations, "anti-trust") or be industry-specific (rates of production, exports, the direction of new investment).'[11] The cases discussed here represent both types of exceptional instances, both general and specific.

The appointment of R.A. Pringle as paper controller in 1917 reveals clearly the government's effort to localize a specific conflict by establishing an independent regulatory agency that operated outside the context of the established administrative apparatus and traditional partisan politics. Newspapers controlled the politicians' lifeline to the public. Accordingly, their political power was enormous. Yet the newsprint companies had every legal right to refuse to supply them at any price. Moreover, newsprint exports constituted a critical element in Canada's balance of payments position, as well as providing full-time or supplementary employment for a considerable proportion of rural central Canada. Under the circumstances both parties had to be forced to moderate their demands and accommodate their interests to the exigencies of the broader crisis confronting the established political economy, namely war with Germany and the threat of continued war with the enemies of industrial Canada. The paper companies were forced to accept somewhat lower prices for domestic sales, which only accounted for a small proportion of their total revenues, and the newspapers were stopped short of more radical claims upon the newsprint industry and the state. (For example, the newspapers might have

10 Schurmann, *Logic of World Power*, 137-8
11 Mahon, 'Regulatory Agencies: Captive Agents or Instruments of Hegemony?' unpublish paper delivered to the Canadian Political Science Association Meetings, Fredericton, NB, Spring 1977

demanded some form of nationalization, as occurred in the Ontario Hydro case where consumers effectively destroyed the power oligopoly.[12]) It is important to appreciate that while neither side acceded to this compromise willingly, both accepted regulation and, ultimately, accommodation to broader interests so that subsequent interest-group conflicts were played out under the auspices of the paper controller rather than within the politically more fragile cabinet. When Pringle's regulatory system finally broke down, and Board of Commerce regulation proved legally impossible, the cabinet once more intervened reluctantly to arrange yet another compromise based on export restrictions. However, by this time both publishers and newsprint producers recognized the futility of further conflict since neither obviously would gain complete ascendancy over the other, and both agreed to an informal and voluntary resolution of their struggle. The government, fearful of offending American interests hostile to continued export restrictions, gladly withdrew its proposed legislation and the state apparatus was remade once again in conformity with the changing political economy.

The appointment of the Board of Commerce in 1919 represented the search for a much broader accommodation of interests than existed in the case of the paper industry. Producers and consumers each demanded price stability (although their interests and their understanding of stability clashed), while the government sought to defuse the widespread class conflict that culminated in the Winnipeg General Strike and the sympathetic strikes across the country accompanying it. While individual interest groups, such as the sugar refiners, struggled to achieve their particular ends under the aegis of the board's authority, the government could only point to modest gains in terms of its broader programme.[13] For example, from March 1919 to June 1920, the cost-of-living index rose by over 40 per cent, from 131.5 to 185.0. Since the main causes for this increase were higher food and clothing prices, both areas that fell under the board's jurisdiction, and since the bulk of these increases occurred after the board became operative in the fall of 1919, the board's practical accomplishments were limited. In part, this failure was attributable to international economic instability, for as one observer commented: 'it is difficult to see how this price inflation from mid-1919 to mid-1920 could have been prevented without concerted and co-operative international action.'[14] At the

12 H.V. Nelles, *The Politics of Development* (Toronto 1974), chaps. 6-7
13 T.D. Traves, 'Some Problems with Peacetime Price Controls: The Case of the Board of Commerce of Canada, 1919-20,' *Canadian Public Administration*, 17, 1 (1974)
14 A.W. Turner and B.H. Higgins, 'Sequence and Timing of Economic Events in the Last War and Postwar Period, 1914-1923,' Advisory Committee on Reconstruction, Studies and Factual Reports, no 1, 1943, mimeo., pp. 33, 16

same time, however, the board's achievements reflect both the level of institutional development within private and public organizations and competing pressures from within the political economy and the state.

Despite their anxiety to secure regulatory support Canadian manufacturers always remained ambivalent about the regulatory experience. While promotional support had long been an established government responsibility, regulation represented a new direction in the organization of the economy. Even leading manufacturers had relatively little experience with the bureaucratic imperatives of economic integration. As J.A. Corry has pointed out:

Large sectors of business activity must first have centralized themselves before the situation is ripe for centralization under the government. Large-scale organization had already made great strides but it had not yet settled down to a bureaucratic routine. It was still flexible, controlled by the resourceful men who built it up, and who were easily attracted to the adventure of producing war supplies. In short, the Canadian economy in 1914-18, because of its character and the character of the men who had the largest share in its operation, was not amenable to central direction ...[15]

As a rule leading Canadian businessmen enjoyed their formative organizational experience within authority structures that proved highly amenable to their personal direction. A.D. Chandler and Louis Galambos argue that during the war industrial mobilization for these men 'involved an emphasis upon loose federations which arranged compromises (where possible) but did not really direct the activities of their constituency bureaucracies. When the wartime agencies were staffed with these men and began to deal with the primary [corporate] organizations, the result was a de facto decentralization of power and responsibility.'[16]

Co-operation and co-ordination, rather than economic integration, reflected Canadian manufacturers' experience, and hence their preference. Wartime bureaucrats, such as Paper Controller Pringle, were really judges, not administrators. They did not regulate an industry by reorganizing the various factors of production, such as labour, raw materials, and capital equipment, which were themselves regulated as to price, supply, and distribution, within a large model of the industry and an even larger model of the industry's place in the economy.

15 Corry, 'The Growth of Government Activities in Canada, 1914-1921,' Canadian Historical Association, Historical Papers, 1940, p. 63
16 Chandler and Galambos, 'The Development of Large-scale Economic Organization in
   Modern America,' Journal of Economic History, 30 (1970), 213-14

Rather, administration and decision-making were decentralized and regulation consisted of judicial-style decisions on prices and distribution patterns. During the boom period of the latter war years this approach proved politically acceptable and administratively effective, but when the economy first over-heated and then rapidly contracted during the reconstruction period this approach provided neither the political power nor the bureaucratic techniques required to forestall rapid deflation and economic dislocation. Only after the modern corporation itself developed much more sophisticated administrative techniques to control internal production procedures could the state hope to apply similar techniques on an industry-wide basis.

For its part, the Board of Commerce had neither the manpower nor the authority required to attempt an extensive price control programme. Initially the board decided to divide its activities among major directorates covering its principal areas of jurisdiction. The operating experience of the Economic Division was typical. The board originally wanted to hire a professional economist with some practical business experience to head this division, but such men were hard to find in 1919, so in time this plan was abandoned altogether and the duties of the director were assumed by the board's chief economist, J.C. Imlay. He divided the Economic Division into four sections covering food products, fuel products, clothing, and general commodities. The food section was personally headed by Imlay, and with a staff of sixteen assistants he was able to bring a wide variety of businessmen under a system whereby monthly data on quantities, costs, and prices were reported. At first many complaints against government interference and red tape were forwarded to the board. However, as the benefits of such supervision were realized, especially in the way of tighter inventory control for smaller businessmen, grumbling fell to a minimum.

No other section of the Economic Division was able to duplicate this achievement. An elaborate plan to place all coal-mining companies and distributors of coal under a monthly reporting system had to be abandoned because the four members of the fuel section could not begin to compute and analyse all the data they received. More seriously, the clothing section had to be abolished completely when the Civil Service Commission blocked the confirma-tion of the board's choice of a qualified technical adviser on the textiles industry. The CSC demanded compliance with its newly established routine of advertising competitive examinations for government positions. The board complained that 'the class of persons most competent to advise us is not such as would answer an advertisement of the Civil Service Commission nor attend at the offices of the Commission as applicants for temporary employment to sign "eligible lists," unless indeed the applicants represented interests subject to investigation at the time.' Such jibes were of no avail. Nor were the board's efforts to find a political solution to its difficulties by means of appeal to a higher authority more successful. When the board approached the cabinet to exempt its *technical staff* from the operation of the Civil Service Act, in a manner similar to that enjoyed by the Board of Railway Commissioners, it made no headway in its struggle against the CSC. Sir George Foster, the acting prime minister, replied that the cabinet 'have come to the conclusion that there are no sufficient grounds in the differentiation of the *clerical work* of your Board from that of other Government services which would justify the exemption of the Board of Commerce from the provisions of the Civil Service Act.'[17]

The ineffectiveness of the Board of Commerce raises serious questions about the government's intentions at the time of the creation of the board. The government's decision to exempt wheat prices from board control and to entrust them to the Wheat Board, also created in 1919, raises similar concerns, for while the Board of Commerce was ostensibly appointed to keep prices down, the Wheat Board was created to keep them up. As W.F. O'Connor complained, it was 'supremely ridiculous' that the Board of Commerce should be empowered to control the pork, cheese, or beef industries while they were unable to control the costs of feeds basic to those industries' cost structures.[18]

By confronting the problem of general price stability with the appointment of the Board of Commerce, the federal government went far beyond the range of economic, administrative, and political problems inherent in its regulation of the paper industry. Specific interest-group conflicts could be resolved by relatively simple compromises negotiated and enforced by traditional regulatory agencies. Price control across the entire economy, however, required the replication of class and interest-group conflicts within the board itself if the legitimacy of the political economy was to be maintained. At the end of the First World War this was impossible. The range of interests was too great and no institutional means existed to rationalize conflicting interests. Therefore, the federal government isolated special interests, such as the wheat industry, which required individual attention, starved the Board of Commerce of personnel in most areas to ensure minimal action against powerful interests such as the textile industry, and used the board to achieve symbolic, or rhetorical, victories rather than real control over prices. Under these circumstances, certain interests, such as the sugar refiners who had a long association with O'Connor, were able to pursue their

17 This account is drawn from Dominion of Canada, 'Annual Report of the Board of Commerce of Canada,' 31 May 1920, Sessional Papers no 205, unprinted, PAC, RG14D2, vol. 74, especially pp. 44, 114 (emphasis added)
18 PAC, Board of Commerce Files, vol. 1, file 1-1-1, O'Connor to H.A. Robson, 15 October 1919.

own goals while the government ignored the board's inactivity on a whole range of equally pressing concerns. However, when the board's activities politically embarrassed the government and threatened the whole political economy through the temporary alliance of small businessmen and outraged working class consumers, government leaders revised their policies and the state's institutions by all but abolishing the Board of Commerce.

It is a striking fact that political and business leaders failed to create a regulatory state at the end of the First World War, while just twenty-five years later they ended the Second World War with the regulatory-welfare state in embryonic form. In part, as already noted, the initial failure reflected specific political defeats and general institutional deficiencies in both public and private organizations. At the same time, however, reconstruction efforts during the First World War period lacked the integrating power and the drive created by a powerful reconceptualization of the ideology of the state. Organizations such as the Canadian Reconstruction Association established their programme of *ad hoc* responses to specific economic and political problems within the framework established by orthodox economic theory. Their revolution, if they actually envisioned one, lay in the political reorganization of the state. Apart from admitting the growing problems of economic concentration they neither developed nor advanced any new economic theories. In this sense the Second World War differed markedly from the First. For along with institutional changes and a different political climate, Lord Keynes' theories provided a powerful ideological impetus and justification for the growth of the state in the peacetime economy.

The appointment of the Advisory Board on Tariff and Taxation introduces another important factor in the analysis of the nature of the Canadian political economy, namely regionalism. Canadian geography and settlement patterns have combined with the historic development of regional staple industries to create extreme spatial irregularities in terms of rates of development and economic structure. Over time these patterns have been reinforced and irregularities exacerbated by national economic policies enacted on behalf of metropolitan interest groups. The process of regional underdevelopment, however, in turn produced forceful political and economic protest movements determined to rectify spatial irregularities through changes in national policies, particularly the tariff.

The history of the automobile and primary steel industries demonstrates the complex interaction between competing industrial, class, and regional interests in the formulation of tariff policies. Political leaders often faced a daunting task trying to reconcile these diverse claims. In 1926, for example, Arthur Meighen was under tremendous pressure from the protectionist wing of his party to denounce the government's automobile policy because it looked like a sell-out of industrial and central Canadian interests to the low tariff programme espoused by the Progressives. Meighen held this view himself, but in order to mollify agrarian and consumer interests within his own party he proposed that the government refrain from any changes until the tariff board was appointed and had a chance to study the proper course to take. This proposal was designed to buy time for the auto makers and to give the Conservative party a chance to stand aside from the conflict between producers and consumers. However, Meighen's Maritime supporters were outraged by this step. For one thing, they supported lower automobile tariffs because they wanted lower prices. More importantly, they did not want to postpone all tariff decisions until after the board investigated because this would delay action on Besco's claims and they wanted an immediate increase in the steel tariff schedule. The automobile producers were unhappy too because they wanted a more forthright defence of their interests. Poor Meighen was torn between these forces and irritated by the narrow views of his supporters. 'The automobile men know ... that as a party we are absolutely sound on this question,' he complained to a colleague, 'and will apply the protective principle to them just as to any business in Canada. If they want more than this from us then they are unreasonable and they cannot get it. The leading of a party is not quite as simple a matter as they conceive it to be.' The creation of the Advisory Board on Tariff and Taxation, however, was designed to make that arduous political task somewhat easier.[19]

The tariff board, of course, was not a regulatory agency; the tariff, however, was probably the single most important element in the Canadian state apparatus, to the extent that it directly transferred wealth from one portion of the community to another. The formulation of tariff policy, therefore, constituted an essential part of the 'daily compromises' needed to maintain the stability of the established social order. During the 1920s demands for tariff changes emerged in all parts of society and from all parts of the country: prairie farmers wanted general reductions, Maritime workers and business interests demanded specific increases, while central Canadian producers were usually divided in their views between the suppliers and consumers of specific industrial commodities. Mackenzie King carefully tried to balance these contending forces by lavishly orchestrated revisions that created a maximum of political advantage for his party with a minimum of economic dislocation for the interests affected by the change. After half a decade of trading minor revisions on farm machinery,

19 PAC, J.W. Dafoe Papers, vol. 3, Grant Dexter to Dafoe, 4 May 1926; PAC, Arthur Meighen Papers, vol. 69, file 42, 38930, W.H. Dennis to Meighen, 27 April 1926, vol. 134, file 168(1), 80807-8, Meighen to Sir Edmund Kemp, 27 May 1926

textiles, sugar, cement, and certain iron and steel products for the ultimate accomodation of western agrarian interests to the traditional political order, King succeeded in establishing a measure of stability and hegemony for the Liberal party across the country.[20] The appointment of the tariff board guaranteed continued stability so long as class or interest conflicts spent their force in tedious and lengthy hearings before the board rather than in the cabinet. The ultimate formulation of the tariff schedule, of course, was too important to be entrusted to a single, 'non-political' agency, so tariff decisions finally were the cabinet's responsibility; but the tariff board provided a forum where contending interests could establish their positions, rebut dubious claims, and perhaps establish an informal consensus on desired changes. Once the map of political and economic dangers was clearly outlined at board hearings, the cabinet felt freer and was more able to chart a safe course between the dangerous shoals and reefs on every side.

These political soundings took time and often produced inconclusive results, however, so that by the end of the twenties Canadian producers in many industries had decided to take measures into their own hands. Labour unrest produced the factory welfare movement and demands for a more comprehensive federal social welfare system; persistent excess capacity produced numerous and varied attempts to limit destructive competition in order to gain monopoly or oligopoly profits. Although the factory welfare movement was less significant than the very high unemployment rates that prevailed throughout the decade as a factor in quelling labour unrest, the movement represented a major departure in capitalist social relations as paternalism buttressed by social engineering techniques emerged as the dominant social form of corporate capitalism. Attempts to control competition enjoyed somewhat greater success. By the early thirties a substantial number of Canadian industries fixed prices and regulated production through powerful trade associations or through more informal oligopolistic practices made possible as a result of the merger movement during the twenties. In other cases, large Canadian firms such as Canada Cement, Canadian General Electric, Canadian Industries Limited, and Imperial Tobacco enjoyed near monopolies in their respective industries. Since these monopolies achieved earnings more than three times the Canadian average during the period from 1927 to 1937, they served as important models for other industries to follow.[21] Despite legal restrictions on price fixing, trade associations, mergers,

20 O.J. McDiarmid, *Commercial Policy in the Canadian Economy* (Cambridge, Mass. 1946), chap. 11
21 Lloyd G. Reynolds, *The Control of Competition in Canada* (Cambridge, Mass. 1940), 60, table 3. According to Reynolds, Canadian manufacturers achieved average earnings of 4 per cent between 1927 and 1937, while ten major monopolistic firms averaged 12.2 per cent earnings over the same period.

and monopolies, all proceeded with only token supervision from the federal government. Between 1917 and 1931 the effort to achieve security through regulation gave way to sporadic attempts to gain security through combination.

Following the war relations between the state and enterprise in Canada suffered many rapid changes. Traditional 'laissez-faire' views gave way to the regulatory state, which many deemed essential to the preservation of corporate capitalism. Although the most important regulatory agencies failed to survive the trials of the reconstruction period, they represented an important evolution in the structure and the role of the state in the political economy. In every society the state is charged with the responsibility of reconciling the short- and long-term interests of its citizens; in a capitalist society, this task is defined in terms of capitalist values and is based on capitalist social relations. In other words, the Canadian state is a structure or system of institutional and power relationships within which class and group interests establish the compromises required to perpetuate the capitalist order in Canada. Between 1917 and 1931 organizations such as the Canadian Reconstruction Association and the Canadian Manufacturers' Association attempted to instruct their members in their wider responsibilities, but these informal attempts to shape group interests around class interests never mustered the discipline necessary to produce harmony out of dissidence. Only the state possessed sufficient coercive powers to guarantee discipline and institute critical compromises. The development of the state and changes in the political economy, however, did not follow any predetermined pattern during these years. At each stage business and government leaders, as well as a host of lesser figures, acted upon their perceptions of the complex balance between self-interest and social stability in the face of numerous changes in markets, private and public institutions, and political alignments. In many quarters misery and discontent persisted, but the system survived, and these halting steps to deal with risk, uncertainty, and instability provided subsequent generations with a measure of experience to guide them along the same path.

Index